blue
flame

blue flame

WOODY HERMAN'S LIFE in MUSIC

Robert C. Kriebel

Purdue University Press

West Lafayette, Indiana

99   98   97   96   95   5   4   3   2   I

∞ The paper used in this book meets the minimum requirements of American National Standard for Information Sciences—Permanence of Paper for Printed Library Materials, ANSI Z39.48-1992.

Printed in the United States of America
Design by Anita Noble
Cover photograph of Woody Herman courtesy Thomas Cassidy, Inc.

Library of Congress Cataloging-in-Publication Data
Kriebel, Robert C., 1932–
        Blue flame : Woody Herman's life in music / Robert C. Kriebel.
            p.   cm.
        Includes bibliographical references (p.   ) and index.
        ISBN 1-55753-073-4 (pbk.)
            1. Herman, Woody, 1913–1987. 2. Jazz musicians—United States—Biography.
    I. Title.
    ML419.H45K75 1995
    781.65'092—dc20   95-6045
        [B]   CIP
                                                                         MN

WHEN *the* WORLD *goes* WRONG,
and I'VE GOT *the* BLUES,
HE'S *the* MAN *who* MAKES ME
get OUT BOTH *my* DANCING SHOES.

—"Doctor Jazz," Jelly Roll Morton

contents

acknowledgments

*t*he recording companies that preserved the music and the writers who have chronicled the times and captured the words of the bandleader Woody Herman are the sources of much information in this book. The primary record companies are Decca, Columbia, Capitol, MGM, Mars, Verve, Everest, Crown, Philips, Cadet, Fantasy, Century, and Concord. Numerous other firms have undertaken reissues of titles and albums or produced their own. Those who wrote album notes, magazine articles, newspaper columns, reviews, and books dealing with, or referring to, Herman are catalogued in my bibliography. It is my intent that they be given full recognition and praise.

The research and writing efforts of a specific few deserve singular mention: Leonard Feather, Charles Garrod, Richard Gehman, Gary Giddins, Ira Gitler, Ralph J. Gleason, George Hall, Gene Lees, John McDonough, Gunther Schuller, George T. Simon, Terry Teachout, James A. Treichel, Stuart Troup, Steve Voce, Leo Walker, and Herb Wong.

I am indebted to J. William Siefert, Chubby Jackson, Frank Tiberi, Ingrid Herman Reese, Bill Byrne, A. J. Julian, Edward Soph, and George Hall for advice, additional information, and manuscript review.

INTRODUCTION

*t*he story of America's big bands has many heroes. Some found immortality by writing new music for bands to play, others just by leading bands, playing instruments, or singing. Some led bands only for a while, then faded from view owing to death or their brusque refusal to change with the times or because of the stress of travel and management woes or because of the uncertainties and the occasional bankruptcies caused by the fickle market for their music. Some quit while they were ahead. Others died too soon. The most durable of them got to know America better than other entertainers or even presidents. Years after their deaths, many of their names are still familiar: Les Brown, Bob Crosby, Tommy and Jimmy Dorsey, Benny Goodman, Harry James, Gene Krupa, Kay Kyser, Jimmie Lunceford, Glenn Miller, and Artie Shaw.

Three band leaders occupy a special place in the annals of big bands for their complex mixture of talent, drive, savvy, personality, and leadership: the urbane pianist, composer, and arranger Edward Kennedy "Duke" Ellington; the laid-back pianist William "Count" Basie; and Woodrow Charles Thomas "Woody" Herman, singer of blues, ballads, and novelties and player of clarinet and saxophone. Song tributes have been composed, and countless stories written and told, about "the Duke" and "the Count," and more are sure to come. Woody Herman may be less remembered than they, but he outlived and outled and outworked them both. Ellington rated Herman as "the one bandleader whose beliefs and music follow the true tradition and direction of our people's music."[1] Basie considered Herman "a marvelous leader . . . his bands always swing, full of fine soloists. I don't know how he does it!"[2] Herman himself viewed his accomplishments with characteristic modesty: "All we do is try to create some kind of mood, and hope somebody digs it."[3]

Herman played in bands nearly sixty years and led his own for more than fifty. That is more than half the life of jazz itself. His was a career productive more of music, friends, and stacks of records than of fame or money. For two glittering years he led arguably the best jazz big band ever, of any era, any musical style. But often he also half-joked that "except for my 1945–46 band [my career] was all downhill."[4]

Among his many achievements, Woody Herman kept putting a smile on the blues until he died in 1987. Before age, injury, emphysema, and heart trouble forced him to hobble onstage using a cane, Herman for an incredible fifty years and four months led a variety of always changing, always young and exciting bands. And he did so with style. Personal problems plagued Herman in his cloudy final years. The good bands he pulled together broke up; fresh ones formed and broke up again. The Internal Revenue Service dogged him about back taxes because of a manager's neglect.

Herman condemned the business end of band life as "a big pain . . . you're victimized before you even start, and it never lets up. There is no life, there is no home."[5] Passion for the music, music-making, musicians, and fans, not money or ego, kept Herman going.

Few band leaders were stubborn or strong enough to survive changes after World War II. After Basie died in 1984, there was only the one left: Woody Herman stood proudly, at age seventy, "as obsolete as a buffalo, and just as grand," as Gary Giddins phrased it.[6] Near the end Herman often was asked to explain his endurance. He had no pat answer. Others offered various opinions: "Woody must be one of the least-disliked persons on earth." "He loves the music." "He owed the IRS. He could [only] change one prison for another."

In any event, Herman struggled on, and several times when it seemed that he was finished, he picked himself up and started over, saying, "I'll go down swinging"—a phrase packed with meaning in baseball, in music, and in life.

chapter one

the
LEARNING
years

*t*he curtain went up for Woodrow Charles Thomas Herman on May 16, 1913, in Milwaukee, Wisconsin. Show business waited in the wings, but not for long. He was the only child of Otto and Martha Herman—"kind and beautiful" parents, he said, who "let me try to do anything I wanted." In no way stagestruck, Martha had emigrated from Poland. But American-born Otto, of German descent, was "a terrible ham who would have loved working onstage instead of [in] a shoe factory,"[1] to hear the son tell it. Otto had been a vaudeville singer of modest acclaim with an obscure act called the White City Four. Otto coaxed Woody toward music with phonograph records and a player piano and coached him in dancing. "My father was a frustrated singer to some degree," Herman later recalled, "and decided I would be the completion of his ambitions."[2]

In the summer of 1920, Otto took the dressed-up lad to an audition for a kiddie revue. Woody won a part in a low-budget troupe directed by a grade-school teacher. He worked his first summer vaudeville tour (Wisconsin and Michigan) at age nine, studied dancing, and practiced piano and violin before settling on the E-flat alto saxophone and clarinet. He bought the reed instruments with his performance pay.

After a summer touring for money again in 1923, Woody faced public-school educators who objected to his musical activities. Through a Milwaukee juvenile court, they threatened to take his working permit. Their negative attitude "bugged me and I decided to do something about it," Herman recalled. So in the fifth grade, he transferred to St. John's Cathedral School in downtown Milwaukee. There, he said, broader-minded Roman Catholic teachers were "more interested in individuals."[3]

As a preteen, Woody toured as "The Boy Wonder." His song, dance, and clarinet imitations of vaudeville star Ted ("Is ev'rybody happy?") Lewis paid as much as fifty dollars a week. With a comedian and a four-woman chorus line (singing off-color lyrics), the troupe at times played two theaters a night, two shows per theater.

As his tastes matured, Woody became intrigued by jazz, with its daring rhythms, range of emotion, and rich, on-the-spot invention. He began collecting records by an eight-piece group called The Washingtonians, led by the then unknown Ellington. "It was the first time I ever heard what sounded like jungle music," Herman said, "and it knocked me out."[4] The Washingtonians first recorded in 1925–26 for the Perfect and the Gennett record companies. Ellington's distinctive style was even more pronounced in "Jungle Jamboree," "Snake Hips Dance," "Black and Blue," and "Maori," which were recorded for Okeh, Brunswick, and Vocalion during 1929–30. Herman also heard recorded jazz by clarinetist Jimmy Noone (Vocalion, 1928–30) and bands led by trumpeters Red Nichols and Louis Armstrong and by pianist Earl Hines. To his parents' dismay, Woody pined to become such a "hot" player and make jazz records.

As a singer, he learned the styles of Russ Columbo, Lee Wiley, and William "Red" McKenzie. Columbo—a heartthrob along the lines of Bing Crosby and Rudy Vallee—sang straight, popular romantic ballads and made no dent in jazz. But Wiley, an Oklahoma runaway who starred at seventeen in New York and Chicago clubs, sang and recorded blues and torch songs with Leo Reisman and with the Casa Loma band, broadcast with Paul Whiteman, and performed with Dixieland combos. Her husky, erotic warmth and wide vibrato made hers one of the most distinctive feminine voices in jazz. McKenzie sang both jazz and zany novelties and played the kazoo in a manner he called "blue blowing." He added a banjo player and a second kazoo to make up the Mound City Blue Blowers for his 1924 records for Brunswick. Some of them—"Arkansas Blues," "Blue Blues," "San," "Red Hot," "Barb-Wire Blues," "Wigwam Blues," and "Tiger Rag"—became late-1920s favorites.

Herman began taking sax and clarinet lessons with a jazz-oriented teacher. Then the slender, pleasant, clean-cut high-school freshman landed a sax-section job in a Milwaukee theater's house band. This provided more chances for him to hear traveling bands playing the area. He soon found better jobs, with Myron Stewart's and Joey Lichter's Milwaukee bands of about a dozen men. Lichter's band worked a ballroom, and the fifteen-year-old Herman was proud to be "the youngest cat in the band by far."[5]

By the time he was sixteen, Woody could play the clarinet and the alto, tenor, and baritone saxes for money and sing ballads, blues, and novelties. He was also old enough to drive— and well-heeled enough to buy—his first car, a Whippet roadster. With his new wheels, he could get around to paying jobs at Milwaukee-area roadhouses, such as the Blue Heaven, Pick's Club Madrid, and the Modernistic.

After his sophomore year in high school, Woody joined a band that spent part of the summer of 1929 in Tulsa, Oklahoma. The group played "in a kind of auditorium that held several hundred teenagers," he recalled. "People would pass a little joint, a stick of marijuana. It was universal among a great number of high school kids in that area." He tried smoking marijuana but didn't like it.[6]

Herman as a young performer, at about about age fourteen. (Jack Siefert Collection)

Anxious to cash in on his talent, experience, grin, and good looks, Woody left St. John's Cathedral High School in his senior year—January 1931—to join the touring San Francisco professional band of Tom Gerun (Gerunovitch). Gerun, who had recorded for Brunswick since 1928, featured such artists as singer Virginia Simms and vocalist and saxophonist Al Morris in his band. (Their fame came later: Simms as Ginny Simms, with Kyser's band, and Morris as singing star Tony Martin.) Herman debuted with the band while Gerun played the Schroeder Hotel in Milwaukee; then they moved on to the Chez Paris in Chicago and the William Penn Hotel in Pittsburgh. The easy-going Herman took music more seriously than he took himself, saying his sax playing "sounded like Bud Freeman [the 1930s Chicago jazz star] with his hands chopped off."[7]

Herman reached San Francisco with Gerun in 1931, playing first the Noon Club, then the Bal Taberin. One evening the cast of a musical called *Nine O'Clock Revue* poured in for an opening-night party. There Herman spotted "a beautiful dancer with flaming red hair" named Charlotte Neste, also seventeen, and, as he put it, "we were attracted to each other from the start."[8] The actress-dancer-comedienne, who performed as Carol Dee, hailed from North Dakota. She and Herman—who was by then called Woody—kept up a long-distance courtship for five years, at times working thousands of miles apart.

Gerun played safe, popular music and recorded little jazz. His 1928 "My Gal Sal" and "There's a Rainbow 'round My Shoulder" did make some discographies, as did a recording made on August 2, 1932, on which Herman sang "Lonesome Me." "It was not a very good band," Herman said long after he left Gerun, "but sometimes we got swinging."[9] Yet Gerun taught Herman the discipline that marked his future bandleading career. And working for Gerun opened up a world of travel and experience for him. Herman explored New Orleans in 1932 with Gerun's band: "We played the Club Forest in Jefferson Parish. Sidney Arodin, the New Orleans clarinetist, would take me on the bayous in his boat and we'd drink home brew and talk about music."[10] And once, while Gerun played the Grenada Cafe (rumored to belong to mobster Al Capone) in Chicago, two thugs set upon Herman and two well-oiled friends, who were joyriding before dawn (after catching pianist Earl Hines playing at the Grand Terrace Cafe) in Herman's new Pontiac roadster. In a scuffle at a stoplight, as Herman told it, "my right leg got in the way—I still have the scar where the bullet went in, and where it came out." He said a doctor "put me into one of those South Side hospitals that took care of things like small shootings, and I got out the next day."[11]

After three years of touring with Gerun, boredom inspired Herman to form his own band, and in late 1933, at the age of twenty, he returned to Milwaukee with the idea of doing so. One biographer has written that he did indeed start a short-lived band called Woody Herman and His Syncopators.[12] But sensing that he was not quite ready to be a band leader, Herman joined pianist Harry Sosnick's ritzy orchestra for two months, then Gus Arnheim's better-known crew for ten weeks of theater bookings. Sosnick played mainly commercial dance music and later got into radio and motion pictures. But Arnheim, based in Los Angeles's Cocoanut Grove, led the top West Coast band in the early 1930s. Arnheim's hard-driving, well-rehearsed outfit ventured into jazz, with the full band following a score while horn soloists took prearranged turns "jazzing up" the number by making up tunes to harmonize with the orchestra's part.

Herman was working in Pittsburgh with Arnheim's band (for one hundred twenty-five dollars a week less road expenses) when some friends recommended him to Isham Jones, whose band played even more jazz. From 1920, Jones's bands recorded more than four hundred numbers for the Brunswick and Victor companies. Jones, who played tenor sax, had also made two short motion-picture soundtracks and had signed with the new, budget-priced Decca Records.[13] Herman joined Jones at Elitch Gardens in Denver in mid-1934. After Denver, the band went to New York City for a long stand at the Lincoln Hotel. During Herman's three-month wait for a membership card in Local 802 of the American Federation of Musicians, union rules prohibited him from playing an instrument for pay. He sang, but sometimes he crouched under a piano, playing the clarinet or sax in the shadows.

Jones fronted one of the nation's better eighteen-piece bands in 1934, but he tried for broad appeal at the expense of focus. Fans and critics debated whether the term "jazz" applied to his repertoire. In Charles Delaunay's *New Hot Discography*, a 1948 book billed as "the standard directory of recorded jazz," Jones is unlisted. A 1955 discography from England, *Jazz Directory*, names fifty Jones records, with the rather lackluster remark that they "may be of interest to some jazz fans."[14] Gunther Schuller confessed that while writing *Early Jazz*, published in 1957, "I was not quite aware of Isham Jones's outstanding accomplishments, or of his remarkable influence. Though he led a 'dance band' rather than a jazz orchestra, I should have included mention of his pioneering work."[15] Schuller liked Jones's ability to combine an old-time, two-beat rhythm with a more modern four-beat pulse. Regardless of whether the rest of the band's rhythm section was playing two or four beats to the bar, Jones had the guitarist play four.

Herman (third from right) in the Isham Jones band at Steel Pier. (Courtesy Duncan P. Schiedt)

Herman made friends everywhere with his humor, talent, and forgiving nature. When encouraged by Jones to develop a small Dixieland unit within the Jones band, his enthusiasm proved contagious. His musicianship, energy, mastery of the Dixieland idiom, and easy rapport with audiences showed his natural leadership ability. In the spring of 1936, Jones's group recorded about twenty tunes and a medley for Associated Transcriptions and broadcast *Good Evening Serenade* radio shows, which were sponsored by United Cigar Stores.

Jones and his band were popular with the public and respected by their colleagues. Jazz drummer, record producer, and critic George T. Simon wrote: "For pure, ungimmicked music and musicianship, there were few bands to match the one led by Jones. What thrilled me was their wonderfully rich ensemble sounds. In the 1930s the band ranked as one of the most popular and polished of all the big bands, [with many] future stars."[16] Among those future stars was Gordon Jenkins, who wrote many of the arrangements. Joe Bishop, who doubled on tuba, penned some scores, too, plus several original songs, including "Blue Prelude." However, Herman found his dreams of jazz stardom no closer to reality than under Arnheim. He complained: "I didn't get any chance to do [enough] jazz. I still liked to think of myself as a jazz musician."[17]

Jones's retirement in 1936 provided Herman with the opportunity to branch out into more congenial, more challenging areas. As Jones's royalties from hit songs piled up, he longed to retire to his new ranch near Denver to write. (Eventually, "I'll See You in My Dreams," "It Had to Be You," "On the Alamo," "Swinging down the Lane," and other popular songs resulted.) Jones worked the first nine months of 1936 before quitting. Before he left, the Dixieland group organized by Herman, Yoder, and others in the band recorded for Decca as Isham Jones's Juniors. This group was made up of trumpeter Chelsea Qualey, trombonist Sonny Lee, tenor saxophonist "Saxie" Mansfield, pianist Howard Smith, guitarist George Wartner, bassist Walter Yoder, drummer Walter Lageson, vocalist Virginia Verrell, and Herman. This band-within-the-band recorded "I've Had the Blues So Long," "Slappin' the Bass," and "Nola" on March 25, 1936, returning in six days to do "Take It Easy," on which Herman sang; "Tormented," starring Verrell; and the fast novelty "Fan It," featuring Herman's Red McKenzie–style singing. The Decca company marketed these artists both as the Swanee Swingers and as Isham Jones's Juniors. The records became collector's items.

Even before September 1936, when Jones broke up his band after their gig at the Claridge Hotel in Memphis, Yoder had campaigned to keep performing with a jazz-oriented group modeled after the Juniors using some of the band's more progressive members. Yoder, Herman, and several others soon worked out plans for a cooperative band. They also took over Jones's contracts with the General Artists Corporation booking agency, the Rockwell-O'Keefe publicity firm, and Decca. Jenkins, Bishop, guitarist Chick Reeves and James "Jiggs" Noble began donating musical arrangements. The co-op members elected Herman president, Bishop and Yoder vice presidents, and trombonist Neal Reid treasurer. Other shareholders were violinist and arranger Nick Hupfer, Mansfield, Noble, trumpeters Clarence Willard and Kermit Simmons, and drummer Frankie Carlson.

The versatile Bishop, who had played tuba for Jones, switched to the flugelhorn, which was rarely used in 1930s dance bands. The most mature member of the new band at twenty-nine, Bishop had left Arkansas and played tuba with the Louisiana Ramblers, mellophone with Mart Britt, and tuba with Al Katz and Austin Wylie before his five-year stint as writer and player with Jones.

Carlson, a New Yorker, would stay with the new band seven years, providing stability and lifting the whole band's quality. (The drummer is the crucial "heartbeat" of dance and jazz orchestras. Count Basie once said, "you may think you're the boss, but that drummer is *really* the head man. When he's not feeling right, nothing is going to sound good."[18]) Yoder, who was from Kansas, was also a unifying influence because of his temperament, experience, and maturity. He had worked with Joe Haymes and bands led by the Dorseys before joining Jones's group. Reid had played in a band in his native Arkansas at age twelve, studied at the University of Illinois, then joined Dick Cisne's band before playing with Jones. His crackling trombone solos, in the style of the famous Jack Teagarden, topped the few "jazz voices" in the co-op.

These musicians added alto sax players Murray Williams and Don Watts, tenor saxophonist Bruce Wilkins, and pianists Norman Sherman and Horace Diaz to form a standard dance band. And they chose a name: Woody Herman and His Orchestra. Some speculated that the men elected Herman as front man because, in the wake of Goodman's 1935 breakthrough to fame, a clarinet-playing leader seemed a good commercial bet. But as Herman saw it, he was made the leader because of his performing experience—fourteen years, going back to child-star days.

Truly good leaders have to have many skills. They hire the players, take charge onstage, set tempos, call solos, adjust volume. Good leaders have intuition about audiences' moods and desires for slow, fast, sweet, or hot music.[19] It is more than making out a program. Good leaders have to dominate rehearsals and establish nuances of phrasing, dynamics, and such subtle devices as pitch sags, variations in attack, and falloffs. Although never written into the music—other than as casual marginal notes—such details are critical for the heat, pulse, and personality in jazz.

Herman could handle it all—and play strong clarinet and sax, sing blues and novelty numbers, croon a ballad in period style, and flash crowd-wowing smiles. "The guys . . . knew I would be a more personable front man than Isham," Herman said. "He was a good musician and great songwriter, but in front of the band he was . . . a flop."[20]

Amid the excitement of grooming this new band for a debut in New York City (the best place to find jobs, add musicians, and make records), Woody Herman and Charlotte Neste married on September 27, 1936, before a justice of the peace. They honeymooned in New York City. Then, after six weeks of rehearsals in space donated by the Capitol Hotel, the band opened Tuesday night, November 3, 1936. The locale was the Brooklyn Roseland at Fulton and Flatbush Avenues, the job more or less a tryout for the Roseland Ballroom in Manhattan. Herman received seventy-five dollars per week, and the other players fifty. "But the main thing was that we were a hit," he said.[21] After three weeks, owner Lou Brecker booked the band into the more prestigious Roseland in Manhattan through May 2, 1937.

The band made its first Decca records on Friday, November 6: the ballads "Wintertime Dreams" and "Someone to Care for Me," both sung by Herman. On Sunday, November 8, it broadcast from the WHN radio studio. It played Bishop's "Blue Prelude" as a theme song, a new ballad called "The Goose Hangs High," and such evergreens as "Liza," "Royal Garden Blues," "Rose Room," "Basin Street Blues," and a medley composed of "Exactly Like You," "Three Little Words," and "Linger Awhile."

The musicians returned to Decca—a cramped and stuffy studio displaying a banner asking "Where's the Melody?"—on November 10 to record four ballads, all with Herman singing: "The Goose Hangs High," "Now That Summer Is Gone," "I Can't Pretend," and "Old-Fashioned

Swing." In a session at Decca on December 3, Herman sang "Better Get off Your High Horse," and the band recorded its first instrumental, a piece then making the rounds called "Mr. Ghost Goes to Town."

"Soon after we opened at Roseland, the management hired a band to play on the other bandstand facing us," Herman recalled. "And that was my introduction to the great Count Basie."[22] Basie's road to Roseland had paralleled Herman's in some ways. Basie had played piano in many settings before landing with Bennie Moten's big, swinging Kansas City band. In October 1936, Moten alumni Carl Smith (trumpet), Lester Young (tenor sax), Walter Page (bass), and Jonathan "Jo" Jones (drums) joined Basie and blues singer Jimmy Rushing to make "Shoe Shine Swing," "Evenin'," "Boogie Woogie," and "Lady Be Good" for Vocalion Records, which called the co-op Smith-Jones, Incorporated. Basie then added trumpeters Joe Keyes and Buck Clayton, trombonists George Hunt and Dan Minor, alto players Jack Washington and Caughey Roberts, tenor-sax players Herschel Evans, and guitarist Claude Williams. The new Count Basie Orchestra had filled dates only in Chicago and Buffalo before the Roseland gig. By January 1937, the Basie crew would launch a big recording career for Decca with "Pennies from Heaven," "Swinging at the Daisy Chain," "Honeysuckle Rose," and the aptly named "Roseland Shuffle." But success came slowly for both the Herman and the Basie bands.

"We were definitely not a hit in the Roseland," the thirty-two-year-old Basie said. "Another new band was also there, led by this young guy Woody Herman. He and his guys had been there a few weeks so they knew what it was all about, and they were playing their things cool. They knew exactly what they were doing, and Woody was helpful and generous to me. 'Just take it easy,' he said, 'just relax if you can, and everything will be all right. Just don't worry about it too much.'"[23]

It irritated Basie, though, when Reeves "used to grab me every time I'd come offstage, sweating like hell, and saying something like, 'Hey, what you sweating for, man? . . . Stop working so hard.' I wanted to kill him. We just thought we'd go in there and play our behind off, lay on them, play hard. But the people didn't know what we were doing. It was a bitch."[24] Basie implied that Herman, with his relaxed style, excelled at crowd-pleasing—not jazz. But long after his own place in the jazz hall of fame was secure, Basie became a musical conservative, rarely straying from what had worked for him in the beginning. Herman in contrast, always risked income and popularity by breaking new musical ground—surprising and at times repelling fans.

Simon's recollections of 1930s bandleaders depict a fascinating and diverse group of artists: the moody, introspective, yet sometimes immensely warm Goodman; the wild and witty Tommy Dorsey; brother Jimmy Dorsey, more relaxed and self-deprecating. Then there was Shaw, who was "bright, garrulous and self-centered," and the "charming, urbane, self-assured . . . Ellington." Herman and Basie, he said, were in many ways alike—relaxed, receptive, and exceptionally considerate of those around them.[25]

As 1937 arrived, the future was bright for the high-school dropout from Milwaukee. His school had been the stage, the road, the spotlights, the paying public. He had learned how to hire and fire, program shows, sing and play, arrange, compose, audition, keep books, and emcee. He had been trained in the intricacies of publicity, travel arrangements and logistics, radio broadcasting, and the recording industry. And he had accumulated a legion of helpful friends and contacts. Woody Herman and His Orchestra were ready.

chapter two

the BAND *that* PLAYED *the* BLUES

*a*fter the Roseland openings and the first broadcasts and Decca record-ings, Woody Herman's band remained intact for nearly a year. Its co-op nature and Herman's friendliness promoted unity, a rare commodity in traveling bands.

Musical conservatism dictated those first Decca decisions, but that was common. Basie had to record the motion picture hit "Pennies from Heaven" and "The Glory of Love," reflecting neither the spirit nor talent of his band. Like Herman, Basie did not yet have the stature to dictate his terms and thus agreed to record bland popular tunes so as to be able to record jazz with such skilled soloists as Evans, Young, and Clayton. It was the same with Tommy Dorsey, who also recorded a flock of short-lived pieces. For Dorsey and Basie, though, acclaim was near, and with fame they would gain more control over what they could record. In late January 1937, Dorsey's rising band, inspired for a few weeks by the dazzling but booze-loving solo trumpeter Bunny Berigan, recorded the smash hits "Marie" and "Song of India." And just ahead for Basie was his masterpiece with Decca, "One O'Clock Jump."

Metronome magazine, a swing music monthly, gave the Herman co-op its first mention in January 1937; Simon reviewed the band's New York Roseland appearance, grading it A-minus (while giving a B to Basie's crew). It impressed Simon that Herman had so soon acquired radio time. Radio helped any new band build a following. For those buying ballroom tickets, records, or sheet music, airtime implied, however incorrectly, that a band was good.

Simon regarded the band's book, or repertoire, of arrangements as thin but growing. Bishop, Hupfer, Reeves, Jenkins, Diaz, and the freelancers Claude Thornhill and Dave Torbett had hurriedly beefed it up after the summer of 1936. Herman rated the band "an excellent staff, especially in view of the fact that we could not afford to pay for arrangements." Simon realized that the band was "scuffling"—that is, was low on money. Still, he rated the saxophones "good," the overall sound "excellent," the musicianship "good," the rhythm section "plenty fine." And Bishop's flugelhorn "really makes the brass section because of its range [and] broad tonal qualities." Simon had high praise for Herman: "Woody plays tempos that are danceable and never too extreme. [The band makes] a good appearance, and possesses an excellent front man in Herman. He's a clean-cut looking lad with a nice smile. He sings nicely and plays good clarinet; and he's a gentleman and all-around nice guy. This Herman outfit bears watching."[1]

"I think Joe Bishop probably influenced that band most," Herman recalled. "We became [for promotional purposes] 'The Band That Plays the Blues' and that was [the influence of] Joe Bishop all the way. Neal Reid made the excitement. Frank Carlson played drums with abandon. Walt Yoder was the father confessor."[2]

Musicians always prefer playing their own choices of music, striving for unique sounds and styles. In Herman's case, the choice was blues. But unless and until they could gain fans and dollars with a hit record, they lay at the mercy of public taste. Promoters, agents, and hall owners all tended to request mainstream numbers, which true jazz players condemned as "cornball."

But then the leader with a hit record faces a dilemma: whether to continue to play new material and grow creatively or to cater to a nostalgic public's requests to hear the old hits again. Jazz players are in some ways harmed by success: a hit brings in the money needed to live, but repeating the same thing chokes creativity. A balance must be struck.

With the security that steady work, radio time, Simon's A-minus, and stable personnel bring, Herman's band sounded considerably looser in the Decca recordings made April 26, 1937. This time their sound was more distinctly rooted in jazz—"Dupree Blues," "Doctor Jazz," "Trouble in Mind," and "It Happened in Dixieland." "Doctor Jazz," Jelly Roll Morton's musical telephone call, interpreted and sung by Herman, was good enough to merit reissue fifty-four years later in a Decca album by "legendary masters." Herman soloed on clarinet, and Reid did on trombone. The fourteen men played what one critic called a "New Orleans-cum-vaudeville" style.[3] The song about Dupree, who robbed a jewelry store to give his Betty a diamond ring, featured Herman in a novelty-song vein, while "Trouble in Mind" was a blues vocal.

Herman's band finished its gig at the New York Roseland a week after making these records and throughout the spring and summer played one-nighters, mixed with longer stints at the Normandie Ballroom in Boston, the Willows in Pittsburgh, the Nicollet Hotel in Minneapolis, the Trianon in Cleveland, and the Netherlands Plaza in Cincinnati. The band played at Guy Hunt's Ocean Pier in Wildwood, New Jersey, for a week in July 1937. There on July 4, Herman struck up an acquaintance with J. William "Jack" Siefert, a local from near Philadelphia, during intermission. Siefert, a nineteen-year-old band junkie, was a neighbor of Herman's aunt, Pauline Traub, who had moved from Milwaukee. "Every afternoon," Siefert said, "the band played right on the beach to drum up business for the evening. It built a real strong following, and was held over for a second week and, eventually, for the summer."[4] Siefert, who later became an electrical designer and one of Herman's closest friends, began collecting Hermania—records, articles, reviews—and keeping files, indexes, and scrapbooks. "Whenever I want to know anything about Woody Herman," Herman once kidded on a Larry King radio interview, "I call Jack Siefert down in Philadelphia."[5]

The management and booking contract with General Artists Corporation was of little or no help to the struggling band. Both Herman and Miller were threadbare GAC clients in 1937. "I was twenty four and optimistic," Herman said, "Glenn was older and sour. He had already blown a ton of money with three bands, and was full of sad stories. GAC apparently didn't think much of either of us at that point."[6] But Cy and

Charlie Shribman did. Guardian angels in the swing band business of the 1930s, they had started in the 1920s running a ballroom. Both loved music and appreciated musicians. When they found new bands in which they believed, they booked, financed, and otherwise encouraged them. Sometimes this meant booking them for ballrooms in their own growing chain so that the bands would have enough work to keep going. They booked Herman's band for five more weeks back in the Normandie.

By August 10, the next recording date for Decca, some charter members of the band had begun to leave the co-op. Newcomers Dean Kincaide, an alto sax player and arranger with several name bands, and pianist Tommy Linehan helped the most to fill the gaps. The Decca recordings—of the popular ballads "Stardust on the Moon," "Lady from Fifth Avenue," "Don't You Know, or Don't You Care?" and "Double or Nothing"—still showed the band's lack of distinction. With none of the fiery soloists it would later acquire and with its bland repertoire, it sounded like so many other bands. But Herman remained determined. One fan recalled that "Woody was willing to take the band anywhere" in order to make ends meet. The rhythm section, at least in Richard Gehman's judgment, was its main selling point. Linehan, Gehman wrote in the *Saturday Review,* played piano "like an Irishman who had deserted his folk permanently," while "Carlson knew how to make the brass section obedient to his beat," and "Yoder laid down the law on the bass line."[7]

On September 23 in New York City, the band recorded sixteen tunes for a company called World Transcriptions. As with the co-op's Decca deal, Herman recorded this material for a flat fee. With transcriptions, recordings made specifically for sale to radio stations, the pay usually amounted to about five hundred dollars, somewhat less than for commercial recordings. Station program managers liked having a backlog of such inexpensive music with which to fill air time and provide program variety. But for bandleaders, there was only money in it, no fame. World assigned Herman the pseudonym Wally Hayes because of his contract with Decca. Thus air play of Wally Hayes's music did nothing to promote the band, but it did help him to meet his payroll. Bands of that era contained mostly eager young men, not unlike struggling young painters or actors, leading a nomadic, nocturnal, low-pay existence—full-time work when a band was clicking, but always with the threat of layoffs ahead. It was a way of life that frequently complicated, prevented, or ruined family life, home-owning, car-owning, even casual romance.

Herman's choices for his World Transcriptions debut—a blend of ballads and "swing" tunes arranged by Bishop, Hupfer, and Kincaide—provide a useful survey of the Herman band's arrangements, strengths (rhythm section and ensemble playing, Herman's singing), and weaknesses (unimpressive soloists, except for Herman on clarinet and Reid on trombone). They also suggest the various moods that Herman sought to create with the hope that "somebody digs it." "Exactly like You," "Am I in Love?" "Remember Me?" "That Old Feeling," "Old Man Moon," "In the Still of the Night," "Stardust on the Moon," "Can't We Be Friends?" "Dream in My Heart," and "Squeeze Me" were the latest romantic ballads, played at easy dance tempos. Sweet ensemble music by the band introduced Herman's pleasant singing, with a debt to Columbo. The best bands created varying moods by playing sweet and hot music, and with humor in novelty numbers. Herman's young band was perfecting all three styles. The band performed "Jazz Me Blues," "Muskrat Ramble," "Ain't Misbehavin'," "Weary Blues," and "Someday Sweetheart" at more fun-loving tempos and with a general Dixieland feel.

In a totally different style was Hupfer's arrangement of the "Meditation from 'Thais,'" by the French composer Jules Massenet, featuring Hupfer himself on the violin. Several mid-1930s arrangers had converted classical music themes into swing band material. Tommy Dorsey's band had performed and recorded Nikolai Rimsky-Korsakov's "Song of India," Anton Rubinstein's "Melody in F," Franz Liszt's "Liebestraum," Felix Mendelssohn's "Spring Song," and Antonín Dvořák's "Humoresque" in 1937. Thus Herman's band was right in step with the times.

Rockwell-O'Keefe advertised in *Down Beat* magazine—a rival to *Metronome*—that Herman's was "one of America's great future bands." The publicity firm now labeled it "The Band That Plays the Blues." In one

1937 photo, the fourteen clean-shaven men in black tuxedoes and starched white shirts resemble a college glee club. Thirteen of them are wearing black bow ties, and Herman a white one.

By October 25, 1937, after Kincaide had moved on to play and write for Bob Crosby's band, a Decca recording session by Herman produced the ballads "I Double Dare You," "Why Talk about Love?" "My Fine Feathered Friend," and "You're a Sweetheart." On November 23, in a novelty mood, the band recorded "Let's Pitch a Little Woo," "I Wanna Be in Winchell's Column," "Loch Lomond," and "Broadway's Gone Hawaii." In terms of record sales, however, Herman was barely treading water. Nothing that he and Decca had agreed to record thus far ever reached hit, best-seller, or even top-ten status. At a second session for World Transcriptions in November, the "Wally Hayes" band recorded sixteen more numbers—ballads, hot pieces, and novelty vocal tunes.

Formal shot of the full Herman band, about 1938. Frankie Carlson is on drums, Walter Yoder on bass, and Herman is directing. (Courtesy Ingrid Herman Reese)

In assessing the band's progress after its first year on the basis of this World Transcriptions recording, we see its imitative nature and its need for jazz solo talent. Goodman's roaring 1937 band could turn loose solo trumpeters James, Chris Griffin, and Ziggy Elman, and showy drummer Krupa, trombonist Joe Harris, pianist Jess Stacey, and Goodman on clarinet. Tommy Dorsey could present saxophonists Freeman and Skeets Herfurt, trumpeter Charlie Spivak, drummer Mo Purtill, and his own silky, pitch-perfect trombone. But Herman lacked that high quality from his "sidemen," as rank-and-file bandsmen were called. Furthermore, the World sessions marked the violin's farewell to Herman's music. Hupfer returned to Milwaukee, his hometown, where later, as Nick Harper, he led a big band. The violin became a little-used luxury in 1930s bands.

Continuing in its quasi-Dixieland style and with soloists of limited ability and a growing book of standards, ballads, and novelties, Herman's band stayed tolerably popular because of his singing. By now the band had made dozens of records and would make many more. But working for Decca at a time when the company assigned the best songs to Bing Crosby, Louis Armstrong, or Ella Fitzgerald, the best swing numbers to Basie, and other good band material to Bob Crosby meant that Herman's co-op groped with such second-rate tunes as "I Wanna Be in Winchell's Column" (a reference to New York syndicated columnist and radio reporter Walter Winchell).

There are many parallels between Herman's band and Bob Crosby's Bobcats. They were of the same size and played with a merry Dixieland lilt, and in terms of voice, Crosby and Herman were virtually indistinguishable. Both leaders were personable, relaxed, versatile. Whatever edge Herman might gain by doubling on clarinet Crosby matched by being Bing's brother. Having started with Decca in the spring of 1935, by the end of 1937 Crosby had recorded eighty-some numbers, including the big sellers "The Dixieland Band," "Little Rock Getaway," and "South Rampart Street Parade." Moreover, Crosby's band could boast such accomplished and popular soloists as Yank Lawson (trumpet), Eddie Miller and Gil Rodin (saxes), Matty Matlock (clarinet), Ray Bauduc (drums), Bobby Haggart (bass), Nappy LaMare (guitar), Warren Smith (trombone), and Bob Zurke (piano). At the beginning of 1938, Herman's band remained stuck a rung or two below Crosby's and several others, while every day more bands stepped onto the ladder, anxious to reach the top. "We became the house unit for Decca," Herman later complained, "having to record any tune that was a hit on another label."[8] At least he had company: Glenn Miller, still two years away from fame and with a going-nowhere fifteen-piece outfit, recorded "My Fine Feathered Friend" for Brunswick Records the same week that Herman did for Decca.

Goodman and Tommy Dorsey led the top bands in 1937. But then in July 1938, Shaw, after experimenting with material and instrumentation for three years, recorded the hit "Begin the Beguine" for RCA's budget-priced Bluebird Records and stayed on top into the 1940s. Bob Crosby and Larry Clinton remained fan favorites, too. Meanwhile Herman's nose-to-the-grindstone band played where it could find a crowd.

Herman's band opened February 17, 1938, at the Hotel Schroeder in Milwaukee, starting a tour of many short bookings. On April 14, it recorded "Calliope Blues," "Twin City Blues," "Carolina in the Morning," and "Saving Myself for You." A novelty, "Laughing Boy Blues," which featured composer Sonny Skylar as a guest (performing laughing-in-tempo spasms with the band's blues backing) was rejected. "Twin City Blues," by Jenkins and Bishop, came off as a bright instrumental with pleasant ensembles broken by solos from Herman (clarinet), Mansfield (tenor sax) and Bishop (trumpet). In "Calliope Blues," Herman played clarinet in a reed-and-flute segment and sang, spoke, and hummed homage to "that ol' CAL-ee-ope man," whose circus music chased the blues away. After a recording session on June 8, an improved version of "Laughing Boy Blues" as well as the smoothly swinging "Lullaby in Rhythm," the ballad "Don't Wake up My Heart," and the jumping novelty "Flat Foot Floogie" reached the nation's record shops. Live bookings that summer included the popular Dunbar Cave (really a cave), near Clarksville, Tennessee, on August 2.

Guitarist Hy White joined the band in another flurry of changes before a Decca session on December 22, 1938. "Indian Boogie Woogie," an attempt to cash in on an eight-beats-to-the-bar craze that stretched to the 1940s, and "Blue Evening"—soon to be a Glenn Miller romantic hit—resulted. Because boogie-woogie featured rhythm piano, Linehan opened and closed "Indian Boogie Woogie." Herman, Reid, and Mansfield soloed, the sections exchanged a few riffs,[9] then let Linehan finish in a minor key, which was presumably intended to add "Indian" mystique.

At the December 22, 1938, session for Decca, a sextet composed of Herman, Bishop, Linehan, White, Yoder, and Carlson also recorded for the first time as The Woodchoppers. The band-within-a band was by then quite common, as in Isham Jones's Juniors. Goodman was pleasing crowds and selling records with both trio and quartet numbers in 1938, and Tommy Dorsey at times rested half of his big band, leaving the Clam-bake Seven standing for Dixieland tunes. The Woodchoppers were formed perhaps to give fans program variety but also to promote soloists. For their recording of "Riverbed Blues," White and Herman, credited as co-composers, provided guitar, clarinet, and vocal touches to this slow, low-down blues. At Decca's behest, Herman's entire band also accompanied the promising Broadway singing starlet Mary Martin on "Who'll Buy My Violets?" and "Listen to the Mocking Bird." White's arrival as the band's guitarist proved important: the rhythm section of Linehan, Yoder, Carlson, and White stayed together while other bands suffered turnover. The four steadily improved, driving and lifting Herman's band and combos for five years.

Herman's motion picture debut occurred in New York in 1938. Warner Brothers filmed a black-and-white *Woody Herman and His Orchestra* short filler for movie houses. The band performed "Carolina in the Morning" and "You Must Have Been a Beautiful Baby" with Herman singing, plus "Two Little Girls in Love," "Jail House Blues," and "Doctor Jazz." This began a decade of bland movies for Herman, alone or with one of his bands. He admitted years later: "There weren't any I want to brag about."[10]

On January 10, 1939, Herman accepted a "house band" job at Decca to help him survive financially. He and his men accompanied an-other of the recording company's star-quality vocalists, Connee Boswell, formerly with a sister act and now working solo, on "Umbrella Man," "They Say," "Thanks for Ev'rything," and "Deep in a Dream." Two weeks later, it backed Martin on "The Maids of Cadiz" and "Il Bacio (The Kiss)" and the Andrews Sisters on "Begin the Beguine" and "Long Time No See"—all "house band" jobs that Herman took to survive financially.

That winter Herman reevaluated the band's music and decided that Bob Crosby was playing better Dixieland, and his own band wasn't in the same league with Lunceford or Ellington as far as jazz or swing was concerned, but it played the blues well. Indeed, the band sometimes took its characterization as the "Band That Plays the Blues" too literally. When it worked Frank Dailey's Meadowbrook ballroom in New Jersey (for which it once received a lowly six hundred dollars for a week in 1938), it filled a remote low-watt radio show almost entirely with blues. Radio stations broadcast dance band programs live from such venues as the Meadowbrook, especially on weekend nights—if they could sell enough commercials to sustain them. Bands received no extra pay for such one-time radio shows in those days, but leaders prized them for their promotional value. Radio helped them sell tickets to future performances and plug their newest recordings. A full program of blues, however, "*was* a little strong," Herman admitted.[11] Simon noted that in fact the early 1939 band struggled on several fronts: with its nonrhythm personnel, its musical focus, its acceptance by the public, and its strong competition from Shaw, Goodman, the Crosbys, the Dorseys, and others.

Herman's stubbornness about artistic integrity impeded the band's success, too. Simon said Herman's was "a loud band, and it wouldn't play rhumbas or sambas or anything except what it wanted to play."[12] And in Houston, Texas, the insensitive manager of the Rice Hotel sent a note to the bandstand: "You will kindly stop singing and playing those nigger blues."[13] Whether at Cincinnati's Netherlands-Plaza, Detroit's Eastwood Gardens, or the Hotel Schroeder in Milwaukee, public reaction amounted to indifference.

Still the "Band That Plays the Blues" pressed on. It introduced "Blues Upstairs," "Blues Downstairs," "Casbah Blues," and its theme song, Bishop's "Blue Prelude." This was what Herman and his friends *wanted* to play. But there were still no hits to inject passion into passive crowds. Jobs became shorter and fewer. By the spring of 1939, the co-op band was flirting with bankruptcy.

In the spring of 1939, Glenn Miller's band struck it rich. "Moonlight Serenade," "Sunrise Serenade," and "Little Brown Jug" became the first of its many hit records. In Glen Island Casino, north of New York City, Miller's band wowed dancers until September. He then thrilled fans with a Carnegie Hall concert and hotel and theater jobs. A *Moonlight Serenade* program hit network radio. A more lucrative record deal, steady bookings at soaring fees, films, and fame followed at stunning speed. It could be done.

But Herman needed more time. He was tempted to give up in 1939, having been canceled his first night in a Chicago hotel for playing "too loud and too fast." But then Goldfarb, Mirenburg, and Vallon moved in. The New York lawyers, who acted as agents for theater acts, heard "The Band That Plays the Blues." When Herman "Chubby" Goldfarb heard bandsmen tuning up on a Bach concerto, he exclaimed to his partners Mary Mirenburg and Mike Vallon: "This is good!" The firm soon began managing Herman's band for the going percentage of gross revenue. Often bands resorted to working dance halls or cabarets owned by lowlifes who would cheat and lie or press for kickbacks. But strong agents could supply both legal and business savvy, which the trusting Herman in some ways lacked, and which GAC had never been willing to wield on Herman's behalf. Right away, Goldfarb, Mirenburg, and Vallon pushed GAC to book more jazz jobs, starting with one at the Blue Note in New York City.

To make the band more marketable, Herman, whose fourth trumpet player brought the total to fourteen members in January, added Sharri Kaye, who was succeeded by Mary Ann McCall in March. A female vocalist widened the range of sights, sounds, and moods that a band could create. In the 1920s, Whiteman had featured Mildred Bailey. In 1934, Goodman presented Helen Ward and a train of successors. By 1939 the field had exploded to include Edythe Wright (with Tommy Dorsey), Bea Wain (Clinton), Marion Hutton (Glenn Miller), Peg LaCentra and then Helen Forrest (Shaw), Marion Mann (Bob Crosby), Helen Humes (Basie), Fitzgerald (Chick Webb), Ivie Anderson (Ellington), June Richmond and then Helen O'Connell (Jimmy Dorsey), and Judy Ellington (Charlie Barnet).

Blue Note patrons would have liked Herman's band, even had it offered no singing. For two years the players had jammed on a series of simple unwritten riffs. Now Herman and Bishop put them on paper for the Blue Note job. The resulting number combined ensemble and section parts, horn solos, and a stretch in which the rhythm section motored along Basie-style. Yoder, inspired by a wood-chopping contest in a sportsmen's show in Boston, named it "(At the) Woodchoppers' Ball." On April 12, 1939, the band recorded it and four other tunes. "Woodchoppers' Ball" became its most requested number; and with this success, Herman began to sip champagne with Glenn Miller.

Horace Stedham "Steady" Nelson had joined the trumpet section for this session, which also featured "Dallas Blues," "Blues Upstairs," and "Blues Downstairs" and McCall singing the inane "Big Wig in the Wigwam." Not yet twenty, McCall had worked with Buddy Morrow's band in her hometown of Philadelphia, and with Tommy Dorsey for a while in 1938. Nelson, a Duke Ellington devotee, added both vocal and "growl" trumpet talent to the Herman band. With its cheerful riff-ensemble foundation, "Dallas Blues" was quite similar to "Woodchoppers' Ball." Herman, Mansfield, and Reid soloed. (At this session, Herman recorded identical clarinet solo phrases in "Woodchoppers' Ball" and "Dallas Blues," a real gaffe for jazz soloists. But the band played so well on both records that Herman let it pass.)

Bishop and Herman collaborated to compose "Blues Upstairs" and "Blues Downstairs," which were alike only in Linehan's piano intros, and which emphasized soloists Herman, Mansfield, White, and Reid instead of full-ensemble playing. In "Blues Downstairs," Nelson responded to Herman's singing with asides intended to be comically imitative of African American dialect. Carlson employed noticeable tom-tomming to suggest "Indian" music in "Big Wig in the Wigwam." A Carlson-Yoder drums-bass duet presaged the same effects obtained by Bauduc and Haggart in Bob Crosby's 1940 runaway hit, "Big Noise from Winnetka." Sounds of good cheer by the ensemble, emphatic soloing, rhythmic undertones, dialect lines, and duets all signaled new styles for Herman's band, changes that were leading to a wider variety in its repertoire.

At first Herman shrugged off the success of "Woodchoppers' Ball." To him it was mere filler. But fans kept buying the record and requesting it in live performances. So Decca went on pressing copies, and in three years sold about two million. "Woodchoppers' Ball"—along with Goldfarb, Mirenburg, and Vallon's representation, brought bigger crowds and better promotion and bookings. Herman eased into an "Ol' Woodchopper" persona with the press and on radio. The band returned to the Meadowbrook at higher pay. And Decca welcomed it anytime, now that it had the hit "Woodchoppers' Ball" on its hands. It gave Decca something to promote and gave Herman more say about what he recorded, a leap forward in his artistic freedom.

On May 24, 1939, the band made "Paleface," "The Sheik of Araby," "Casbah Blues," and "Farewell Blues." "Casbah Blues," with its slow, exotic beat and Herman's soft, warbling clarinet playing in the lower register, laid the blues foundation for his future theme song, "Blue Flame." Herman approached "Sheik of Araby" as a rhythm number for Linehan, Yoder, Carlson, Reid, Mansfield, Nelson, and clarinet solos, continuing his trend away from full-band playing. And then the band did star, in "Farewell Blues," which it played at the fast, frantic tempo that qualified the number as a "flag-waver," in 1930s jargon. Although eclipsed by "Woodchoppers' Ball," "Farewell Blues," with its solos by Herman, Mansfield, Reid, and Nelson, is an impressive ensemble-band piece. In summer radio broadcasts from the Meadowbrook, the band also played "D-flat Blues," and Herman sang the new ballads "Grateful" and "But It Didn't Mean a Thing," while McCall gamely warbled such fluff as "At a Little Hot Dog Stand."

Now that money wasn't quite so tight, Herman began buying charts—written arrangements—from free-lance writers. For example, the band recorded Bob McDonald's "East Side Kick" and Zilmer Randolph's "Jumpin' Blues" for Decca on July 18, 1939. Bright ensemble passages, solos by Herman, Mansfield, Nelson, and Reid, and a brief clarinet-drum duet pepped up "East Side Kick" before a full-band riff ending. "Jumpin' Blues," on which Herman also sang, is a sample of the forty-one-year-old Randolph's crisp writing for the brass instruments. A conservatory-trained trumpeter from Arkansas, Randolph had crossed paths with Herman back in Milwaukee, where Randolph was playing in Bernie Young's band from 1927 to 1931. Over the next four years, he played trumpet backup and arranged for Armstrong, for whom he composed "Ol' Man Mose." Living in Chicago in 1939, Randolph also was writing for Hines, Duke Ellington, Fletcher Henderson, and other leaders. Bishop arranged the instrumental "Midnight Echoes" and "Big Morning," which contained vocals for Herman and Nelson. Fifteen days later the band recorded songs featuring the vocal talents of McCall in "Love Me" and "Love with a Capital 'You,'" Nelson in "Rosetta," and Herman in "Still the Bluebird Sings."

*G*ermany's invasion of Poland on September 1, 1939, started World War II. Far-off war affected American big-band life, song writing, and public taste slowly at first. Business as usual prevailed, but anxious eyes scanned daily headlines from the war zones.

By the end of the summer, as "Woodchoppers' Ball" kept making friends, Herman followed Glenn Miller into Glen Island Casino, then played the Panther Room in Chicago's Hotel Sherman, the New Yorker Hotel, and the Famous Door (the Blue Note's neighbor on Fifty-second Street). With band profits he hired Toby Tyler to team with Reid on trombones. Tyler, who had been with Krupa's band for a while and with Glenn Miller's briefly, gave Herman a sixth brass player, and thus more power and harmonic range. Tyler played lead trombone—the written, mainstream trombone part—for nearly a year for Herman, and Herman went on hiring other lead players to free Reid for jazz improvisations in his solos.

But there were still setbacks. Barnet, needing a replacement for Judy Ellington in his fifteen-member band in late 1939, hired McCall away from Herman. McCall was sax player Barnet's only vocalist, so he gave McCall more and better songs than Herman did. She sang on the first five records that Barnet made for Bluebird in December and on twenty-one more before leaving his group in mid-1940. Herman replaced McCall with Elsa Harris for a few weeks. Still mixing pop songs with jazz pieces at his Decca sessions, Herman recorded "This Changing World" and "It's My Turn Now" on November 20.

Carol Kaye replaced Harris, and Carroll "Cappy" Lewis joined the trumpet line beginning with a Decca session on December 13. From it came "Smarty Pants," "The Rhumba Jumps," "Peace, Brother!" "Love's Got Me Down," and "Blues on Parade." Hats and mutes for the brass, cowbells tapped by Carlson, section passages, Lewis's trumpet solo, better soloing by Mansfield, and Yoder's strong, clear bass marked this performance of "Blues on Parade," played with the loose, happy feel of "Dallas Blues" and "Woodchoppers' Ball." Tyler adapted the number from composer Gioacchino Rossini's 1842 "Stabat Mater," which was used for a time in Roman Catholic churches as Good Friday music. Some church purists urged Herman and Decca to take the record off the market.

War in Europe and China and the brief row over "Blues on Parade" made irony of the title "Peace, Brother!" a brassy ain't-you-glad-you're-livin' number starring Herman's singing with a choir of sidemen. "The Rhumba Jumps" was a Hoagy Carmichael novelty. Carol Kaye starred on "Smarty Pants" and "Love's Got Me Down." Despite being seemingly mired in such average or less-than-average new material, Herman and his band could see signs of rising popularity. By the end of 1939, it had risen to twelfth in the "sweet" category, seventh in "swing," and seventh in "best-band" in the fan magazine *Metronome*'s annual poll.

As 1940 arrived, an early January recording session produced more run-of-the-mill fare: "Careless," "Wouldja Mind," "Pick-a-Rib," and "It's a Blue World." And yet the sound of the band reflected a widening range of talents. "Pick-a-Rib" featured another glee club of band singers, something that Herman and his fans seemed to like. In "It's a Blue World," the saxes played in the smooth, seamless legato fashion polished and popularized by Glenn Miller's reed section, and one could hear White's clear, twinkling guitar notes coming through.

For Herman's band, as well as for the other recording bands, the numbers released as commercial records constituted but a small fraction of the entire book. Many Herman tunes went unrecorded; perhaps he did not think they would be commercial enough, or they relied on visual impact from onstage for their success, or the chart ran too long for the three minutes allowed on recordings, or a contract or the record company limited the number of recordings the band would make. In Herman's case, for instance, his NBC radio broadcast from the Famous Door on January 7 featured four numbers never made into records: "Choppin' Wood," "Faithful Forever," "In an Old Dutch Garden," and "South of the Border." On January 16 the band recorded "On the Isle of May," "Thank Your Stars," "Do I Love You?" and the novelty "Say 'Si Si.'" "Isle of May" came from Peter Ilich Tchaikovsky's String Quartet in D Major. "Thank Your Stars" featured Carol Kaye. "Do I Love You?" with its high register, was a strain for Herman's voice. The chart also contained muted brass and clarinet-led reed passages like Miller's. Herman applied a fast instrumental treatment to "Say 'Si Si,'" a vocal tune in the hands of other artists.

Most bands averaged three or four tunes per session. But Herman's studio session of February 5 produced six: "Give a Little Whistle," "The Sky Fell Down," "Peach Tree Street," "Blue Prelude," "Cousin to Chris," and "Blue Ink." A cornball arrangement—dreaded by jazz players and rare in the Herman book—stocked with whistling, cartoonish clarinet toots, and even some cow-belling by Carlson, temporarily lowered Herman's stature as a jazzman in "Give a Little Whistle." In recording it he clearly was going for another hit by capitalizing on this widely hummed number from Walt Disney's movie *Pinocchio*. And while the effort fell short of hopes in terms of sales, it did display Herman singing for the first time on record in the relaxed style of Bing Crosby. Jenkins and Bishop had composed "Blue Prelude" for Isham Jones, and Herman made it his own band's theme song in 1936. For the recording, Herman now called for dirge tempo and tried singing of pain and anguish, something he never mastered. Randolph's lively "Cousin to Chris" contained section interplay and solos by Nelson, Linehan, and Carlson. On the surface, this song was routine. But as the band gained size and flair, there were significant changes. "Cousin to Chris" stressed dynamics—a strength of such 1940 bands as Duke Ellington's, Glen Gray's, Glenn Miller's, and Lunceford's—to create moods and moments of "swing." Bishop's "Blue Ink" featured the trombones punching out basement-level notes, Nelson, Linehan, and White in solos, and smooth reeds. Herman played a few short alto saxophone notes, breaking in an engraved gold Selmer. Arrangers could now write in solo parts for Herman's alto sax or clarinet or blend him with the other reed players.

Following a February–March stand in the Sherman Hotel in Chicago, the band moved into the Meadowbrook in April. Dillagene Plumb—stage name Dillagene—now sang in place of Carol Kaye. The band made four recordings on April 10, 1940. Randolph's version of "Deep Night" featured muted brass, Herman's clarinet, and solos by Nelson, White, and Reid. Randolph's "Whistle Stop"—a medium-tempo blues—contained soft ensemble riffs similar to "Slow Freight," which Glenn Miller recorded the week before. Randolph's "Herman at the Sherman," built of simple riffs, saluted the hotel that hired name bands in Chicago. The band sounded crisp, relaxed, and happy, an indication of its building momentum.

Herman and Nelson shared the vocal on Bishop's "Bessie's Blues," parts of which were in Nelson's falsetto African American dialect ("hush yo' mouf, hush yo' mouf"). Such elements were not uncommon in 1930s show biz, where matters of race were oppressive and sometimes contradictory. Although the African American Randolph frequently wrote arrangements for "The Band That Plays the Blues," the performers themselves were all white. The races mixed rarely in the big-name bands of that era. Certain riverboat bands had been mixed; Goodman presented the black musicians Henderson, Fitzgerald, Lionel Hampton, and Teddy Wilson; and black saxophone star Benny Carter sat in with Barnet. But the top bands of Tommy Dorsey, Bob Crosby, and Glenn Miller remained all white, while those of Lunceford, Basie, Webb, and Duke Ellington were black bands. Few leaders of either race crossed the color line much in hiring performers. But writers could work "safely" offstage, out of the spotlight. Goodman bought many charts from Henderson; and Tommy Dorsey in 1939 outbid Lunceford for ace arranger Sy Oliver.

"Hush yo mouf" lyrics, however offensive they are today, are a product of their times. Such tunes and lyrics as in "Bessie's Blues"—or others in songs about Hispanics ("Funny Little Pedro") or Native Americans ("Big Wig in the Wigwam") or Asians—may have amused some whites. But World War II united all races of Americans in a life-or-death effort for common survival and consequently heightened sensitivity to such questionable humor. Songwriters poked fun at other ethnic groups far less after the war.

Comparing jazz played by black and white musicians has long tempted writers. In *The Swing Era,* Schuller devotes chapters to Goodman (white), Armstrong (black), and Duke Ellington (black). His chapter "The Great Black Bands" runs 163 pages; "The White Bands" (minus the word "Great") is 148 pages. Schuller colored Herman unique. He regarded Herman—as player, singer, and leader—to be at times as influential as anyone in jazz. His contributions were "generally ignored or suppressed"; but "had Herman and his orchestra been black, the verdict would be quite different [for it was] Woody's dilemma that, being white but knowing and deeply feeling that all the important innovative and creative impulses in jazz derived from black sources, he received little appreciation for striving to pay tribute to those sources."[14]

The four-year-old Herman band of 1940 still played it safe, however. While some charts did contain breaks for horn solos, many listeners typed it as a "singer's band," or at best an "ensemble band." Subtly, though, change continued. It was evident in the works by new talents such as Randolph, and in odd titles: "Laughing Boy Blues," "At the Woodchoppers' Ball," and "Cousin to Chris." Soon came "Jukin'" and "Get Your Boots Laced, Papa." "Jukin'" was a speed-of-light riff piece by freelancer Bob Mersey. Linehan, Herman, Nelson, Mansfield, Reid, and Carlson soloed before

Sidemen from the "Band That Plays the Blues" in February 1940: Neal Reid, trombone; Joe Bishop, flugelhorn; Cappy Lewis, cornet; and Nick Caiazza, tenor sax. (Courtesy Duncan P. Schiedt)

a full-ensemble coda at the fastest tempo that Herman had yet recorded. Different still was "Get Your Boots Laced, Papa," from Bishop and Herman, which ran more than five minutes long. They divided this good-humored piece into two parts with a rhythm-section interval. "Blues Upstairs" and "Blues Downstairs" had been separate pieces linked by related titles and piano intros, but "Get Your Boots Laced, Papa" was one piece broken only by the three-minute limit to one side of a record. Herman and a few sidemen sang while Linehan, Lewis, Mansfield, Yoder, and Reid soloed. Carlson's drum fills and sections over which Herman's clarinet soared marked this relaxed reprise of "Woodchoppers' Ball." Herman's "don't be an ick from Battle Crick" lyrics brought many a smile.

When the band recorded on May 14, 1940, Herman sang "You Think of Ev'rything," "Where Do I Go from You?" "(Can This Be) The End of the Rainbow?" "Mister Meadowlark," and "I'll Pray for You." Romantic tempos prevailed with these tunes. At this period of the band's career, every recording session seemed to result in more innovations. Yoder boldly played the four-beat-per-measure rhythm in "You Think of Every-thing." The rhythm section sounded smoother and the band fuller and surer as it pulled away from its old two-beat Dixieland style. The legato reeds and full ensemble sparkled in "Where Do I Go from You?" while Reid's statement of the "Mister Meadowlark" theme imitated Tommy Dorsey's skill with the muted trombone. Singing in a lower register, Herman mimicked less and created more.

The May 18 issue of *Billboard* contained a story headlined "Herman, the Coming Band," rating him the top contender to take over Goodman's "King of Swing" title. During the summer, for program variety, Herman chose Linehan, Yoder, and Carlson to join him as the Woody Herman Quartet. The four broadcast such numbers as "Going Away Blues" and "Roll 'Em, Pete" in August, when the band started a sixty-day engagement at the Hotel New Yorker. The hotel advertised it as Herman's first big hotel date in the New York area. Late in the Hotel New Yorker job, the band was selected to play the Harvest Moon Ball in Madison Square Garden; and after the hotel job they played for several weeks in the Strand Theater.

The band's next recording session, on September 9, 1940, included a new face: Bob Price joined Nelson, Lewis, and Bishop in a more powerful trumpet section. And in another addition, Herman began play-ing more alto saxophone and hiring sax players who could double on the tenor and alto instruments, giving arrangers more options to expand on the band's many sounds when playing in full ensemble. This session pro-duced "Rhumboogie," which combined rhumba and boogie-woogie rhythms to back Dillagene. "I Wouldn't Take a Million" pleased with its slow tempo, light rhythm, tightly muted horns, and Herman's way of "bending" notes as a vocalist. This technique showed the influence of Frank Sinatra, who was a rising star after a year with Tommy Dorsey's band. Herman again employed Bing Crosby's lazy-day style in "A Million Dreams Ago" as he continued to work at developing a singing style of his own.

During the same session, Herman, Linehan, Yoder, and Carlson (playing as Woody Herman's Four Chips on their Decca recordings) made "Chips' Boogie Woogie" and "Chips' Blues." The boogie rode on Linehan's fast piano, with breaks by Herman's clarinet, and a Yoder-Carlson duet at the end. The blues offered a slow tempo for contrast. Over the years Herman made up nonsense lyrics when testing new blues:

> Got fourteen cousins, all of 'em is dead;
> They had the blues so bad, they was tetched in the head.

The music from these quartets was of average quality and almost unavoidably echoed Benny Goodman Quartet pieces in that a clarinet dominated it. In forming the quartet, Herman intended no challenge to the domain of Goodman, the "king of swing" in those days. But he did achieve parity, in terms of diverse and competitive showmanship, with Goodman, Shaw (Gramercy Five), Tommy Dorsey (Clambake Seven), and others for the allegiance of fans of small combos. A broadcast from the Terrace Room in the Hotel New Yorker, for which Herman programmed "Blues Upstairs," "Blues Downstairs," and "Blue Ink," also introduced "Give a Little Whistle," "Sawdust," and "Jughead Blues."

The full band gathered at Decca on September 27 to record "Frenesi," "Song of Old Hawaii," and the bouncy "Five O'Clock Whistle" and to rough out Noble's rhythmic "The Golden Wedding." Herman sang "Frenesi" with conviction, above sparkling notes from White's guitar. (Both Glenn Miller and Shaw made better-selling records of the number with no vocal part.) "Song of Old Hawaii" plodded, White stating the theme above lush reeds before Herman's lullabying. Dillagene sang the novelty "Five O'Clock Whistle," which featured Herman's alto sax.

On October 10, the boogie rhythm of "Beat Me Daddy, Eight to the Bar," and the ballads "Dream Valley," "What Ever Happened to You?" and "There I Go" rolled from the Herman band in another Decca session. "Beat Me Daddy" came off as a gallop paced by Linehan's piano. Herman sang, and the chart ended with Nelson's falsetto "beat me, papa." The band played "Dream Valley," in which Herman sang about the land of let's pretend, at dance tempo, with muted brass. Yoder's briskly marching bass notes backed Herman on "What Ever Happened to You?" In the impeccable "There I Go," the band performed as well as any then playing. Pleasingly calm, legato, and danceable, the chart's smooth rhythm passages featured muted brass with reeds, reeds alone, and Herman's romantic baritone.

On November 9, the same confident and commanding band recorded the ballads "You're the One," "Love of My Life," "The Stars Remain," and "I Should Have Known You Years Ago," plus a cleaned-up take of "The Golden Wedding." Herman sang the four ballads. As with "Woodchoppers' Ball," "The Golden Wedding" became a big seller with a long life. Carlson carried it with his solo breaks and tom-tomming.

Herman's 1940 recordings continued to reflect his art-versus-profit struggle. He longed to play blues and swing, while Decca preferred the sure sales of pop tunes. So he often succumbed to the song-pluggers' demands. He complained at times that "if I did two for them, I might get to do one [for me] later."[15] "Love of My Life" and "The Stars Remain" were "two for them." "The Golden Wedding"—for Herman—outlived those ballads by decades.

The band's rise continued; the 1940 survey of *Billboard* readers ranked it sixth in sweet music, and the third-best swing band. Great musical and financial success, however, still eluded Herman. Over the course of the year, his band recorded forty-six sides for Decca. Eleven were "his": "Pick-a-Rib," "Cousin to Chris," "Blue Ink," "Whistle Stop," "Bessie's

Blues," "Herman at the Sherman," "Jukin'," "Get Your Boots Laced, Papa," "Chips' Boogie Woogie," "Chips' Blues," and "The Golden Wedding." Overall, this commercial strategy won out. In four years Herman and the co-op band had taken few musical chances in 150 records and transcriptions. The band imitated, shied away from dynamics or daring harmonics, played few extreme tempos.

Among the top-rank critics, Simon alone liked Herman's singing. Simon dismissed McCall, Elsa Harris, Carol Kaye, and Dillagene as "not much more than fair." He opined that "the best singer Woody ever had was Woody himself. He sang a lot of blues, and a good many up-tempoed swingers and novelties, but it was as a ballad singer that he impressed me and many musicians the most. His phrasing was immensely warm and musical; he used his *vibrato* well, and his voice had both a sensuous and sensitive timbre."[16]

Simon wrote a brief social note for the November 1940 issue of *Metronome* in which he described traveling by bus with James's struggling band. In Hartford, Connecticut, a "grand reunion [occurred] between the James boys and Woody Herman's Herd, playing the State Theater there." And with that, Herman's Herd had been invented. The name lived long after "The Band That Plays the Blues" changed colors.

When Glenn Miller opened in the Cafe Rouge of New York City's Hotel Pennsylvania early in 1941, the big-band boom was nearing its zenith. Miller's seventeen—four trumpets, four trombones, five saxes, and rhythm section—played charts mostly by Jerry Gray and Bill Finegan. Saxophonist Gordon "Tex" Beneke and trumpeter Johnny Best soloed. Clarinetist Willie Schwartz led the flawless reeds, while Beneke, Hutton, Ray Eberle, and the Modernaires sang. Soon they would record "Chattanooga Choo Choo" and make the movie *Sun Valley Serenade*. "Chattanooga Choo Choo" would sell millions of copies.

At Miller's opening, Herman, Spivak, Brown, Clinton, and Sammy Kaye posed holding champagne bottles to christen the stylish new bandstand with its rounded corners and "G. M." monogram. And business was booming for them all. Kaye's band, which played sweet music, recorded

"Daddy" that year. Brown would record "Bizet Has His Day" and the summer novelty "Joltin' Joe DiMaggio." Clinton's credits included the hit ballads "Deep Purple" and "My Reverie," with Wain as vocalist, and the catchy "Dipsy Doodle." Spivak started a band with Glenn Miller's backing. Leaders attended one another's shows, parties, and premieres and joined movie stars as willing photo and gossip subjects. National fan clubbers talked lead trumpeters as baseball fans talked leadoff hitters, and rehashed sidemen moves like major-league player trades.

And then there was Goodman, who stayed at or near the top in 1941. His alumni Krupa and James led rising bands. Tommy Dorsey rivaled Goodman. Shaw led thirteen violins, flute, bass clarinet, and oboe. Basie, Duke Ellington, and Lunceford were at their peaks. With his clarinet and alto sax, Jimmy Dorsey led a sterling 1941 band, backing singers O'Connell and Bob Eberly.

Cab Calloway, Carter, Xavier Cugat, Hampton, Phil Harris, Kyser, Guy Lombardo, Vaughn Monroe, Ozzie Nelson, Teagarden, and Lawrence Welk were among the myriad bandleaders touring, recording, broadcasting, and profiting. Young women starred as singers, but rarely as instrumentalists or leaders. Pianist Mary Lou Williams, with Andy Kirk, broke the custom, as did the singing and dancing leader Ina Ray Hutton. Radio's Phil Spitalny led an "all-girl orchestra," as it was called.

On January 22, 1941, Herman added to his Decca catalog with the fantasy "(Come Back to) Sorrento," the pop song "Oh, Look at Me Now," "Boogie Woogie Bugle Boy," and "Bounce Me Brother with a Solid Four." Brass section moves had improved the band's sound after Bishop quit playing to write full-time. Still fifteen strong, the band now contained three trumpets and (for the first time) three trombones, five saxes (counting Herman), and a rhythm section. Singer Muriel Lane succeeded Dillagene. Herman sang the danceable "Oh, Look at Me Now." But "Boogie Woogie Bugle Boy" was bittersweet. War was shattering regions of Europe and Asia. In the United States, draft boards pulled able men into army camps, and songwriters captured wistful farewells in tunes both sad and hopeful. (The "boogie woogie bugle boy of Company B" in the lyrics had been a jazz trumpeter drafted from Chicago.) Decca paired "Boogie Woogie Bugle Boy" with Lane singing "Bounce Me Brother with a Solid Four," a takeoff on "Beat Me Daddy, Eight to the Bar."

The war and the draft were beginning to complicate the entertainment business enough. But a war brewing within the business itself made matters worse. A huge body of previously published and recorded music was banned from radio broadcasts because of the networks' disagreement with the American Society of Composers, Authors and Publishers. Known by the acronym ASCAP, this collector of royalties demanded more money for its members to license their music for radio. Networks refused to pay more and set up Broadcast Music, Inc., which offered good terms and tried to woo new writers plus ASCAP defectors. During the radio-ASCAP battle, good new tunes stayed unknown, and past hits went unheard. Unable to broadcast "Moonlight Serenade," Glenn Miller turned for a temporary theme to "Slumber Song," by his pianist, J. C. "Chummy" MacGregor, which was then published by Miller's own firm, a BMI member. For a time, bands played songs based upon classical or folk melodies in the public domain.

These difficulties forced Herman to make certain changes as well. For transcriptions recorded in early 1941, he selected the non-ASCAP numbers "Up a Lazy River," "What'cha Know, Joe?" and "You'll Never Know," on which Herman sang; "Rockin' Chair" and "There'll Be Some Changes Made," with Lane singing; Noble's "Jughead Blues" and "Minka"; plus "Lullaby from Jocelyn," "One Nighter," "Blue Flame," "Bishop's Blues," and "Fur Trappers' Ball." From these new charts, Decca in February chose to record "Fur Trappers' Ball" (by Bishop) and "Blue Flame" (by Bishop, Noble, and Leo Corday). "Blue Flame" provided a slow blues for Herman's clarinet and Reid's trombone. In mood and tempo, it resembled Bishop's 1939 "Casbah Blues." In fact, "Blue Flame" and "Fur Trappers' Ball" became stand-ins for "Blue Prelude" and "Woodchoppers' Ball," both of which were banned from radio. It proved a lucky break for Herman: "Blue Flame" became a better-known theme song than "Blue Prelude." "Fur Trappers' Ball" teased fans with melodic suggestions of "Woodchoppers' Ball." Brass and reed sections blew assorted riffs, Reid and Mansfield soloed, Lewis played muted trumpet over the reeds, and White, Yoder, and Linehan soloed in the same order as in "Woodchoppers' Ball." After the full band had recorded, The Woodchoppers (here composed of Herman, Lewis, Reid, Linehan, White, Yoder, and Carlson) recorded the non-ASCAP oldies "Fan It" and "South." "Fan It" gave Lewis, Linehan, Herman, and Carlson more solo space. Herman, who had sung the rapid-fire lyrics with Isham Jones, performed them again in this version. Frankie "Half Pint" Jaxon had sanitized this X-rated material to record in 1928. The Woodchoppers played fast, tight Dixieland in this number, with an abrupt change to slow tempo for Lewis's blues-based trumpet solo. The players then resumed a dash to the end. That tempo change stood as a first among Herman recordings. And on Moten's 1920s song "South," the Dixielanders played a tricky ritard coda, also new in Herman's charts.

From the Terrace Room of the Hotel New Yorker, the band broadcast over the NBC Radio Network. A program on February 26, 1941, contained "Blue Flame," "Jughead Blues," "Rockin' Chair," "Chips' Boogie Woogie," "Whatcha Know, Joe?" "Sorrento," "Fur Trappers' Ball," plus "Gentleman Jim" and Herman singing the short-lived ballad "These Things You Left Me." The band's March 11 Decca session produced "Sleepy Serenade," Lane's vocal number "Let's Get Away from It All," and Herman singing "Everything Happens to Me" and "Chloe." The arrival of Sam Rubinwitch and Herbie Haymer gave the sax section a new look for the band's April 4 session at Decca, where they recorded the ballads "You Call It Madness," "Intermezzo (A Love Story)," "Time Changes Everything," and "My Mom," all starring Herman as singer, and "Lazy Rhapsody." Richard Hadlock regards Rubinwitch as a "crack alto man," and Haymer as a "front-rank jazz tenor man of the period,"[17] although these tunes disguised their talents. But before long, Rubinwitch's steady alto sax would lead the reeds, and Haymer would deliver deep tenor sax solos in place of Mansfield's whinier sound.

The band recorded again on April 11, turning out the ballads "G'Bye Now" (Lane singing), "Dancing in the Dark," "Until Tomorrow," and "You'll Never Know" (with Herman), and Noble's "Night Watchman." The last contained a wah-wah trombone theme that was Ellingtonian in concept and sound.

In the spring of 1941, Lowell "Skippy" Martin's and Dave Matthews's writings began enriching the band's book. Matthews, with Herman's blessing, copied Ellington. "With personnel changes caused by the draft, we began to play differently, and I was looking for different kinds of arrangements," Herman said. "Most of our charts had been done by 'Jiggs' Noble, Joe Bishop, Nick Harper and Gordon Jenkins. They were fine writers, but I felt that we were in a rut; we weren't progressing."[18] "Until Tomorrow" showed fresh writing: Herman sang over White's guitar passages and soft stretches of muted brass.

In mid-May, Herman played Philadelphia the same week as Tommy Dorsey. *Metronome*'s Simon reviewed Dorsey's band, which was playing with Elman, drummer Buddy Rich, and singers Sinatra, Jo Stafford, Connie Haines, and the Pied Pipers. He ended up at a birthday party for Herman at 4 A.M. Nineteen years a performer, the slim Herman was still boyish looking; and no wonder—he had only turned twenty-eight! Dorsey at the time was thirty-five. Shaw was thirty-one, Goodman thirty-two, Basie thirty-six, Bob Crosby and Glenn Miller thirty-seven, and Ellington forty-two.

Herman's busy June 5 record cuttings included "Love Me a Little Little" and "Hey Doc" with Lane, and Herman singing "Don't Cry, Cherie," "Prisoner of Love," "There Goes That Song Again," and "Loveliness and Love." Lane received a vocal backup from the band on the rhythmic "Hey Doc." Cappy Lewis's lead trumpet sparkled both in brass-section and full-band passages. Yoder's bass kept gaining force, too, as in "Love Me a Little Little." "Prisoner of Love," which worked well for some artists—including Herman's model, Columbo—proved a waste for Herman. Played at a slow tempo, the chart pitched Herman too high; and as always, he struggled selling lyrics of inner pain. But there was a tenderly muted brass choir and Haymer's mellow tenor sax solo. "Don't Cry, Cherie" vowed that France, which had fallen to German invaders in 1940, "will rise again."

The band's steady rise in 1941 was fueled, Herman said, by turnover. Like so many changes, this one was instituted by the war: "As the U.S. Selective Service began drafting bandsmen for military duty, Woody [hired] stronger players. He bought out each of his partners' shares in the old co-op band as they departed, so that gradually the band became all his."[19]

*E*ver since he had joined Jones's band in 1934, Herman's base had been New York City. "The Band That Plays the Blues" visited Connecticut, New Jersey, Boston, Philadelphia, and Chicago, but always returned. Much the same was true of all the name bands. Big venues paid top money only a short drive from anywhere in New York City. People flocked to the ballrooms (Roseland, Glen Island Casino in New Rochelle, Arcadia, Savoy, Fiesta Danceteria), to the hotels (Taft, Biltmore, Ambassador, St. Regis, Waldorf-Astoria, New Yorker, Edison, Lincoln, Astor, Pennsylvania), to the nightclubs (Famous Door, Blue Note, Metropole), and to the great theaters (Strand, Paramount, Capitol, Apollo, Loew's State, Carnegie Hall). A biographer of Goodman describes the scene dramatically: "One of the most spine-chilling experiences for swing band fans [was] to sit in the Paramount audience, begin to hear the faint first notes of [Herman's] 'Blue Flame' or [Glenn Miller's] 'Moonlight Serenade' or [Goodman's] 'Let's Dance,' and then as the music grew louder watch the band rise slowly and majestically [on the theater's rising bandstand] into sight. It jerked fans from their seats with a roar."[20] Not that it was much fun for bandsmen. New York theater jobs were "like doing time up the river," Herman said. "Some lasted ten weeks and included weekends. It was very difficult, and we'd lose one or two guys every week. There was a lot of panic all the time because the rule was that the show must go on."[21]

Across the Hudson River, there was the Adams Theater in Newark, the Central Theatre in Passaic, the Meadowbrook off Highway 23 in Cedar Grove, Guy Hunt's Ocean Pier in Wildwood, and the Steel Pier and Million Dollar Pier downstate in Atlantic City. Also in easy reach were the Cocoanut Grove and the Bradford Hotel in Boston, the Earle Theater and Fay's Theater in Philadelphia, and the Capitol in Washington, D.C.

En route to good spots in Chicago or Detroit, bands could make money at the Top Hat Club in Toronto; the Westwood Supper Club in

Richmond, Virginia; Myrtle Beach Pavilion in South Carolina; the Knox-ville (Tennessee) Auditorium; Joyland Casino in Lexington, Kentucky; Sandy Beach Park at Russell's Point, Ohio; the Trianon Ballroom in Cleve-land; Summit Beach at Akron, Ohio; Ideal Beach at Monticello, Indiana; the Murat Temple, Indiana Roof, or Circle Theater in Indianapolis; and countless dances in college student unions and gyms.

Good venues in Chicago included the ballrooms (Aragon, Trianon, Dreamland) and hotels (Sherman, Edgewater Beach, Congress, Drake, Stevens); nightspots such as Midway Gardens, the Black Hawk, or the Chez Paree restaurants; and the lavish Chicago Theater. New York bands also played at Detroit's Eastwood Gardens, Arcadia Ballroom, Greystone Ballroom, and Paradise Theater.

And in the summer of 1941, a new, exciting venue was added to the list. Moviemakers offered time on the silver screen and good pay on West Coast stages, which welcomed the eastern name bands. To get there, bands could fly or go by train; or they could go by bus or car and play their way overland, hitting the Chase or the Jefferson Hotel in St. Louis; the Claridge or the Peabody in Memphis; the Roosevelt in New Orleans; the Baker or the Adolphus in Dallas; the Rice in Houston; the Muehlbach or Fairyland Park in Kansas City; King's Ballroom, the Pla-Mor, or the Turnpike Casino in Lincoln; the Paxton Hotel or the Fontenelle in Omaha; the Prom Ballroom in Minneapolis; the Corn Palace in Mitchell, South Dakota; several spots in Denver; the Saltair, the Rainbow Rendezvous, or Hotel Utah in Salt Lake City; Natatorium Park in Spokane; the Trianon Ballroom in Seattle; or Golden Gate Theater in San Francisco.

Herman took his band west the summer of 1941, playing dance halls, pavilions, hotels, and theaters en route and ending in Hollywood for a dash of moviemaking. All about town fans of the big bands packed ballrooms (Palladium, Venice, Plantation, Trianon, Avodon) and hotels (Ambassador, Biltmore) or the nightclubs Zucca's Terrace or Macombo. Some distance from Los Angeles, but worth the trip, were the Mark Hopkins, the St. Francis, and the Palace Hotel in San Francisco; the Aragon Ballroom and Casino Gardens in Santa Monica; the Avalon on Catalina Island; and the Mission Beach Ballroom in San Diego.

Herman's crew appeared in the movies *What's Cookin'?* with the Andrews Sisters and *Quota Girl* and *Wintertime* with Norwegian ice-skating star Sonja Henie. One wag suggested that Herman play "The Skater's Waltz" for a theme song and perform as "Woody Herman and His Gay Blades." That summer, sixteen other bands were filming. Earlier, Goodman's had appeared in *Hollywood Hotel*, Shaw's in *Dancing Co-ed*, and Tommy Dorsey's in *Las Vegas Nights*. In 1941, Glenn Miller finished *Sun Valley Serenade*, with *Orchestra Wives* next.

Since 1940, Herman had been pleasing ever increasing crowds . His July 1941 opening at the Hollywood Palladium was his greatest triumph yet. Tommy Dorsey had drawn 7,200 to his Palladium premiere nine months before; Glenn Miller had pulled 5,200. Herman attracted 4,800. That was no surprise: for several months, Herman had been nearing—and sometimes matching or breaking—marks set by Goodman, Miller, and Dorsey; and in the fan magazines, his band had risen in both jazz and dance polls.

The band and Woodchoppers recorded twenty-some numbers in Hollywood during July, August, and September, beginning with a July 30 session with easy-going Bing Crosby. As in 1938–39, Decca used Herman's as a house band to back Crosby. The Woodchoppers played for Crosby and Lane singing "Let's All Meet at My House" and for Crosby soloing in "I Ain't Got Nobody." Crosby crooned the slow ballad "Humpty Dumpty Heart" with the full band, which also accompanied Crosby and Lane on "Whistler's Mother-in-Law." (In early 1942, working California again, Herman's men backed Crosby on "I'm Thinking Tonight of My Blue Eyes" and "I Want My Mama" with the band, and on the smash hit "Deep in the Heart of Texas" with the hustling Woodchoppers.)

Making the sound track for Universal's *What's Cookin'?* meant more shared stardom for Herman, this time with the Andrews Sisters and singer-actress Gloria Jean. Herman led the band in "Blue Flame" and "Woodchoppers' Ball" and in backing the Andrews Sisters ("What to Do"), Jean ("You Can't Hold a Memory in Your Arms"), and Jean and the Andrews Sisters ("I'll Pray for You"). Herman sang, and men in the band hummed and clapped in a two-beat revival tune called "Amen," which suggested

Oliver's popular "Yes, Indeed!" written for Tommy Dorsey. Simon previewed *What's Cookin'?* for *Metronome* and reported that it "has plenty of laughs and quite a bit of the Herman Herd." Herman considered it his first "feature film," but nothing more than a "routine comedy."[22]

On August 21, 1941, the band recorded six more tunes. "Bishop's Blues" relied on low trombone notes to set the mood for big-band blues. Linehan and Yoder soloed, and Nelson's trumpet playing near the coda saluted the dazzling James. Lane sang the frothy "By-U, By-O (The Louisiana Lullaby)." Skippy Martin's fast "Woodsheddin' with Woody" opened with rhythm-section action, saxes softly riffing, Herman's clarinet playing here and there, and a finish powered by Nelson's ever better trumpet. Herman sang the ballad "Don't Be Blue, Little Pal, Don't Be Blue," another off-to-war song. Herman sang "My Foolish Heart" and—again struggling for high notes—"I Love You More, More Every Day," a ballad in dance tempo.

On August 28, the band recorded "Concerto No. 1" and the new ballad "I'll Remember April." The Woodchoppers cranked out "Too Late" and "Fort Worth Jail." Finally, Herman, Linehan, Yoder, and Carlson, as Woody Herman's Four Chips, produced "Elise." Dick Steinhardt's "Fort Worth Jail" and Jimmy Wakeley's "Too Late" marked Herman's only venture into the "western swing" idiom established by Bob Wills and His Texas Playboys. Wills's style married the charms of the fiddle ensemble in country music and the drums and horn players of the dance bands. These Woodchoppers pieces perhaps resembled "western Dixieland" more than "western swing." "Concerto No. 1," widely known as "Tonight We Love," was based on Tchaikovsky's Piano Concerto in B-flat Minor and featured Linehan's elegant piano and White's guitar; midsong the band shifted the mood from concert-hall longhair to a jitterbug tempo.

*g*rowing fame brought growing visibility and a more frenetic life-style. In fan magazines one could turn a page and see Herman laughing with bandleader Louis Jordan, talking shop at a nightclub with Goodman and Monroe, gabbing with Tennessee Williams, posing with the Andrews Sisters and actress Claire Trevor, dining with Judy Garland, chatting with Joe

DiMaggio at some ballpark, cheering with Mel Tormé at a motor speed-way, reading music with pipe-puffing Bing Crosby, or mending a torn chart in a Scotch tape ad. The pace meant success for Herman, but stress for his wife. Expecting their first child, Charlotte Herman left their apartment in Queens to stay with her parents in Los Angeles while the band played California. There, on September 3, 1941, she gave birth to their daughter, Ingrid.

Just two days later, with war jitters shaking the neutral United States, the Herman band recorded "Misirlou," free-lancer Pat McCarthy's "Three Ways to Smoke a Pipe," and Skippy Martin's swinger with the timely title of "Ten Day Furlough." Martin's chart and Rubinwitch's lead alto sax made the reeds sound the strongest yet. The futuristic "Three Ways to Smoke a Pipe" featured Haymer, Cappy Lewis aping Duke Ellington's trumpet star Cootie Williams, and Herman honking a few alto sax notes. It was one of those "different kinds of arrangements." But Herman's sunny voice was wrong for exotic and passionate lyrics about hot sands and oases in "Misirlou." This complex number, written in a minor key, was "different," too, offering only a brief flash of swing. Some punsters in audiences around the country are said to have called it "Misery Lou" because of its doleful disposition and love lyrics of inner pain. It seemed doubly out of place in Herman's mostly keep-smiling repertoire. But overall, Herman kept gaining fans. Simon crashed a Herman rehearsal and took in the band's Palladium performance with singer Martha Tilton, reporting that the band was in "its usual fine form."[23]

On September 10, Herman's band recorded two soon-to-be-famous Harold Arlen and Johnny Mercer songs, plus the ballad "I'd Love You Again" and "Hot Chestnuts" by free-lancer Bob Hartsell. "Hot Chestnuts," which relied more on rhythm than melody, continued the experimentation shown in "Three Ways to Smoke a Pipe" and "Ten Day Furlough." The band sparkled in Arlen and Mercer's "Blues in the Night." Mercer stood by, echoing lines sung by Herman, who said, "We both sounded like barroom singers." For the flip side of that record, Herman and a choir of bandsmen sang Arlen and Mercer's "This Time the Dream's on Me." Herman said they "worked for hours, having the whole band singing and making backgrounds"[24] for what proved to be a fine song, although it was always topped by "Blues in the Night." Both ballads soon debuted in Warner Brothers' movie *Blues in the Night.*

After the band had finished recording, the Four Chips played Noble's "Yardbird Shuffle" to pair with "Elise," which had been made in August. "Yardbird"—the word is slang for "chicken," and alto-sax player Charlie Parker acquired the nickname at about the same time—contained tight, fast ensemble playing in the style of the Goodman Quartet. Simon, sitting in on this recording session, was amused that Herman still was "so excited about being a new papa he spoiled one master after another."[25] Soon after a radio guest appearance on Bing Crosby's *Kraft Music Hall,* Herman steered his "herd" back east.

In Chicago on November 13, with a singing trumpeter from Montana, Elizabeth "Billie" Rogers, the band recorded the ballads "'Tis Autumn" and "I Guess I'll Be on My Way," the instrumental "Las Chiapanecas," and "Even Steven" for Decca. The latter showcased Rogers's singing and trumpet playing. Rogers performed with Herman until mid-1943. "'Tis Autumn," a widely recorded ballad, featured a vocal duet full of high notes for Herman and Carolyn Grey, Lane's successor, backed by a chorus of bandsmen. Skippy Martin arranged the Mexican dance "Las Chiapanecas," which was punctuated with hand-clapping. Like "The Golden Wedding," this tune spotlighted Carlson's drumming and the brass section, now seven strong with Rogers.

Trumpet player Billie Rogers in a GAC promotional photo, autographed for Herman's mother: "A swell Mommy with a swell son—Billie." 1942. (Jack Siefert Collection)

The band reached New York City in late November. With the United States as yet uninvolved in World War II, the bandsmen were all anxious about being drafted and about the disruptions in lives and careers that induction might create. Later, of course, after Japan's attack on Pearl Harbor, patriotism and outrage inspired a substantial number of draft-age men in all walks of life to leave peacetime jobs and volunteer to fight. Meanwhile, hernia surgery in New York kept Herman off the bandstand for a couple of weeks and out of the draft. Simon visited him for a November *Metronome* item, writing that Herman "looks fine after his operation and insists he wants to have one every year, just for the relaxation thereof."[26] But there was a plot beneath the "hernia operation." In a pre-draft exam, a doctor purposely poked Herman's hernia zone hard enough to require surgery and assure "unfit" draft status. Herman quoted the doctor: "You're doing more good on the outside than you could ever do in the service."[27]

On December 18, the band recorded "Someone's Rocking My Dream Boat," "Rose O'Day," "Night of Nights," "I Think of You," and "Fooled" at Decca. Herman and Grey sang about the Irish lass in "Rose O'Day," which was subtitled "The Filla-Ga-Dusha Song." With its double-talk lyrics, it became a modest success in radio and in record and sheet music sales. "Someone's Rocking My Dream Boat," a pop song, projected fine reed and full-band sounds. "Night of Nights," subtitled "Tura Lura Li," again teamed Herman and Grey with serenading bandsmen.

As 1941 passed, Herman and "The Band That Plays The Blues" could look at their achievements with satisfaction. "Blues in the Night" became their second-best seller after "Woodchoppers' Ball." The band sounded better than ever. It was playing fresh charts from new writers. It had mastered ritard codas and tempo changes and could offer quartet and septet music for variety. It could boast a female trumpet player who could sing, competent soloists in Lewis on trumpet, Reid on trombone, and Haymer on tenor sax, and the veteran rhythm section. Sometimes the band sounded daring, like Duke Ellington. Fans saw the band in movies, heard it on radio, bought its records, talked about it. Its acceptance matched any band's. If number of recordings is an indicator of popularity, Herman's band had few rivals: in 1941, Glenn Miller recorded fifty-one numbers for RCA Bluebird; Tommy Dorsey sixty, Shaw thirty, and Ellington twenty-four for RCA Victor; Goodman fifty-seven, James fifty-six, and Basie forty for Columbia. Herman made fifty-seven at Decca, while Bob Crosby slipped to only twenty-two.

But the New Year would bring new, different anxieties, and not just for Herman's band. Just weeks after Japan's attack on Pearl Harbor in December 1941 and the U.S. entry into World War II, able young men in all walks of life were enlisting or awaiting draft calls. The bands suffered irreparable drains of star talent and consequent loss of box-office appeal, and fans were talking rifles more than riffs.

One musician recalls that "in the first few weeks [after Pearl Harbor] pandemonium reigned. One-nighters were canceled by blackouts, with bands on the stand ready to play. War news bulletins broke into their broadcasts. The shock left few in the mood for night clubbing or dancing. Business dropped off drastically."[28] But the war also created an entertainment boom. Defense personnel had money to spend. Whether relaxing in USO (United Service Organizations) clubs, off-duty in training camps, or home on leave, they craved fun. Military bases competed with hotels, nightclubs, ballrooms, and theaters to hire bands. For top bands, one-nighters, even in out-of-the-way places, paid record fees. Major venues hedged against band shortages by booking them months ahead. Some leaders took "for-the-duration" (of the war) contracts. Tommy Dorsey and Horace Heidt bought their own ballrooms.

Wartime changed the band business in other ways. With a national curfew in effect, dancing and liquor service stopped at midnight. Events started and finished earlier. And loyalty to country prevailed. The president of the American Federation of Musicians, James C. Petrillo, ordered all members' broadcasts and public jobs to end with "The Star-Spangled Banner." Sidemen and leaders volunteered for military or war-related service to build morale. Some two hundred bandleaders offered to play for USO shows, with Kyser leading the way.

*I*t seemed the worst of times for doing so, but a new company joined the recording field in the spring of 1942. RCA, Columbia, and Decca dominated pop recordings. Still, in April, Mercer and other backers founded Capitol Records. Based in Hollywood, Capitol recorded Whiteman's and Stan Kenton's bands, Mercer, and a few other artists.

For Herman, a Decca session in war-jittery New York City on January 28, 1942, produced typical "yes-but" results:

> Yes, the band recorded "A String of Pearls" with power, precision, and Haymer's virile tenor sax solo. But Goodman's (Columbia) and Glenn Miller's (RCA Bluebird) recordings of it sold better.

> Yes, the band played and Herman sang a slow, danceable "Skylark." But Bing Crosby's version sold far more copies for Decca.

> Yes, Herman, band, and vocal ensemble recorded "Lamplighter's Serenade." But Sinatra, who was about to leave Dorsey to star alone, made a bigger hit of it for RCA.

> Yes, Herman, Grey, and background singers recorded "You Can't Hold a Memory in Your Arms." (Jean had sung the pedestrian love song in *What's Cookin'?*) But it was no one's favorite. Herman's band, much as it had improved with Reid, Haymer, and Cappy Lewis, still lacked top solo talent. And when appendicitis sidelined Carlson, drummer Dave Tough had to be summoned to sit in.

> Singing? Bing Crosby, Ray Eberle, Bob Eberly, Sinatra, O'Connell, Forrest, and Billie Holiday all surpassed Herman.

> Soloists? Herman's loyal sidemen were outmatched by Glenn Miller's tenor saxophonist Beneke and trumpeters Billy May and Best and by Goodman's trumpeters Billy Butterfield and Bernie Privin, trombonist Lou McGarity, saxophonist Georgie Auld, pianist Wilson, and guitarist Charlie Christian. Basie's 1942 band—starring Lester Young and Evans (tenor sax), Trummy Young and Dickie Wells (trombones), Clayton (trumpet), Freddie Green (guitar), Page (bass), and Jo Jones (drums)—also boasted more solid solo talent.

Clarinet playing? Herman trailed Goodman, Shaw, Noone, Pee Wee Russell, Edmond Hall, George Lewis, Johnny Dodds, and Barney Bigard.

Duke Ellington's 1940–42 band, meanwhile, sustained a creative level unmatched in big-band jazz. Starting with "Ko-Ko" and "Jack the Bear" in March 1940, that band made nearly a hundred classic recordings, ending with "Mainstem" and "Johnny Come Lately" in 1942. Its galaxy of star players included the trumpeters Cootie Williams, Rex Stewart, and Ray Nance; trombonists Lawrence Brown and Juan Tizol; saxophonists Johnny Hodges, Harry Carney, and Ben Webster; clarinetist Bigard; bassist Jimmy Blanton, guitarist Freddie Guy, and drummer Sonny Greer. Add to all that Ellington's piano playing and composing and Billy Strayhorn's arranging. Most musicians admired Ellington, his stars, and all of the music they made, as Herman did. No band matched Ellington's talent.

Still, chosen for a new *Spotlight Bands* coast-to-coast radio broadcast series in early 1942, Herman cheerfully pressed on with his lesser talents, and the band made seven records on April 2: "There Are Rivers to Cross (before We Meet Again)," "We'll Meet Again," "She'll Always Remember," "A Soldier Dreams (of You Tonight)," "Amen," "Whisper That You Love Me," and "Deliver Me to Tennessee." "Amen," from *What's Cookin'?* provided a loping hit in which Yoder played strong bass and the brass and ensemble work reflected power, with Herman singing and scatting and the bandsmen handling the spiritual lyrics, sometimes in falsetto. The band's clipped unison phrasing echoed the emerging style of young Kenton's brassy California crew. The drowsier "Deliver Me to Tennessee" starred Herman as singer, with Reid's blues trombone and rich full-band passages.

Three pieces painted sentimental portraits of men leaving for war. "She'll Always Remember" featured Grey with a male chorus, and Herman sang "A Soldier Dreams (of You Tonight)." The upbeat "We'll Meet Again" starred Rogers's singing and trumpet playing. Hers was a low, clear voice, and her vocal manner was more rhythmic than melodic. "There Are Rivers to Cross," another till-we-meet-again song, reflected new arranging ideas. The Matthews chart assigned the four-beat rhythm to Yoder and offered stirring reeds, Herman's clarinet playing and singing, Haymer's tenor sax, and sparkling brass.

On April 23, 1942, the band recorded "Don't Tell a Lie about Me, Dear (And I Won't Tell the Truth about You)"—another Rogers song-and-trumpet number—plus "Story of a Starry Night" and "Just Plain Lonesome." Then there came a high-humor novelty, performed by Herman, Grey, Rogers, and a male chorus, pronouncing phrases from "Rose O'Day" and "Chattanooga Choo Choo" backwards. Herman called it "Ooch Ooch A Goon Attach (The Backward Song)." Its whimsical premise was that a party was getting dull, so participants played their favorite records in reverse. The Woodchoppers belted out a snappy "Three Little Sisters" to finish the session. Herman sang it and the serious ballads.

Despite second-tier players, the Herman band's following grew. Better and longer bookings came its way. With fees often tied to a cut of ticket sales, bigger crowds meant more money. Herman kept recording, too. But radio appearances were particularly sought after, as they created demand for records. An appearance on *Spotlight Bands* might pay poorly, but Herman could plug soloists, writers, new charts, and bookings and sell his nice-guy personality. Airtime always raised tour revenue.

And apparently those radio appearances were doing the trick: *Make Believe Ballroom* listeners rated Herman's band the nation's "most improved band," and the show's host, Martin Block, presented Herman with a commemorative plaque. Then as now, polls were topics for fans to debate. *Billboard* printed annual Collegiate Choice of Orchestras polls. Goodman's band won in 1938, Shaw's in 1939, and Glenn Miller's in 1940, 1941, and 1942. The Tommy Dorsey and Kyser bands always ranked high, as did James's by 1942. Herman's band rose to tenth in 1942. The magazines *Variety, Billboard, Band Leaders, Orchestra World,* and *Down Beat* conducted polls, picked all-star bands, printed ads for musical instruments and booking agencies, and ran features about the bands, musicians, singers, even their itineraries. The dry figures of the trade journals actually told much about band life: in 1939 the Bob Crosby band made 31 percent of its revenue from theater dates, 29 percent from one-nighters, 16 percent from locations (i.e., hotels, ballrooms), 14 percent from radio broadcasts, and 9 percent from records and royalties. In 1942, 30 percent of James's income came from motion pictures, with another 30 percent from one-nighters; locations, records, theater, and radio made up about 10 percent each.

Records seemed a can't-lose outlet for bands; yet Whiteman and Fred Waring, leader of the Pennsylvanians, claimed that disc-jockey radio shows were detrimental to the bands, as shows competed with live radio programs, which paid more. Petrillo, who despised that scene even more, hired Ben Selvin, a bandleader and recording exec, to survey the effect of records on union members. Selvin's report to the union's 1941 convention drew a standing ovation. Figuring that the record industry would cost musicians more than $3 million in paying jobs that year, Selvin urged finding ways to pay players more for making records. The record companies stood firm, the bandleaders caught in the middle. To break the impasse, in early 1942 Petrillo threatened to order union members—sidemen in most name bands—to stop recording. If record companies couldn't devise some system whereby musicians would be paid for the use of their records on radio shows, then he wouldn't let them record at all. Bandleaders, who made far more than the sidemen from records, and radio moguls mostly bucked the union, so Petrillo ordered a ban to begin August 1.

The international front was equally gloomy: on June 5, the United States declared war on Bulgaria, Hungary, and Romania, and on June 21, German troops seized Tobruk in North Africa. The outcome of the war remained anyone's guess. Petrillo's deadline, imposed on a war-jittery industry, had the unexpected effect of causing a stampede into recording studios as leaders sought to backlog tunes. Even while talks to negotiate an agreement were under way, Glenn Miller recorded an astounding thirteen in three days.

Herman, again touring cross-country, reached Decca/Hollywood (minus Haymer) for beat-the-deadline sessions on July 24, 29, and 31. The result was eleven salable records and three rejects. On the twenty-fourth, the band rushed through "Four or Five Times" (a much requested Matthews chart), "There Will Never Be Another You," "Down Under," "Dearly Beloved," "Please Be There," and "Gotta Get to St. Joe." "Down Under" marked Herman's first dealings with the future trumpet superstar

Dizzy Gillespie, then twenty-five, who wrote and arranged it. "Swing Shift," another Gillespie piece, went unrecorded, as did "Woody'n You." Herman sometimes did play "Woody'n You" to back dancers in stage shows. Gillespie said that Herman was the first bandleader to pay him one hundred dollars for an arrangement.

The up-tempo "Down Under" contained a number of experimental elements that Gillespie was testing, as a remedy against boredom, with small groups of mixed black and white players on New York City side-street stages. The fast tempo, four-beat measure, loud and wild brass passages, reeds played in unison instead of parts, dissonant chords, full-octave jumps, and weird rhythmic accents of this tune blew in like a fresh wind. There were brief solos for Herman on clarinet and for Cappy Lewis. With "Four or Five Times," the band returned to the old two-beat sound, along with singing (some falsetto) by Herman and backers.

On July 29, still racing to record as much as possible before Petrillo's ban took effect, Herman recorded "Let Me Love You Tonight," "Singing Sands of Alamosa," the never issued "If You Only Knew," and "You Were Never Lovelier" for Decca. The usually tame-sounding brass section flared in the opening of "Let Me Love You Tonight," and the sections and ensemble backed Rogers's singing. Herman and a chorus of bandsmen sang in "Singing Sands of Alamosa," Grey sang "If You Only Knew," and Herman took the vocal solo in "You Were Never Lovelier."

Just hours before the deadline, the band finished "Santa Claus Is Comin' to Town," "Jingle Bells," and two novelties that became modest hits: "I Dood It" and "Be Not Disencouraged." The band took "Santa Claus Is Comin' to Town" at a peppy tempo. Herman sang, and the sections swung. "Jingle Bells," performed in the same cheery spirit, gave Grey and the male chorus vocal time. "I Dood It"—the title is a reference to Red Skelton's radio routine punch line—contained a vocal duet with Herman and trumpeter Chuck Peterson, who had sung such novelties as "The Skunk Song" with Tommy Dorsey in 1941. Ironically, "I Dood It" ended up plugging a Jimmy Dorsey movie, the musical comedy *I Dood It,* which also featured Skelton, dancer Eleanor Powell, and singers Patricia Dane, Hazel Scott, and Lena Horne.

The two-beat "Be Not Disencouraged" was a patriotic tune that displayed Grey's singing, Herman's falsetto humming, and a male chorus singing and clapping. Its stirring message, reminiscent of revival meetings—was "we will change conditions." Decca released "Singing Sands of Alamosa," "Gotta Get to St. Joe," and the Christmas pieces early on but eked out the other July hurry-ups to last through the silent night of the record ban.

The ban was not allowed to affect the important business of entertaining America's troops, however. Early in the war, sustaining troop morale became vital, especially in remote parts of the world. Short-wave radio shows by the better bands helped. The Armed Forces Radio Service (AFRS), founded in mid-1942, grew to encompass more than nine hundred stations (private, military, foreign, and short-wave). Its programming included original shows made for the AFRS, reruns of domestic shows, and recorded music. Building a music library—the starting point for programming—began in 1942. First the military acquired transcriptions. Artists and the recording industry, forced into inactivity, were eager to cooperate, and new AFRS music hit the air fast. The singers Simms, Dinah Shore, and Frances Langford and the bandleaders James, Goodman, and Herman performed in the first AFRS Basic Music Library releases. With Decca's consent, AFRS engineers adapted Herman's "Four or Five Times" and "Woodchoppers' Ball," the latter into the sixth of what would be hundreds of transcriptions. Herman also rerecorded "Four or Five Times," along with "Taking a Chance on Love," "In the Blue of Evening," and "Take It from There" for AFRS in late July. In all, Herman made about twenty such donations.

The Herman band stayed in Hollywood after the ban set in so as to play jobs and make *Wintertime.* Herman also kept bringing in new charts, some of them heard on a CBS broadcast from the Hollywood Palladium on August 20. That show contained "Mr. Moto Flips His Queue" (anti-Japanese propaganda), Grey singing "Somebody's Thinking of You To-night," Rogers singing and playing the trumpet in "I Can't Get Started," and "I Want to Be Happy" and "Blue Lou." Mixed in were plugs for Decca's "Let Me Love You Tonight," "Amen," and "Singing Sands of Alamosa."

In the early fall of 1942, the war was again changing the big-band business. As gasoline and tire rationing restricted travel, the chartered bus became widely used. Like all Americans, the bands had to cope with food shortages, and bandleaders had to raid one another for talent to make up for losses caused by the draft. (These troubles seemed tame, though, alongside September 16 dispatches reporting that German armies had swarmed into Stalingrad.)

By late 1942, Shaw started working for the USO to form bands for camp shows; he then joined the navy. Orrin Tucker and Eddy Duchin followed Shaw into service, as did Thornhill. Clyde McCoy and nearly his whole band enlisted. Vallee joined the Coast Guard. Glenn Miller, accepting a captaincy, broke up his band in September and took the army oath on October 1. Those who did not enlist donated their talents without reserve at USO shows, at fund-raisers, and at war-bond rallies. For a while, a wartime law set a $25,000-a-year earnings cap for salaried employees (bandleaders and sidemen alike). With the resulting cash surpluses, some leaders hired more musicians, even violinists. War again intervened by causing a shortage of shellac, needed in certain crucial wartime products—especially as a protective finish on vehicles and arms—which hit the recording industry. Big companies asked fans to turn in old records to dealers, who then passed them back to be reused.

Petrillo's ban did not bar singers from recording solo after August 1, which was a considerable factor in their rise—at the expense of the bands that nurtured them. Stars such as Sinatra, Forrest, Boswell, Shore, the Andrews Sisters, Bing Crosby, Stafford (from Tommy Dorsey), Perry Como (from Ted Weems), Doris Day (from Les Brown), Peggy Lee (from Goodman), Anita O'Day (from Krupa), O'Connell and Eberly (from Jimmy Dorsey), Eberle and the Modernaires (from Glenn Miller), and Dick Haymes became stars.

The war kept draining away band musicians, and "The Band That Plays the Blues" began dissolving slowly. For years Herman had entertained with a repertoire of blues, ballads, novelties, and Dixieland. But Whitney Balliett, writing in the *New Yorker,* took the band lightly, dismissing it as one that played pop, novelty, and blues like self-conscious Dixielanders.

He considered the full ensemble playing weak and, while exempting Cappy Lewis and Reid, accurately panned the band's other soloists.

Unflattering—but it didn't matter. Americans had mostly quit dancing to Carlson's beat anyway; they had begun marching—grim-faced, arms locked, and in step—to the drums of war.

chapter three

TRANSITION

*I*n the face of success, some bandleaders were tempted to enjoy fame and coast. But it was as a serious artist with a sense of history that Herman measured a career. Since his vaudeville days, Herman had come to distrust the public's susceptibility to musical fads: "you can't play down to [fans]. If you do, you may make a million dollars, but you've lost."[1] And so instead of imitating "Woodchoppers' Ball" to his grave, Herman peered ever ahead in search of the new.

Draft notices for his sidemen forced changes, one of which could be seen as well as heard: Herman sometimes filled vacancies with black musicians. This practice was rare at the time, but Herman was more interested in the music than in prejudices. He wanted the best players he could find. For the same reason, he had bought charts from Randolph and Gillespie and looked for more. But Gillespie's idiosyncratic trumpet playing—still in embryonic stages in the forties—was too much, even for Herman: "Dizzy played with us for a short time—I think it was for a week at the Apollo Theater," Herman recalled. "And after I'd heard him, I advised him to stick to writing and give up the trumpet! Thank God he ignored me."[2]

Gillespie's writing was complex and extreme in its use of dynamics, dissonance, scales, rhythm, and harmony. The seemingly simple "Woody'n You," an experiment in scales and harmony, was based on piano-chord progressions, but it was by no means grade-school music. In Gillespie's words, "The melody came from a minor sixth chord to the dominant seventh. B-flat minor sixth with a sixth as the bass to a C. A-flat minor sixth with the sixth the bass to B-flat. It's a natural progression in fourths. From G to C is one fourth. You jump down to F, which is a fifth from C, to another fourth and then jump down a fifth to another fourth, and then the tonic, which is D-flat, and that's the key you're in. Looking at the notes in my right hand, I discovered a counter-melody. I didn't try to express anything, just music, what the chords inspired."[3]

Gillespie called his piece "Woody'n You" because Herman had liked his charts, if not his trumpet playing. The piece also went by the name "Yenta," and Gillespie's 1947 big band recorded it as "Algo Bueno." By the time Herman recorded "Woody'n You" in 1979, it was known as a minor classic because so many jazz groups, large and small, had recorded it. Herman might have recorded it in 1942, but for more than a year after the Petrillo ban commenced, major record companies did not employ union musicians. The companies produced only a thin trickle of discs by singers, either soloing or with choral backgrounds. The shellac shortage further weakened the industry, while the rising costs of material raised record prices.

In February 1943, still playing the Los Angeles area and with several new members, Herman's band recorded four tunes for *Wintertime.* In the 20th Century Fox film, Henie played a Norwegian ice-skating star who came to Canada with her uncle, who bought a faltering resort hotel. The band played "I Like It Here," "Later To-night,"

20th Century Fox publicity still from Wintertime. *showing Herman with clarinet and five saxophonists, including Vido Musso on the far left, early 1943. (Courtesy Ingrid Herman Reese)*

"Wintertime," and "Dancing in the Dawn." The team of Herman, Grey, and the chorus sang of their hopes that after the war the world would dance in the dawn of a new day. Herman sang "Wintertime" and "Later Tonight," while Carol Landis and Cesar Romero sang "I Like It

Here." (In *The Dance Band Era,* Albert McCarthy chose a photo of Herman's band on the *Wintertime* set, mistakenly referring to Rogers as "an unknown lady trumpeter sitting in.") Herman saw moviemaking as good PR but barely worth the trouble: "I had to do a little acting in some of the films, but not much," he said. "They were all nothing pictures. Making the movies was hard work, and the finished products were disappointing. Of eight or nine feature length films we were in, the only good-budget picture was *Wintertime.*"[4]

by 1943, AFRS shows linked thousands of overseas Americans to the life they left behind. Program sources still included commercial recordings made before the ban (some of them unissued alternate studio takes), mostly from Columbia, Decca, and RCA files; radio shows (or rehearsals); concerts; and the AFRS's own recording sessions. Tunesmiths kept writing in spite of the ban on recording. The AFRS and commercial radio helped such songs as "My Ideal," "The Old Music Master," "Moondreams," "Pistol Packin' Mama," "G.I. Jive," "I'm Gonna Sit Right Down and Write Myself a Letter," "Shoo-Shoo Baby," "Poinciana," "Mairzy Doats," and "Bésame Mucho" become wartime hits.

That summer Grey left Herman's band, and he hired O'Day for a few weeks. A first-rate jazz singer from Chicago with a throaty style and a great feel for rhythm, the twenty-three-year-old O'Day had starred with Krupa in 1941–42. Hit records, among them "That's What You Think" and "Let Me Off Uptown," a duet with singing trumpeter Roy Eldridge, assured her reputation. A wild soul who lived on the edge, O'Day had figured in a feud with Eldridge. Then in 1943, when police jailed Krupa for possession of marijuana, O'Day and the band all needed jobs. O'Day was Herman's best hired singer yet, but she recorded nothing because of the ban. In broadcasts from the Chase Hotel in St. Louis, Los Angeles venues, and Mitchell Air Force Base near Milwaukee, she sang "I Lost My Sugar in Salt Lake City," "Slender, Tender and Tall," and "Let Me Off Uptown," in which Herman sang Eldridge's lines.

Rogers became the veteran of the trumpet section as the men kept answering draft calls. May, a twenty-six-year-old trumpeter/writer who had played with Barnet and Glenn Miller, was a member of Herman's band for a brief time in 1943. Reid still anchored the trombones, but with ever changing partners. The sax section presented both a new sound and a new look with alto players Chuck DiMaggio and Les Robinson and tenor players Vido Musso and Pete Mondello aboard, augmented by Skippy DeSair on baritone sax. The draft split Herman's rhythm section, a team since 1937. Carlson and White remained on drums and guitar. But Linehan had to be replaced by pianist Jimmy Rowles, and Yoder by bassist/arranger Gene Sargent. Rowles, twenty-five, had worked with Goodman and others and became a favorite of Herman's, but the draft soon snatched him, too. The 1943 broadcasts also featured new tunes, such as "I Don't Believe in Rumors," "Don't Cry," "Stormy Weather," and "Let's Get Lost," on which Rogers sang and played; Herman's singing of the ballads "Cabin in the Sky," "As Time Goes By," "Sunday, Monday or Always," and "With My Head in the Clouds"; and instrumentals, such as Gillespie's "Down Under," plus "Spruce Juice," "Ten Day Furlough," "C.G.C. Jam," "Starlight Serenade," "The Golden Wedding," and Duke Ellington's "Don't Get Around Much Any More."

In September 1943, Decca agreed to pay the American Federation of Musicians the royalty it demanded for all future records released. Capitol followed in October. Bands led by Kenton, Jenkins, Carter, Freddie Slack, and Paul Weston soon built Capitol's toehold in the business. Kenton's recordings "Harlem Folk Dance" and a version of Duke Ellington's new "Do Nothin' Till You Hear from Me" became hits. But RCA and Columbia, large, rich, and with most of the big-name bands under contract, fought on. Late in 1943, the federal War Labor Board sided with the companies and urged that the ban be dropped. But Petrillo refused. Even when President Franklin D. Roosevelt asked, Petrillo stood firm.

By the fall of 1943, mostly with Matthews's charts, Herman had led his band into an "Ellington period," even to the point of borrowing Ellington's soloists for the resumption of recording. Herman explained the change in direction: "We were getting one-slotted. I felt there was more to music than what we were playing." Herman admitted to being "terribly impressed" with the voicings of the Ellington band. "We had reached a certain level before the war; but then things came to be determined by forces beyond our control," Herman said. "Everybody got drafted, and even though we started as a co-op band, finding replacements became my job. That's when I started making drastic changes. Miller, Artie Shaw, Goodman, and some of the others had tremendous equity in their pre-war successes. I didn't have that much to lose by radical change. That's why we started attracting a different kind of young jazz player than would go to, say, Benny Goodman. Arrangers, too. We came up with great people. It became a band guys wanted to be part of."[5] But the draft and other factors kept the musical chairs going. Rogers left to form a band. May and Rowles departed for the war. A tenor sax player from New York City, Joseph Edward Filipelli—"Joe Flip"—sometimes subbed. Exhausted from the strain of keeping the band intact, Herman collapsed while the band was playing the Earle Theater in Philadelphia; he was laid up nearly two weeks. Recovering in the suburban home of his friends Jack and Mary Siefert, Herman kept worrying. "I can just picture those guys," he said. "One band with thirteen leaders."

In the view of Balliett, the *New Yorker*'s jazz critic, Herman's band faltered during the early years of World War II, then made a string of Decca records showing Herman's fondness for Duke Ellington. (Balliett noted that Barnet and Hal McIntyre had emulated the Duke's music as well.) He conceded that Herman did at least brighten otherwise run-of-the-mill recordings during 1943–44 by borrowing from Ellington's ensemble the black star soloists Webster (tenor sax), Hodges (alto sax), and Tizol (trombone).

The keenest listeners could also detect Ellington trumpeter Nance playing without credit on Herman records. And Budd Johnson, a black sax player and musical director with Hines's band for many years, wrote and subbed a few times. As for the "Ellington influence," Herman explained: "Webster, Tizol, Nance, and Hodges approached me about recording with us [after Decca prepared to record again, a year before Victor, with Ellington under contract, made its peace with Petrillo]. It didn't bother Duke. He told me: 'If you can make a buck, go ahead.'"[6]

On November 8, 1943, Webster played on the first of Herman's sessions for Decca and World Transcriptions after the ban was lifted. That session, which took place in World Studios, New York City, produced three ballads: "The Music Stopped (But We Went On Dancing)," "I Couldn't Sleep a Wink Last Night," and Matthews's chart of Duke Ellington's "Do Nothin' Till You Hear from Me." Nine days later, the band recorded a ballad, "By the River of the Roses," Sargent's riff-and-rhythm chart of "Basie's Basement," and a pop novelty from Ellington known as "Who Dat Up Dere? (Who Dat Down Dere)?"

These tunes are a good indication of the band's change during Petrillo's ban. In August 1942, at the ban's outset, the sixteen-member "Band That Plays the Blues" had featured four trumpets, three trombones, Herman playing clarinet and alto sax, a four-man reed section composed of two alto and two tenor saxes, and a rhythm quartet of piano, string bass, guitar, and drums. Now it presented vocalist Frances Wayne in place of O'Day, and eighteen players:

> five trumpeters, including veteran Cappy Lewis;
>
> three new trombonists;
>
> Herman (playing clarinet and sax) and five sax players (two altos, two tenors, and the added baritone);
>
> a modified rhythm quartet, with pianist Dick Kane in for Rowles, drummer Cliff Leeman for Carlson, Greig Stewart "Chubby" Jackson (for Sargent) plucking a bolder, five-string bass, and White strumming an amplified guitar.

Those who felt Herman overdid the Duke Ellington sound were not hearing everything. His revamped band now outnumbered Ellington's by two. Herman's addition of the baritone sax did enable arrangers to copy more accurately the Ellington band's reed sound and to write richer, deeper section parts. But the power of Herman's trumpet quintet suggested James's band rather than Ellington's. And charts like "Basie's Basement" owed their inspiration to Basie.

However, the Herman band resembled Barnet's more than any other, not least because four recent Barnet players were now with Herman.

Five months Herman's junior, Barnet, a man of wild parties and many marriages, was pistachio to Herman's vanilla. Before he was seventeen, he had played chimes in Duke Ellington's 1930 recording of "Ring Dem Bells" and later, as a leader, dared to front racially mixed bands. In 1939, three months after Herman's "At the Woodchoppers' Ball," Barnet scored with "Cherokee." "Cherokee Charlie" left RCA's Bluebird to sign with Decca and rushed ten tunes onto the market in three months before the Petrillo ban. After Decca gave in, Barnet raced back to the recording studio. On October 21, 1943, his eighteen-man band (plus vocalist Virginia Maxey) recorded "Strollin'," "The Moose," "Pow-Wow," and "Sittin' Home Waitin' for You." But Decca, more interested in profit than art, only issued "Strollin'" and "Sittin' Home Waitin' for You." It shipped the other two off to its corporate kin in Great Britain, which issued them on the English Brunswick label and exported them back to the United States. Thus "The Moose," a seminal modern jazz piece, written by young Ralph Burns and featuring seventeen-year-old piano whiz Michael "Dodo" Marmarosa, barely reached American ears.

The young 1943 Herman and Barnet bands were near carbon copies, the only differences being in the trumpet-trombone balance (four-four with Barnet, five-three with Herman). Twenty-one-year-old trombonist Eddie Bert played in Barnet's "The Moose," then jumped over to Herman for a few weeks. "Woody wanted the latest stuff," Bert said, "and wanted all the great players. He wanted his band to be loose and swinging, but he also rehearsed a lot because the arrangements were intricate, and he wanted tight ensemble. When you worked for Woody you were part of his family."[7]

Leeman, at thirty, functioned as a big-brother figure in Barnet's band. A native of Portland, Maine, he had played with his hometown symphony orchestra at thirteen, toured as a vaudeville xylophonist, drummed for Shaw from 1936 to 1939, Tommy Dorsey in 1939, and Barnet from 1940 to 1943. Two of the arrivals from Barnet were the nineteen-year-old Boston vocalist Wayne—born Chiarina Francesca Bertocci—who debuted with the combo of her brother Nick Jerrett in New York City and joined Barnet in 1942; and Jackson, a boisterous, high-energy bassist. A twenty-five-year-old New Yorker, Jackson had started playing the bass at seventeen, and from 1937 to 1941, he worked with the bands of Mike Riley, Johnny Messner, Raymond Scott, Jan Savitt, Terry Shand, and Henry Busse, whose trademark "shuffle rhythm" demanded a dominating bassist. Barnet began featuring Jackson's rhythmic bass in 1941. Typical basses have four strings, tuned to E, A, D, and G; Jackson added a fifth string, tuned to C. "This gave the player a fourth more range on the fingerboard," he said. "It became quite popular, put out by the Kay Bass Company in Chicago. A number of bassists took off the low E and it again became a four-string bass."[8]

After Jackson joined Herman in September 1943, Jackson turned talent scout for innovative new players, luring fellow Barnet alumni, as well as others who fit the mold, over to Herman. Why the exodus from Barnet? For one thing, Herman was a practical, honest, affable, generous, appreciative, understanding, and musically knowledgeable man. But also, as former Barnet trombonist Trummy Young said, "Barnet would keep a band only so long. When the band got popular, he broke it up because he said it was interfering with his pleasure."[9]

Although Wayne was no match for O'Day, her voice was lower, sultrier, silkier yet more worldly than those of the vocalists employed by Herman before the war; she sang "The Music Stopped" and "I Couldn't Sleep a Wink Last Night" for the November 1943 Decca session. After working with Barnet for most of 1942, she endured the terrifying experience of losing her voice. She took an eight-month rest and was working as a soloist in a Boston nightclub when Herman heard her. Two days later, she was with his band.

Webster played one of his rolling tenor-sax solos on "I Couldn't Sleep a Wink." Herman sang the sugary ballad "By the River of the Roses" and "Do Nothin' Till You Hear from Me." His melodic clarinet and the more vigorous saxes elevated "By the River of the Roses." Matthews's slow-paced Ellingtonian arrangement of "Do Nothin' Till You Hear from Me" also teased with Cappy Lewis's suggestions of Cootie Williams's trumpet playing, Kane on piano, and Webster in two solos. But it exposed weak, poorly rehearsed trumpet playing. The most innovative feature of this chart was Jackson's syncopated "walking" bass, which laid down a pulse loud enough to sound like drum beats. Jackson, a rotund show-biz ham, would also slip in two notes where one was expected and make fast runs on a scale for effect.

Jackson's bass also propelled "Basie's Basement," which was taken at a relaxed tempo with piano, muted brass, and reed-section and full-band passages. Webster soloed and Herman played clarinet. But Decca also exiled the toe-tapping "Basie's Basement"—a playful reference to Macy's Basement—overseas for release on English Brunswick. Ellington's "Who Dat Up Dere?" is marked by Amos-and-Andy dialect lyrics, wah-wah brass reminiscent of Ellington, and Herman and the bandsmen in back-and-forth vocal exchanges (by then a cliché). Webster soloed, and Herman played alto passages while Cappy Lewis blew muted trumpet. "Who Dat?" became an overnight success, but Herman regretted that Decca gave Webster no credit on the record. Moreover, "Duke took some heat from the NAACP about that tune, and asked me what I could do to get it off the air,"[10] Herman said. All he could do, though, was quit playing it on the bandstand. Decca paired "Who Dat Up Dere?" with "Let Me Love You Tonight," a 1942 recording.

Clearly, Herman's old dilemma of having to play two songs for "them" so as to play one for himself still applied, and "Do Nothin' Till You Hear from Me" and "Basie's Basement" were his ration this time. But for astute fans of Herman, "The Music Stopped" enthralled most. Jackson again drove the band with his bass, while now and again the reeds played something subtly new. In certain passages the chart called upon alto sax players to switch to tenors. This gave the reed section a deeper, mellower chorus of four droning tenors harmonizing above a baritone. As this euphonious scheme gained favor in 1940s bands, some called it "tenorizing." Most five-sax bands used altos so that arrangers could work with a broad range of notes. Without altos, the sax parts were written within a narrower range. The sound was refreshingly new.

Before 1943 ended, Herman's band transcribed eight newer tunes from its book for the AFRS. Wayne sang "I Don't Believe in Rumors," "I Lost My Sugar in Salt Lake City," and "Don't Cry." Herman and the guys sang and played "Who Dat Up Dere?" and banged out "Spruce Juice," "Bishop's Blues," "Starlight Souvenirs," and "G.C.G. Jam." The new year began with what Herman called "an especially important acquisition": arranger Burns, another Barnet alumnus.

"I worked exclusively for Woody for about five years, and for another ten while writing for singers and other bands," Burns said. "I think my first chart for Woody was 'Happiness Is Just a Thing Called Joe.' I have no idea how many pieces I did altogether, but it was at least two or three a week during the first few years. Woody taught me so much about writing. His big thing was that [music] wouldn't swing if there were too many notes. A lot of stuff is overwritten when you're young and eager."[11]

As Herman recalled it, "Ralph's first arrangement was 'I've Got the World on a String.' I guess Chubby Jackson must have advised him to 'write a couple of vocals for the old man—that'll get you in solid.'" In any event, Burns and Herman clicked. Hailing from a Boston suburb, Burns, twenty-one, quiet and shy, had studied at the New England Conservatory and played in Boston-area bands. Like Wayne, he moved to New York City with Jerrett's band. Burns then wrote and played for Barnet and sold charts to vibraphonist Red Norvo. He came to consider Herman "the best bandleader I ever worked for. He gave everybody a chance, he never hogged the spotlight."[12]

Burns prepared four numbers for Herman's January 8 session in World Transcriptions' studios: "Noah," "I'll Get By," and the Cole Porter show tunes "I've Got You under My Skin" and "I Get a Kick out of You." World liked them, but Decca waived all four for release on English Brunswick. "Noah," like "Be Not Disencouraged," "Amen," "Dancing in the Dawn" and "Who Dat Up Dere?" was in the pop-spiritual genre. Webster and Cappy Lewis soloed, and Herman sang in the style he called "Milwaukee gospel." World also recorded (and sold for radio) "Don't Believe Everything You Dream," "Speak Low," "Just Dreaming," "Starlight Souvenirs," and "Crying Sands." Jackson had written the last of these—a simple, pretty ballad.

In a few weeks the band took a quick trip to Hollywood and recorded sound-track music on February 13 for United Artists' *Sensations of 1945.* Powell, Dennis O'Keefe, Calloway, and Sophie Tucker acted in the movie, which had a show-biz story line. One skit marked W. C. Fields's last frames on film. The Herman and Calloway bands played minor roles. Herman's "Wake Up, Man! You're Slippin'," "Our Love," "The Kiss Serenade," "No, Never," and "Spin Little Pin Ball" impressed fans of both music and film, even if they weren't as memorable as "Amen," "Noah," and "The Golden Wedding," which were taken for the AFRS library from a Hollywood radio broadcast the same week.

When the army drafted Cappy Lewis, Herman hired Neil Hefti, who offered trumpeting and songwriting talents, as well as a 4-F draft status, thanks to injuries sustained in an auto crash. From Hastings, Nebraska, Hefti had played and/or written for Barnet, Hines, Spivak, Heidt, and Bobby Byrne. All the while, the draft went on robbing Herman of his band. For two weeks, one kid named Lenny Garment filled a draftee's sax chair. Years later, when he was President Richard M. Nixon's White House counsel, Garment remained a staunch Herman fan.

Hefti remembers the frenetic pace of 1944 with a shudder: "So many people were drafted in Woody's band that every night it was almost like a new band sight-reading the book. It got to the point that Woody couldn't call out his real swinging numbers. The band couldn't read [them] so we started faking."[13] Back in New York City for a March 23 session with Decca and World, the reed section housed former Glenn Miller sideman Ernie Caceres and guest tenor sax player Johnson (for Webster). Johnson could play clarinet and tenor, alto, and baritone sax, and write. The thirty-three-year-old Dallas native had toured with Armstrong, Wilson, and Hines. This session produced English Brunswick versions of "Cherry" (Matthews's chart of a 1942 James hit) and "It Must Be Jelly" (Burns's cover of a romp that Glenn Miller had done for RCA Victor in 1942), plus Decca releases of Don Raye and Gene DePaul's "Milkman, Keep Those Bottles Quiet" and their steamy ballad "Irresistible You."

"It Must Be Jelly ('Cause Jam Don't Shake Like That)" tapped Herman's and Wayne's talents singing novelties. "I used to go into that falsetto bit when I didn't know what else to do," Herman said. "You might say I was a sort of a Ray Charles with a small voice."[14] On "Cherry,"

Herman played the clarinet in its lower register, while Johnson and Burns soloed. (Sharp-eared Herman fans could notice that Burns reused his sprinkling-of-piano-notes ending on "Cherry" for an intro when arranging Duke Ellington's "I Ain't Got Nothin' but the Blues.")

Burns's arranging touches and distinctive piano playing could be heard in both of the Raye-DePaul tunes. "Milkman," which was based on the premise that a night-shift worker in a defense plant needed daytime sleep, featured Hefti's growling trumpet and Herman singing the topical lyrics. The chart also used Jackson's double-timed walking bass and tenorized saxes in spots behind soloists. Burns and Leeman added still another touch that would catch on: a coda that, by design, started strong then fell apart, as though—oops!—Leeman's drums and cymbals had gone spilling down a flight of stairs. Similar free-for-all codas in brass began to make it into modern charts for several bands—a stunt known among sidemen as a "train wreck." "Irresistible You," with tenorized reeds backing Wayne, featured more of Jackson's wandering bass, muted brass, Herman's alto sax and clarinet, and Johnson's tenor sax. And in this coda, Jackson sprinted up and down the scale, as he had in "Do Nothin' Till You Hear from Me."

On March 29, with Auld on tenor sax substituting for Johnson, the band recorded the ballads "Say So," "Refuse It," and "Goin' Home," with Herman singing; and Matthews's ballad "Ingie Speaks"—a tribute to two-and-a-half-year-old Ingrid Herman—which featured solos by Herman and Auld and a duet by White and Jackson. Herman only rarely brought his family into his public life. However, his own music publishing company, Charling, was named after Charlotte and Ingrid. Formed in 1942, when Herman composed a dance tune called "Lazy Rhapsody"— with lyrics by his friend Don George—Charling, which was a member of the ASCAP stable, published about two dozen numbers, mostly band instrumentals, during the next five years.

Decca did not choose to issue the four ballads, probably because of their length. The four-minute "Goin' Home" was the first of Herman's thirty-some "V discs," longer-playing vinyl discs manufactured solely for the benefit of military personnel. The ten-inch prewar discs produced by such companies as RCA Victor, Decca, and Columbia were stamped into brittle composition material and coated with shellac. These seventy-eight rpm discs had several drawbacks: they used materials required by the war industry, and their playing time was limited to about three minutes and fifteen seconds per side. Transcriptions were records up to sixteen inches across, to be replayed and broadcast on high-tech radio studio equipment at much slower speeds, allowing up to thirty minutes of playing time. V discs were twelve-inch, unbreakable vinyl discs that went only to military bases. The time limit on the seventy-eight-rpm V discs was nearly six minutes. Some V discs contained one long number per side, others two short ones. The bright red, white, and blue labels with the artsy V disc logo warned in fine print:

> War Department—Music Section—Entertainment & Recreation Branch
>
> Special Services Division—A.S.F.
>
> This record is the property of the War Department of the United States and use for radio or commercial purposes is prohibited.

The army authorized Simon—who held the rank of private—to make V discs by "anyone I wanted to, wherever I wanted to—provided, of course, I could get them to record for the troops free. Fortunately, I had made many friends during my *Metronome* days so, combining my contacts with the prevalent patriotic feelings, I had little difficulty lining up recording stars. In addition, various radio shows let us record dress rehearsals and actual broadcasts."[15]

Because Petrillo still banned union musicians from recording with Columbia and RCA, V discs boosted any leader who needed to stay in the public eye. The union waived royalties on V discs as a contribution to the war effort, but Petrillo insisted that the masters be destroyed to prevent copying and public sale after the war. Tommy Dorsey's name went on about a dozen V discs, mostly reissues of his best RCA Victor tunes; Goodman and James—waiting out the ban with Columbia—made about forty V discs apiece.

Herman's band, a shadow of its former self due to the draft, recorded next on April 5. Tizol, Nance, and Hodges, guesting from Duke Ellington's band, sparked Herman's lineup. So did Herbie Fields, substituting for Auld, and electric guitarist Billy Bauer, replacing White, the last sideman from the "Band That Plays the Blues." Now twenty-eight, the self-taught banjoist Bauer had switched to electric guitar, mastered modern chording, and played for Jerry Wald, Dick Stabile, and Abe Lyman. When Leeman left, Theodore "Red" Saunders, a fellow Milwaukeean a year older than Herman, sat in at the drums for a few weeks.

But strain between Herman and Decca, evident in the unproductive March 29 recording session, resurfaced when Decca rejected, for reasons unknown, versions of "Blue Lullaby" and Wayne singing "As Long As I Live" (both taken by World Transcriptions). Furthermore, the record company decided to defer release of Matthews's chart of Tizol's 1942 "Perdido"—which featured solos by Hefti, Fields, Tizol, and Hodges— to its distant cousins at English Brunswick. Decca did keep for U.S. release the best: Duke Ellington's new ballad "I Didn't Know about You," in a gorgeous arrangement by Burns that highlighted Herman's tender singing and Hodges's alto-sax solo. Played at medium tempo, it packaged echoes of Ellington, a walking bass, tenorized saxes, and Burns's bold piano chords. Herman also played a soft, low clarinet part for the piece which, except for bland brass playing, promised a new sound for his band.

"With our music [getting to be] more diversified in mood and sound, we were even able to play the 'black theaters,'" Herman said. "In fact we were one of only two 'white bands' doing that regularly—the other was Barnet's—in Baltimore, Washington, and New York at the Apollo."[16] Since he resumed recording in November 1943, Herman had led his rapidly changing lineup through twenty-one commercial sides. But only five— "The Music Stopped," "Basie's Basement," "Milkman, Keep Those Bottles Quiet," "Irresistible You," and "I Didn't Know about You"—presaged the full changes that Jackson, Burns, and Hefti would soon effect.

Jackson's bass playing and on-the-job cheerleading made him unique enough; but his forte was finding talent. "What an immense influence he had on us," Herman reflected. "And what enthusiasm! He used to get around to hear everything. He was always screaming about some musician. He'd been with Barnet with Ralph Burns, Neal Hefti and Frances Wayne, and kept telling me I should hire them. So I did, and you know how much they meant to us!"[17]

So it is not surprising that when Herman hired Tough in May 1944 to replace Saunders, Jackson asked: "Do you think he'll fit?" But after Tough had been with the band only a couple of days, as Herman told it, "Chubby decided he *invented* Davey!"[18] At thirty-six, the Chicagoan Tough was the oldest Herman bandsman and had played with Goodman and Tommy Dorsey and been a member of Shaw's navy band since mid-1942. But now, a chain smoker prone to illness, alcohol abuse, and (some said) melancholy, Tough held a medical discharge. (His weight stayed around one hundred pounds.) Unlike many who were known as "modern" in the 1940s, Tough played simple, basic drums. But so firm and swinging was his beat, and so subtle the little throw-ins he invented on the spot, that musicians of all stripes voted him their favorite. Tough, like Herman, cared little for nostalgia or acclaim. He looked ahead to what was new, and to mastering it. Just before he joined Herman, Tough visited a number of New York City jazz joints on Fifty-second Street and heard such musicians as Kenny Clarke, Mary Lou Williams, Thelonius Monk, Gillespie, and Parker jamming. Once, he said, "as we walked in, those cats snatched up their horns and blew crazy stuff. One would stop all of a sudden and another would start for no reason at all. We never could tell when a solo was supposed to begin or end. Then they all quit at once and walked off the stand. It scared us."[19] But as jazz historian Marshall Stearns points out, Tough right away began injecting into the Herman band some of those things that "scared" him.[20] Tough knew modern art and read and tried serious writing. But he was a born jazzman. To him the drums were "a rhythmic palette on which he held in readiness the right color for each soloist."[21] Fellow drummer Shelly Manne, twenty-four in 1944, remembered how "Davey was very flexible. He could play with Bud Freeman one night and play with Woody Herman the next with the new Herd. He had the permanent thing that drummers have to have—they have to swing. If a drummer can swing, he can play with anybody."[22] Jackson's assessment of Tough's talents reflects the crucial role that a good drummer plays for a band: "He joined our band *harmonically*, and changed the whole rhythm focus. I learned how to play a whole new kind of time. I could actually feel the band growing behind me!" Herman added: "Davey . . . could propel a band and put everybody into a relaxed position. He was a dynamic time-keeper, who took great pride in his cymbals, the sound of each one, the heads on his drums. And he kept you musically straight. Time-wise, you were always at home, no matter where you were."[23]

In June 1944, when Herbie Fields moved on, Herman reacquired Filipelli, a strong tenor sax soloist. The deadpan Brooklyn native—good as a booming jazzmaker or a soft, sensitive balladeer—had played with a Hickory House band in New York City during 1942–43 and sat in briefly with Goodman's, Norvo's, Herman's, Wingy Manone's, and Russ Morgan's bands. Herman had to persuade Filipelli, who, he said, "didn't want to leave Russ Morgan—*that* represented security!"[24] With Herman, Filipelli performed as "Flip" Phillips and soon became Herman's best in-house sax star since Haymer.

While the band was playing Chicago in June, Herman signed with the Columbia Broadcasting System to replace pianist Frankie Carle's band and to costar with singer Allan Jones on eleven weekly national radio shows for Old Gold cigarettes, starting July 26. And soon the acquisition of three more talents gave the band a preaching—that is, powerful, original, and emotional—trombone soloist—William Palmer "Bill" Harris, twenty-seven, from Philadelphia—and two trumpeters from Mishawaka, Indiana: the brothers Walter Joseph "Pete" Candoli, just turned twenty-one, and Secondo "Conte" Candoli, who at seventeen would need to return to high school in September. Harris had been a power trombonist but was a poor sight reader, a failing few leaders condoned. He played with a number of bands, served a Merchant Marine hitch, and worked in a defense plant. Returning to the trombone, he played for Buddy Williams, Bob Chester, and Goodman during 1942–44. By then, having improved his reading, the taciturn, prank-loving Harris soloed on the sound track of Goodman's movie *Sweet and Lowdown*. Back in New York City in early 1944, the emboldened Harris led his own sextet at Cafe Society Uptown, then rejoined Chester for a short stint until Jackson recruited him for Herman. Pete Candoli was a prodigy who had blown big-band trumpet for Goodman, Barnet, Tommy Dorsey, Sonny Dunham, Will Bradley, Ray McKinley, Freddie Slack, Alvino Rey, and Teddy Powell.

Now in mid-1944, the band came into its own. The years of imitating were over. Burns and Hefti wrote fresh, lively charts that made the band sound like none before it. The main catalyst? Herman always pointed to Jackson, who said:

> The younger soloists [Phillips, Harris, and Pete Candoli] started to come into the band addressing ideas like [Gillespie] and Parker. . . . As the band left its "Ellington Period," those soloists started to fly around like Charlie and Dizzy. Neal Hefti started to write some of his ensembles with some of the figures that came from that early be-bop. We were really one of the first outside of Dizzy's that flavored be-bop into the big band—different tonal quality and rhythms, and the "drum feeling" started changing, and that was the beginning of it. When bop first came out it amazed all of us. We were used to milky alto saxophones of Benny Carter, Willie Smith and Johnny Hodges and more melodic-type passages. Then the staccato concept came through, and at first it was a little raucous. It was cooking, but it was so strange, and it seemed that you had to play double time all the time to get a raised eyebrow. I fell in love with it, and I finally got into playing it with the big band because [Hefti] had it down.[25]

Herman, however, considered Burns the stronger arranger "because he was so versatile; he could go in any bag and make it happen." Herman said that while Hefti did bring in "unison choruses based on early bop things [he] really didn't do a great deal of writing, but he was constantly coming up with ideas. He was invaluable in that department, because a lot of our things were based on heads anyway."[26] With Burns, Tough, Jackson, Bauer, Hefti, Phillips, Pete Candoli, and Bill Harris all improvising, the Herman band by July was belting out thunderous, highly creative instrumentals and giving sparkle to ballads.

Private Simon, moonlighting for *Metronome* when he could, felt "considerable shock" the August night he drove to Pleasure Beach in Bridgeport, Connecticut, to hear Herman's 1944 band. "What I heard gave me one of the big thrills of my life, and I said as much in a rave review that appeared in the September *Metronome*," he said. "It began: 'Before you can have a really great band,' Woody Herman once told me, 'you've got to be able to play really fine music all night long. You can't just coast on a few arrangements and play average stuff the rest of the evening.' Herman's band [now] qualifies as a really great band." Simon marveled at the rhythm section's "massive, swinging beat" for a "batch of brilliant soloists." In Simon's view, the band could "jump like mad" or play "really pretty, moodful ballads, featuring either its leader or else arrangements that spot interesting modern chords and voicings." Furthermore, he rated the reed players "a section that's fast becoming one of the best in the business" and raved about "the amazing Bill Harris." The trumpet section disappointed Simon, but he could not praise Burns enough: "One of the greatest arrangers to come along in years." The review also lauded Herman ("the greatest all-around singer in the business today [whose] clarineting continues to improve") and Wayne ("a smooth-working stage performer.") Offstage, Simon found Herman "ecstatic" because the band pleased him musically while listeners were swept away by its spirit and excitement.[27]

Herman's relationship with Decca was sour, but fortunately, the Old Gold shows rapidly widened Herman's following. He shared the bantering, scripted thirty-minute broadcasts each week with Allan Jones and the drawling announcer Red Barber (future Hall-of-Fame baseball broadcaster). "That summer, fall and winter were turning points in the band's history," Herman said, "and things began to happen!"[28]

chapter four

the
<u>FIRST</u> <u>HERD</u>

*t*he name Herman's Herd had been coined by Simon in 1941, but by mid-1944, Herman led a far better herd, playing wild, unfettered stampede music. This band and its arrangers tested harmonies and rhythms, spicing the written book with whoops and shouts, quintuple-fortissimo horns, brass-section "train wrecks," and ritard and tumble-down-steps codas. In jazz history this band became known as Herman's First Herd—a handy name to separate it from the others that followed. The First Herd played for a rollicking and moneymaking twenty-nine months before attrition and market conditions silenced it.

Because Herman's Decca deal was dissolving in 1944, the eleven Old Gold radio shows provided the first nationwide exposure to the First Herd and stirred up demand for it. Between August and year's end, in a splurge of good fortune, the band also played top venues in New York City and Hollywood, worked in another movie, made V discs, AFRS shows, transcriptions, and its last Decca records.

Before the Wednesday night Old Gold shows, Herman and the band, Allan Jones, and Barber practiced the scripts and checked timings and sound balance. Some high-quality rehearsal music went onto V discs and into AFRS broadcasts.

For the radio series, Jones sang pop and semiclassical songs such as "Let's All Sing about Suzie" and "Thine Alone." Herman and Wayne, too, endured their share of middling fare, such as "If There Is Someone Lovelier than You" and "How Blue the Night." And Herman dipped into his modest cache of past hits: "Woodchoppers' Ball," "Blues on Parade," "The Golden Wedding," "Four or Five Times," and "Amen."

In spite of pressure to be "commercial," Herman seized the chance to do more on network radio. In 1944, fans were lapping up the topical lyrics of "Milkman, Keep Those Bottles Quiet." "Is You Is or Is You Ain't My Baby?" which Herman broadcast on August 2, was another fun-with-jazz number. Imitations followed immediately: Nat "King" Cole's trio's hit "Straighten Up and Fly Right" (August 9) and Mercer's "G.I. Jive" (August 16) and "There'll Be a Hot Time in the Town of Berlin" (September 20).

The First Herd, about 1945. As the full band plays, Herman encourages bassist Chubby Jackson. (Courtesy Duncan P. Schiedt)

The First Herd supported Herman's singing with a pulsing rhythm section in which Jackson beat time on the bass, while Burns and Bauer supplied piano and guitar chords, and Tough laid down a foamy carpet of cymbals. Since the street-march days of early Dixieland music, big drums had driven bands. But now Clarke, Max Roach, and others were perfecting—and Tough was mastering—ways to propel a band by stirring cymbals with hand-held wire brushes, with oddly timed accents or "bombs" coming up from the bass drum. It was the difference between thunder and soft rain. With Hefti and Pete Candoli, the trumpet section sounded crisper, more in tune, precise and higher-pitched, whether playing muted- or open-horn passages. Hefti tore into daring, bop-inspired solos while Candoli urged his trumpet to wild high notes. Bill Harris's trombone solos became pieces to be studied and copied, and he led the three-man trombone section with a throaty bravado. Phillips could blow sledgehammer or velvet-glove tenor solos, and the reed section sounded solid, sure, and able to create many moods.

In this band's hands, Burns's chart of "Is You Is," with its inane pop lyrics from the movie *Follow the Boys,* became a model jazz piece, with Tough's cymbals, Jackson's driving bass, trombone eruptions, muted brass, solos by Phillips, Pete Candoli, and Bill Harris, nine dissonant staccato trumpet-section blasts from nowhere and for no reason, Burns's silky piano playing, and one of those tongue-in-cheek, fall-to-pieces codas. The same could be said of "Flyin' Home" and a "Woodchoppers' Ball," both broadcast on August 2. Worked out in 1941 by Hampton, "Flyin' Home," with Phillips and Herman—on clarinet—wailing over the rhythm section and Candoli playing high above the others at the finish, came to function as a head chart. The rehearsal version became a V disc. Hefti, meanwhile, altered the basics of "Flyin' Home" twice more, creating "Helen of Troy" that fall and "The Good Earth" in 1945.

On the Old Gold show of August 9, Herman introduced "Apple Honey" and "I Ain't Got Nothin' but the Blues." On August 16 there came the swinging "Red Top," followed in a few days by the stunningly modern "125th Street Prophet" and Hefti's bold, booming composition, known both as "Jones Beachhead" and "Half Past Jumpin' Time." These numbers, all put together in about a month, constituted a rare burst of creativity. Taken at a slow beginner's tempo (which increased as the band learned the number), "Apple Honey" opened with a crashing brass figure (Hefti's borrowing from Duke Ellington's "Drop Me Off in Harlem"), then unison reeds played a linear driving theme, in the style of bop. Muted brass introduced a strong Phillips solo, backed by Burns's bold piano chords. A trumpet-section figure softly came to life in the background, then Bill Harris soloed over the reeds, the full band blasted away, Phillips returned, and Pete Candoli and Tough held a trumpet-drum conversation in half-measure phrases before Candoli led an ending that finished on one note held for eight beats. The title "Apple Honey" came from Old Gold's trademarked name for a flavoring for its Turkish latakia tobacco. Herman, credited as composer, used the name to promote the cigarettes on the air. Herman called the piece "one of [our] many head arrangements . . . based on 'I Got Rhythm,' one of the better B-flat tunes."[1] For the next five minutes the band dazzled listeners to that broadcast with Burns's chart of Ellington's new "I Ain't Got Nothin' but the Blues." Herman sang and soloed on clarinet, backed by Phillips and Candoli.

"Red Top"—named in honor of Barber—was a rhythm number. Unique among most jazz numbers up to that time, "Red Top," like Hartsell's 1941 "Hot Chestnuts," had a basic chord structure and fast tempo, but no central melody. It opened with twelve strong notes from the brass, then settled for a while into a brisk quartet for Burns, Bauer, Jackson, and Tough. Strong, rhythmic chords by Burns then led to a clarinet solo by Herman and a full-band shout of "yaaaaahh!" Jackson urged things on with his own excited "yeahhhh!" before the brass entered with a complex rolling figure (written out by Hefti), followed by a series of solos—Phillips over the brass, Phillips over the piano, and Harris over the reeds. Next came brass-and-clarinet riffing and Pete Candoli blowing sky-high as all sections played a hypnotic riff to the end.

On August 21, 1944, the band opened at the Cafe Rouge in New York City's Hotel Pennsylvania. CBS radio broadcast an opening-night program consisting of a short "Blue Flame," played as a theme song, Wayne singing "Irresistible You," and the new, four-minute Phil Moore piece called "125th Street Prophet," a reference to a street in Harlem. Moore, a twenty-six-year-old composer, singer, and pianist from Oregon, had written for Barnet, among others. This oddly swinging "musicians' music" relied on minor chords and rhythm breaks, powerhouse drumming, and great blocks of full-band and section playing. Another glittering part of that show was Burns's chart of "I've Got the World on a String." Herman sang and played clarinet, and Phillips blew a mellow tenor sax solo. Wayne returned to sing "It's a Cryin' Shame," a pop tune big with Tommy Dorsey at the time. In the "Blue Flame" closer, Bill Harris treated Herman fans to some of his variations on the 1941 theme.

As the band played it on the Old Gold show of August 23, an edited "Red Top" came out faster and smoother, with Burns less bossy on piano, his chords lighter, a different reed riff behind Bill Harris's solo, and Pete Candoli soaring just as high but with better control at the finish. Herman also programmed Burns's chart of "G.I. Jive," which honored the lowly army private. Herman sang Mercer's amusing lyrics.

On August 28 from the Cafe Rouge, Herman's radio fans heard "125th Street Prophet" and "I Ain't Got Nothin' but the Blues" in a seven-piece set closed by the rumbling "Flyin' Home." On the August 30 Old Gold show, Herman and the band—after some radio-script humor, cloying perhaps even in 1944—introduced Hefti's jarring "Jones Beachhead." Like "125th Street Prophet," it was bold, powerhouse jazz. And like "Basie's Basement," its title had special meaning: those who followed war news knew "beachhead" as an invasion term, yet Jones Beach was a mecca for urban New Yorkers in search of sea and sand. The title also honored Allan Jones. "Jones Beachhead" featured full-band ensemble playing, with driving drums to keep it moving. Burns's strong chords, Pete Candoli's muted trumpet peeps, and Phillips playing over the muted brass gave it variety.

Six days after broadcasting "Jones Beachhead," the band recorded it for a V disc, together with a scorching "Red Top" and two ballads, "I Can't Put My Arms around a Memory" and "Happiness Is Just a Thing Called Joe," sung by Herman and Wayne, respectively. The band played the V disc version of "Jones Beachhead" more slowly than it had for radio and added a tenor sax solo to fill the five-minute allowance. (To make V discs less attractive to thieves, the War Department coupled contrasting kinds of music on them. Thus it matched "Red Top" with "Poor Little Rhode Island Girl" and "Come with Me My Honey" by Lombardo's sweet-music band.)

On September 10 in Liederkranz Hall, the band recorded three more V discs: the pop ballad "Time Waits for No One," starring Wayne; an infantry-flavored Irving Berlin ballad, "There Are No Wings on a Fox-hole," with Herman singing; and "Apple Honey." Eddie Sauter, alumnus of the Glenn Miller and Goodman bands, arranged "Time Waits for No One," from the 1944 film *Shine On Harvest Moon*. But Sauter and Herman did not mesh musically. Sauter's many advanced ideas did not swing in Herman's style.

Many of the band's jazz numbers began exceeding three minutes, to the joy of fans and players alike. But unless they heard broadcasts or V discs or attended performances, fans missed those stretched-out pieces. The First Herd never recorded "Red Top," "Jones Beachhead," or "125th Street Prophet" commercially, probably because the band did not care to cut them to three minutes. Clearly no Decca executive liked the music. Many years later, with the technical advantages of long-playing records, cassette tapes, and compact discs, the tunes did at last reach the marketplace.

For the September 13 Old Gold show, Herman again chose "125th Street Prophet" and sang Burns's dreamy treatment of "Some-body Loves Me." The September 20 Old Gold show's broadcast of "Basie's Basement" showed much better talent than the crew who recorded it in December 1943, enabling us to document the First Herd's superiority over the earlier band. This performance revealed a greatly improved rhythm section, overall smoothness, and better solos, such as Bauer's guitar play-ing. And whereas the old version tiptoed to a piano-and-bass finish, the new one reached that point, then had Tough blast out a drum break before a loud full-band coda.

On the September 27 Old Gold show, Herman turned loose a new Woodchoppers group, adding vibraphonist Marjorie Hyams, whom he heard and recruited in an Atlantic City boardwalk tavern in early Au-gust when his band was playing Hamid's Steel Pier and he was out with Siefert. Hampton had taken up vibes for jazz recordings in 1930, but after fourteen years only he, Hyams, Norvo, and a few others played vibes in jazz settings. The new Woodchoppers played "1-2-3-4 Jump," which was borrowed from a group led by Norvo. This Woodchoppers number had bop elements, beginning with the lineup of trumpet, trombone, tenor sax, clarinet, vibes, and rhythm section and employing the abrupt staccato rhythm figures variously termed in casual conversations and a few song titles as "re-bop," "be-bop," or "mop-mop." Phillips and Hefti played tight unison sax-trumpet passages, with solos assigned to Hyams, Phillips, and Jackson. (Phillips and Burns had played on Norvo's 1943 V disc of "1-2-3-4 Jump.")

On October 4 the full band gave "Apple Honey," by now rounded into better shape, another radio airing in its final Old Gold show, as it did Burns's treatment of "Sweet Lorraine," a ballad adapted by a number of jazz musicians during the war, and the dance tune "Somebody Loves Me." Both charts called for Herman to play the themes on alto sax, then sing.

After the band ended six weeks in the Hotel Pennsylvania, it played a few one-nighters in and around New York City. It also put on five studio shows for AFRS and *Treasury Star Parade* transcriptions. Highlights from these included Burns's charts of "The Man I Love," "Two Again," and "Always," sung by Wayne; the pop ballads "There Is No Greater Love," "Golden Earrings," "The Trolley Song," "Evalina," and "Right as the Rain," sung by Herman; and "Red Top," "125th Street Prophet," "1-2-3-4 Jump," "Helen of Troy," and "Jones Beachhead," which was introduced as "Half Past Jumpin' Time."

Then they embarked on a westward theater tour before opening in the Hollywood Palladium on October 12, where the band stayed six weeks. CBS Radio broadcast the opening night, noting on the air that Herman's was the first band ever booked four times in the lavish dancing palace since its opening in 1940. At the Palladium Herman played "Who Dat?" which, despite Duke Ellington's pleadings and the NAACP's displeasure, had become a Decca hit and was to be featured in the band's next movie, Republic's *Earl Carroll Vanities*; "'T'ain't Me," a good rhythm vehicle for Bill Harris's solo trombone and Herman's singing; and "Let Me Love You Tonight," another of Sauter's charts for Wayne; and "I've Got You under My Skin," "Time Waits for No One," "Somebody Loves Me," and "Come Out, Come Out Wherever You Are," a hit sung by Sinatra and

Gloria DeHaven in *Step Lively*. A five-minute-forty-five second "Wood-choppers' Ball" followed, with solo slots going to Phillips, Hyams, Bill Harris, Hefti, and Pete Candoli. (Hefti wrote out his solo for all the trumpets to play in "Caldonia" three months later.) Other Palladium shows repeated "1-2-3-4 Jump," "Who Dat?" "'T'ain't Me," "Red Top," "Apple Honey," "I'll Get By," "Somebody Loves Me," "It Must Be Jelly," and Sauter's gloomy "I'll Walk Alone" for Wayne. Short-lived material tested during this stretch included Herman singing "I'll Remember April" and "There Goes That Song Again," Wayne's "And Then You Kissed Me" and "Up, Up, Up," and the Woodchoppers' sprightly "Skyscraper," which Phillips and eight pals recorded before leaving New York City.

The AFRS copped several Palladium broadcasts for its *One Night Stand* shows. During the day, the band filmed scenes and recorded its sound track for *Earl Carroll Vanities*. This ninety-one-minute musical, directed by Joseph Santley, featured Dennis O'Keefe, Constance Moore, Eve Arden, and Otto Kruger as Carroll. *TV Guide*'s movie guide called it "nit-written, with no style, but an engaging cast." It did show the First Herd playing "Apple Honey," "Rock a Bye Boogie," "You Beautiful Thing You," "Who Dat?" and "Riverside Jive."

*P*etrillo's ban on the commercial record companies finally ended in November 1944 when Columbia and RCA agreed to pay royalties to his union for all records released. Petrillo called it "the greatest victory . . . in the history of the labor movement."[2] The greatest losers were the big bands. Simon wrote that after the recording blackout, which lasted twenty-seven months for Columbia and RCA, the bands "found that they were no longer champions of the recording field; while they had been down, the singers had taken over, and record-making would never again be the same."[3]

Victor's and Columbia's star bandleaders did rush back to the studios. In three sessions for Victor between November 14 and 22, Tommy Dorsey made nine tunes, among them "On the Sunny Side of the Street" and "Opus No. 1," two of his best sellers. On November 16, Goodman recorded "Every Time We Say Goodbye" and "After You've Gone" for Columbia with a quintet and vocalist Peggy Mann. James arrived at Columbia on November 21 with a thirty-two piece band (the regulars plus a dozen violinists and two cellists) for "I'm Beginning to See the Light" (a smash hit with vocalist Kitty Kallen) and others. On December 1, Duke Ellington brought his sixteen-piece crew to Victor to record "I Ain't Got Nothin' but the Blues" and "I'm Beginning to See the Light." Basie, at Columbia on December 6, recorded "Taps Miller," "Jimmy's Blues," and "Red Bank Boogie."

On December 11, still playing in southern California, Herman's band cut its last sides for Decca, ending the eight-year deal, which failed because of marketing, artistic, and technical issues. Decca released just four of the twenty-four sides that Herman made during the year. Herman felt that other companies, especially Columbia, made higher-quality records, permitted more creative freedom, and helped their artists more with marketing and promotion.

For his Decca farewell—cold business—Herman recorded "As Long As I Live," "Saturday Night (Is the Loneliest Night of the Week)," and "You Took Advantage of Me," all featuring Wayne; the ballad "Please Don't Say 'No'" and "I Ain't Got Nothin' but the Blues," sung by Herman; "Flyin' Home," played by the full band; and "1-2-3-4 Jump," featuring the Woodchoppers. On Burns's "Saturday Night" chart, Wayne sang to smooth reeds, Herman's alto sax, and a memorable solo by Bill Harris. Burns, Herman, and Decca saw it as a brooding, romantic piece, while at Columbia, Sinatra, backed by a bouncing big band, treated it as upbeat. As Herman sang "Please Don't Say 'No'" and "I Ain't Got Nothin' but the Blues" one can imagine him gritting his teeth in defiance of Decca wheels, who wanted the "Band That Plays the Blues" to live on. Herman had newer and better material to play. He could find some artistic satisfaction in the Duke Ellington number, "I Ain't Got Nothin' but the Blues," but it had to be hacked to three minutes from the five in Burns's sublime chart used on radio. It was an unproductive session, to say the least: Decca handed over "As Long As I Live" to English Brunswick, dealt "You Took Advantage of Me" to World Transcriptions, waited several years to issue "Please Don't Say 'No,'" and rejected "Flying Home" and "1-2-3-4 Jump."

The band then played its way back east, opening at the Paramount Theater in New York City on December 27. There Herman landed another big talent: trumpeter Sonny Berman, who came on because Hefti stayed in Hollywood. Since turning sixteen, the free-spirited wunderkind Berman had played with the big bands of Louis Prima, Tommy Dorsey, Dunham, Auld, James, and Goodman. He would blossom into a warm, graceful solo star in the First Herd. Back in New York City, Simon approached Herman about making more V discs sometime during his Paramount job or in early 1945, when he would be playing the Meadowbrook. "Both times," Herman patriotically said. "It's the least we can do."[4]

*a*s 1945 began, the U.S. and Allies seemed to be winning the war. Major Glenn Miller, who had been pleasing troops with V discs, concerts, and broadcasts of a hand-picked Army Air Force band for two years, had made plans for after the war. His civilian band's first booking, undated as yet, would be the Paramount Theater for a record fifteen thousand dollars a week for six weeks. But on December 15, 1944, as Herman's band played the Paramount, Miller's single-engine airplane vanished over the foggy English Channel en route from a field near Bedford to Paris.

One January night during his Paramount job, Herman guested on a radio show hosted by "the incomparable Hildegarde," a sassy singer with an appealing French accent. Of course, he did not play "Apple Honey" on Hildegarde's *Raleigh Room,* which was sponsored by rival Raleigh cigarettes. On January 24, Herman, Bill Harris, Phillips, Hyams, Burns, Bauer, and Jackson joined Webster, Hodges, and others to record V discs in the Vanderbilt Theater. Some V discs labeled the eleven players "Woody Herman's V Disc All Stars." They played "The Jeep Is Jumpin'," "Stompin' at the Savoy," "Somebody Loves Me," "John Hardy's Wife," "J. P. Vanderbilt IV," "Just You, Just Me," "Billy Bauer's Tune," and "Northwest Passage." Herman joined this all-star roster more as a leader-singer than a player. In his one starring role, in "Somebody Loves Me," he tapped out a medium-slow tempo and sang. Harris soloed on trombone; then Phillips, the rising star, and Webster, the master, played relaxed tenor solos.

The First Herd finished six weeks at the Paramount in early February 1945. It then played a week at the Adams Theater in Newark and moved upstate for two weeks at the Meadowbrook. The band also made four V discs in Liederkranz Hall in mid-February: "The Golden Wedding," a spinoff called "Wedding In Gold," "I've Got the World on a String," and Roger Segure's "Yeah Man!" which was based on the 1941 "Amen."

The band broadcast on the *Let's Dance* radio show for Columbia Broadcasting System on February 18 from the Meadowbrook. The show opened before a small, subdued Sunday-night crowd with Tough's impish bolero beat in "Blue Flame," then moved on to the flame-throwing "Red Top." Jackson, who was looser outside the studio, shouted a Brooklynese "Woody Hoimannn!" during "Blue Flame," and a cheerleading "yeahhh!" in the opening bars of "Red Top." Hyams's vibes solo lent a certain sparkle that was missing in the earlier version. Wayne repeated the brooding "Saturday Night," which was recorded for Decca in December. Then the First Herd cut up a bit with "Chubby's Blues," with Herman modifying the lyrics of "Chips' Blues" and adding that Jackson looked sad and weird with a fat face and funny little beard. The sections played in counterpoint, and Jackson plucked double- and quadruple-time scales, supporting Pete Candoli's obbligato of bop-influenced flatted fifths. "I was [Herman's] foil onstage where he insisted I wear a uniform that had nothing to do with the rest of the band," Jackson said years later. "He [also] gave me the go-ahead to wear the colorful looking Van Dyke beard on the stand."[5] Wayne sang a version of "Happiness Is Just a Thing Call Joe" that ran for more than four minutes, counting Herman's glowing alto sax interlude. Next Herman sang "I Didn't Know about You," recorded nearly a year before. He ordered a faster tempo now, and this far better band gave a grand performance. The band closed the half-hour broadcast with one of its new head arrangements, with trumpet parts by Hefti. CBS announcer Sidney Barry, steeped in the radio-script jargon of the times, called it a "hep trip up the rhythm road called the 'Northwest Passage.'" The Herd started the tune too fast and wobbled, like a cold engine running rough before smoothing out, only to have network engineers fade it as time ran out.

On February 19 the band debuted at Columbia Records, producing "Laura," "Apple Honey," and "I Wonder." "We cut those first sides in the wonderful old Liederkrantz Hall studio," Herman said. "I liked the Columbia *sound*, and they gave us a free hand. My idea with Columbia was not how much money or how many pressings we could make, or any of the things that were difficult in wartime. I did ask for the same publicity as their top stars, Frank Sinatra and Dinah Shore."[6] Founded in 1888 by Edward Easton, the Columbia Phonograph Company had prospered until his death in 1915 but was out of business by 1923. Bought and revived by a Canadian owner, it collapsed again in 1931. The American Record Company bought it in 1934 but struggled. CBS acquired American in 1938, and with radio network backing, a strong new Columbia Records Division began to soar in 1939. It signed top bands and singers, recording them often and well and promoting their music in ways that profited all concerned. That year alone, Basie left Decca, Goodman left Victor, and James and Krupa skipped Brunswick, all for Columbia. Soon Kyser joined Columbia, as did the Latin star Cugat, pianist-leader Carle, and Les Brown, who switched from RCA Bluebird. Singing stars Sinatra and Shore followed.

Herman considered getting the 1944 Old Gold radio shows a major break. But he said that "the biggest shot in the arm was signing with Columbia." In the wartime economy, companies could press only a limited number of records for an artist before moving on to another and could sell only a limited number of copies of any tune, no matter how great the hit. But because Columbia had agreed to Herman's request for promotional parity with Sinatra and Shore, every time it put an ad for them in a trade paper, the First Herd got one. "That drove the other bandleaders crazy," Herman said. "We became Number One in the country because of that as much as anything. It pushed us to the very peak of popularity."[7]

Burns's chart of "Laura"—David Raksin's haunting theme from the 1944 movie starring Dana Andrews, Jean Tierney, Vincent Price, and

Clifton Webb—featured both Herman's voice and his alto sax. It also paired Hyams's vibes with Bill Harris's trombone for a duet played over warm reeds. Herman saw the movie, liked the music, and loved Mercer's lyrics. "Laura" became the band's greatest recorded hit since "Blues in the Night" and "Woodchoppers' Ball." Herman gave the credit to Mercer; he pictured himself merely as a novelty, blues, and rhythm singer, hardly the voice for romance. Indeed, Herman claimed that Columbia had made ready to push James's instrumental "Laura" without Mercer's words, and the record company did toss Herman's first take of "Laura" to the V disc people. However, Columbia made a solid-gold copy of the second take as a souvenir for Herman, even though it did not sell a million copies until after wartime production limits had been lifted.

As with "Red Top," the band had experimented with "Apple Honey" for six months and played it in *Earl Carroll Vanities.* Two Columbia takes featured Jackson's strong bass under Phillips's opening solo, and the cheerleading effect made by bandsmen shouting behind Bill Harris. These elements carried the number, along with Hyams's vibes, Pete Candoli's high note on the trumpet, and Tough's crashing cymbals. "Apple Honey" became a standard, played for decades by Herman herds, but the 1945 Columbia master was repeatedly reissued in anthologies and remains an enduring classic. Herman rerecorded a modified "Apple Honey" in 1955, played it as "Monterey Apple Tree" at a California jazz festival in 1959, and led off with it at his fortieth anniversary concert in 1976. In 1984, a Time-Life album surveying Herman's Decca/Columbia years contained Columbia's alternate take, which was dulled by Herman's and Phillips's weak solos. That version turned up again in 1990 in Columbia's album *Woody Herman,* part of its "Best of the Big Bands" series.

"I Wonder," a short-lived popular ballad of early 1945, featured Herman's slow singing, and an in-your-face solo by Bill Harris. Columbia rushed the "Laura"/"I Wonder" pairing onto the market on March 10. "Amen!"—which Herman sang in *What's Cookin'?* and recorded in 1942— had gained a following by 1945, when Oliver adapted it for Tommy Dorsey's band. Herman recorded Segure's update of "Yeah Man!" for Columbia on February 19, but it stayed off the market until 1984.

The First Herd recorded again on February 26, starting with new ballads with Mercer lyrics from the film *Out of This World*. Wayne sang Burns's beguine-like arrangement of the title song. Herman sang and played alto sax on "June Comes Around Every Year," a livelier chart with a vibes solo and big, brassy ending. Next the band recorded the jazz novelty "Caldonia" and "Happiness Is Just a Thing Called Joe." Burns wrote an opening and ending for "Caldonia"; the rest was a head arrangement. "We were at the Meadowbrook, and somebody had heard Louis Jordan do 'Caldonia' at the Paramount, and said we ought to get on it right away," Herman recollected. "We put it together on the job the night before the recording session. The unison trumpet passage was a thing of Neal Hefti's we were using in a blues, and we put it in. That's why we changed key. Then the supervisor said that the bass and rhythm passage at the end was anti-climactic, so I just started talking on the next take: 'You look so *sweet* tonight, Caldonia, talk to me, tell me everything, mmmmmmm.' I've always thought that the essence of jazz was its spirit of abandon, and that's the spirit that Phillips and Harris got when they came shouting in on this one."[8] Tough ended "Caldonia" with another of his rattle-trap drum codas; and there were shouts by the full band, hard-driving rhythm segments, Hefti's unison trumpet stretches, and Herman's mile-a-minute questioning of what made Caldonia's head so *hahhhd*. An alternate take, more ragged and with milder solos, did make its way into the record stores over the years, but is of value mostly for comparison and shows that even top soloists and bands do not play well every time. "Caldonia" and "Laura" ran neck-and-neck as 1945 top record sellers.

"Happiness Is Just a Thing Called Joe" had to be trimmed to three-plus minutes, so out went the alto sax solo that Herman had played at the Meadowbrook. After Columbia released it, Herman dropped the solo altogether, believing that listeners and dancers preferred to hear "Happiness" as it sounded on record. Many ranked this as Wayne's best recording and, along with "Laura," as one of the First Herd's best ballads.

On a roll, the Herd recorded two more jazz-hall-of-fame entries, "Goosey Gander" and "Northwest Passage," and two pop songs, "A Kiss Goodnight" and "I've Got the World on a String," on March 1, 1945.

Herman said that the beginning of "Goosey Gander" "was based on 'Shortnin' Bread,' but then, like so many other things, it went into the blues." Softly played at a medium-fast tempo, it featured Herman's clarinet answering the saxes, followed by Phillips, Bill Harris, and screeching Pete Candoli solos, surprise starts and stops, dissonant chords, a raucous trombone chorus at a faster tempo, and nearly the same section interplay that ended "Chubby's Blues." Herman explained that the "little extra drum tag that Davey Tough put on the end [was] one of those things we liked to do in one way or another. We hated to cut arrangements short, the way most of the big bands were doing, so we usually let about three more things fall."[9]

"Northwest Passage" displayed the First Herd's distinctive stampede momentum. Odd enough, with its rasping, almost dissonant intro by saxes and trombones and its guitar solo over the rhythm section, it glided into something like a Goodman sextet when Herman joined on clarinet. But then solos by Burns, Hyams, and Herman and the five unison trumpets (playing another of Hefti's segments) ignited a Phillips tenor sax solo and sax riffs for Bill Harris's ripping trombone. This stirring mix of fun and fury was continued with all-out brass screaming, a blasting ensemble with Berman soloing above it all, then a ritard ending, quietly dying out with four after-the-fact drum taps from Tough. Columbia credited Herman as composer of "Northwest Passage," but he said that it really "evolved on the job . . . beginning with that little thing around rhythm and vibes. We kept adding and changing it around."[10] An alternate take of "Northwest Passage" with tamer solos is of less musical value and was only issued by Columbia in 1990.

Burns's chart of the 1945 pop tune "A Kiss Goodnight" showed how a great writer and band could elevate bland songs. Six attention-grabbing blasts by the trumpeters led into Herman's singing, then Berman soloed over the reeds and trombones. The full band played a toe-tapping segment, Herman sang a second chorus, and Berman took a second turn with his spicy trumpet before the whole matter came to an end amid a single chord by the brass section.

In "I've Got the World on a String"—which the band had played since the fall—Burns, Herman, the band, and Columbia reached the sublime. Played at a medium-slow tempo, it was simply a great chart. Herman never sang better or sounded sunnier, Columbia captured the band's commanding force, Tough and Jackson drove the number with controlled power, and the full band playing was crisp, explosive, dynamic. And Phillips, so vigorous in up-tempo pieces, waxed elegant in his solo. Had he lived, Glenn Miller would have been top bandleader. Yet no band could match Herman's. Not musically. Not in 1945.

Simon ranked Herman's first Columbia records great because of the band's musicianship and spirit. Tragically, the First Herd worked for more than five months before recording again. So superior was this band, one wishes that every note it ever blew—at dances, concerts, radio shows, even rehearsals—could have been taped for pleasure and study. For it soon began to come apart. It closed at the Meadowbrook and "headed out" (as they said when leaving metropolitan New York) for a theater tour in the Midwest and four weeks (March 16–April 12) in the Hotel Sherman in Chicago. A CBS broadcast from the Sherman on March 27 included "Goosey Gander," "Happiness Is Just a Thing Called Joe," "I Wonder," and "Apple Honey." The band guested with Hildegarde on another *Raleigh Room* on April 10.

It returned to New York City for a few weeks of short jobs, rest, and rehearsal before nine weeks at the Cafe Rouge. But in June, three trumpeters left, and Hyams resumed small-combo work. Herman waited several months before he could find another vibist who could work with a big band. He was soon looking for a pianist as well, as Burns left the band. He continued to supply the Herd with top arrangements, shipping two or three charts a week from Jackson's place in Freeport, Long Island. Among the first were "Bijou" and a three-part suite entitled "Summer Sequence." Wartime law required Herman to offer the piano job first to Rowles, the 1943 draftee he lost, but Rowles was still on army duty. So Tony Aless (Anthony Alessandrini) replaced Burns. A New Jersey native just turning twenty-four, Aless had performed with Berigan, Johnny McGhee, Teddy Powell, Monroe, and Spivak.

The Cafe Rouge job ran from July 16 to September 19. Radio shows from there and the Ritz Ballroom in Bridgeport, Connecticut, mixed old and new. Herman plugged his several new Columbia records— "Happiness Is Just a Thing Called Joe," "A Kiss Goodnight," "Goosey Gander," "Northwest Passage," "June Comes Around Every Year," "Apple Honey," "Out of This World," and even reached back for "It Must Be Jelly." But the summer ballads "I Don't Care Who Knows It," "And There You Are," "There, I've Said It Again," and "On the Atchison, Topeka and the Santa Fe" made the airwaves, too, as did a short-lived novelty, "Katushya," and Burns's new "Bijou." The trivial "Katushya" was done up by Burns as "Russian" music, with novelty lyrics, solos by Phillips, Aless, Bill Harris, Berman, and Herman on clarinet. Herman played the number for a while during 1945, then it was dropped from the band's repertoire. But "Bijou" was another matter. Burns wrote it as a Latin rhythm show-piece for Harris. Tough's rhumba-like beat underscored the intro with Bauer's guitar and Herman's alto sax before Harris's swooping entry and solo choruses over cascading reeds.

In a Cafe Rouge broadcast on July 28, Herman fans heard "Good, Good, Good" and "There's No You" plus "Don't Worry 'bout That Mule," another novelty borrowed from Jordan. Herman fans wished that he had recorded "Mule" for Columbia, as he had for a V disc, for in this chart by Burns, they enjoyed Herman's singing and clarinet playing, Berman's shouting trumpet, and full-ensemble swinging.

On August 10, 1945, with the end of the war in sight, the band recorded the minor ballads "Love Me" and "No Time," the witty "Put That Ring on My Finger (Put That Piece of Paper in My Hand)," and Hefti's "The Good Earth." Herman whimsically recollected that CBS was "using two theaters at Seventh Avenue and Fifty-Third for radio shows and recording. The theaters were back to back. We were in one and Frank Sinatra was in the other. When we were there, there was a big crowd of bobby-soxers outside Frank's stage door, and one lonesome chick outside ours. One of Frank's fans asked her, 'Who's in there?' 'Woody Herman,' she said, rather defensively. 'Don't get excited,' the other kid said, 'we're sympathizers.'"[11] Herman sang "No Time," which was based on a theme by Frédéric Chopin, and Wayne starred in "Love Me." Herman played alto sax segments on both. "Put That Ring on My Finger" started out with a vocal by Herman, then Berman soloed, Harris worked in a "Song of the Volga Boatmen" quote, and the full band roared out a fourteen-chord coda. "The Good Earth," mostly written out, impressed Herman as "a wonderfully constructed piece [that] succeeds in saying something and getting it well said all in three minutes."[12] It was a loose, airy chart for full band, with solo space for Phillips and Herman. On August 20, the band rerecorded "The Good Earth" without improving it and made "Bijou (Rhumba A La Jazz)." The earlier version of "The Good Earth" and "Bijou" added to Herman's string of enduring jazz classics. The second "Good Earth," with its weaker solo by Phillips, reached collectors in the 1980s.

Bill Harris and his slide trombone found stardom with "Bijou." "Bill didn't play a valve trombone as some critics stated when it first came out," Herman said. "This number—and recording—really established Bill. I gave it the 'Rhumba A La Jazz' subtitle to explain why we were 'abusing' the Latin rhythm."[13] As *Look* magazine's "Record Guide" editor Michael Levin wrote, "There are records which only sell; there are those few which shape the styles of music and musicians for years to come." Duke Ellington, Tormé, Herman, and Cole all rated "Bijou" among their all-time favorite records, reflecting the influence it had on music generally. "The strong use of South American beats, the rhythm section wandering by itself doing solos, the touches of [classical composer Igor] Stravinsky in the brass scoring all mark a new era in American dance music," Levin said. "It is a flat denial that jazz can be played in only one rhythm and with one type of scoring. All over the country bands are abandoning the pile-driver concept of rhythm for lighter, more fertile fields first mapped by Ellington and here made crystal clear by Herman."[14]

*G*ermany surrendered in May, and Japan on August 14. On August 22, the nation still euphoric over the hard-won peace, the First Herd recorded four more V discs. After all, millions of Americans still wore uniforms—in camps, on ships, at air bases, and overseas as occupying forces. Simon supervised as the band recorded "125th Street Prophet" and "Lover Man (Oh, Where Can You Be?)" with Wayne, "Don't Worry 'bout That Mule," and a new piece that Herman introduced: "Fellas, this is Woody Herman. We got a V disc here we just finished a few minutes ago. It's a very beautiful thing. Matter of fact, I'm sure all you fellas from Brooklyn, and other places south of the border, will appreciate this tune. It has a very touching title: 'Your Father's Mustache.'" With that, the band pounded out one of its strangest pieces yet. It featured throbbing rhythms, Jackson's tempo-setting bass, a raucous trombone trio, big ensemble chords, and solos by Berman, Herman on clarinet, Aless, Bill Harris, and Phillips. Near the end, in a reed-section riff, Herman cried: "Sweet love!" The men then sang in beer-hall harmony "Ah, your father's mustache" four times before a full-blown finish and Tough's tumbling coda. Nearly five minutes long, "Your Father's Mustache" was a weird stew of serious jazz and tongue-in-cheek fun—another of those group efforts. Columbia soon recorded it, too, crediting Harris and Herman. But Herman claimed that "the melody was Bill's, and the ensemble parts Neal Hefti's. I was only responsible for the title; me, with my stupid sense of humor. I threw in the vocal one night on a job, and it stayed."[15] After the band finished, a septet called Chubby Jackson's Mad Mob (Jackson, Hefti, Berman, Harris, Phillips, Aless, and Tough) made "Meshugah" for a V disc.

A broadcast from the Cafe Rouge on August 23 started with "Out of This World" and Hefti's "Black Orchid," first cousin of "The Good Earth." Completing the show were the new vocals "I Can't Believe My Eyes" and "I'm Not Having Any This Year," featuring Herman and Wayne, respectively, and "Good, Good, Good," with Herman's singing and the band's romping spirit. It opened shows for several weeks.

The slow scattering of the First Herd, which had begun in June with Burns's departure, continued when Tough's health problems worsened, eventually forcing him to leave the band. At first, when Tough could not perform, Herman found subs, and he rented Rich for one recording date. Rich, as well as Norvo on vibes, played with the First Herd at Columbia on September 5. The band backed Wayne singing "Gee, It's Good to Hold You" and recorded a brisk "Your Father's Mustache," reduced to three minutes by means of a faster tempo and fewer solos and repeats. This new version became an often requested number. Herman praised Rich for "a tremendous job" on short notice, which included playing Tough's trademark coda. Berman, Bill Harris, Phillips, and Norvo soloed.

Norvo, thirty-seven, joined the First Herd in stages—in and out in 1945 and staying several months in 1946. An Illinois native, he had led a marimba band at seventeen and toured in vaudeville playing xylophone and tap dancing. He had worked NBC network radio, married Bailey, and led a twelve-piece band playing mellow "chamber jazz." In 1942–43, Norvo switched to vibraphone and led a combo, at times helped by Burns, Bert, or trumpeter Shorty Rogers. By early 1945 he was touring with Goodman.

In a September 6 broadcast from the Hotel Pennsylvania, without Norvo this time, Herman programmed a number of old favorites, a new ballad called "Can't You Read between the Lines?" with Wayne, and Mercer's new "On the Atchison, Topeka and Santa Fe" with Herman singing. On September 8, with Tough back, the band tried without success—according to Herman's high standards—at Columbia to record Herman singing the new ballad "You've Got Me Crying Again" and a chart that Hefti named "Wild Root."

When Tough fell apart next time, Simon only hinted at his troubles obliquely: "Even before Tough's victory in the 1945 *Metronome* Musicians' Poll as Best Jazz Drummer appeared in print, the little drummer—he weighed scarcely 95 pounds—departed from the band, the victim of the same trouble that had hounded him during his Dorsey and Goodman days."[16] Later, between breakdowns, Tough worked in both Dixieland and modern groups. In 1948, on leave from a veterans' hospital in New Jersey, he fell on a street in Newark, fractured his skull, and died.

*t*he First Herd closed at the Cafe Rouge on September 9, 1945, and began a five-week theater tour of Alabama, Georgia, South Carolina, and Virginia. Along the way, at Berman's urging, Herman hired twenty-five-year-old Don Lamond as his drummer. An Oklahoman reared in Washington, D.C., Lamond had studied at the Peabody Institute in Baltimore and had played in Dunham's and Boyd Raeburn's little-known wartime bands. Lamond's own small band was out of work, and he was jobbing around Washington when Herman's manager called.

Returning to New York City on October 13, the First Herd launched a thirty-nine-week radio series sponsored by Wildroot Cream Oil, a hair product for men. (A rival company selling shampoo sponsored a *Fitch Bandwagon* show.) Herman's breezy Saturday broadcasts, held before cheering crowds in theaters, dance spots, and on college campuses, ran through July 5, 1946, on American Broadcasting Company stations. Many shows aired from the 400 Club or the Chesterfield Supper Club, but ABC also followed the band to bookings at such widely scattered venues as the Riverside Theatre in Milwaukee, the Adams in Newark, the Palace in Toronto, the Murat Temple in Indianapolis, the Lincoln Auditorium in Syracuse, the Teen Timers Club in Philadelphia, the University of Nebraska in Lincoln, the Hotel Sherman in Chicago, and the finale from the Casino Ballroom in Fort Worth.

While the band's Columbia recordings certainly pulled in new fans, the Wildroot shows flashed its talent and verve worldwide via the AFRS. Herman used the shows to plug records and band members and to test new charts:

> jazz pieces for the full band—"Superman With a Horn," "Ee-Ba-Ba-Lee-Ba," "Blowin' Up a Storm," "Wild Root," "Great Northern," "Back Talk," "Hallelujah," "They Went That-a-Way," "Tico Tico," "Liza," "Non-Alcoholic," "Twelfth Street Rag," "Crazy Rhythm"
>
> music by an all-new Woodchoppers combo—"Sergeant on a Furlough," "Pappiloma," "Flip the Whip," "Glommed," "Gung Ho," "Heads Up," "I Got Rhythm," "Steps," "Lost Weekend"
>
> light-hearted numbers—"Put That Ring on My Finger," "Caldonia," "It Must Be Jelly," "Don't Worry 'bout That Mule," "Katushya," "No, Don't, Stop!" "Hubba Hubba Hubba," "Chubby's Blues," "Panacea," "Mabel! Mabel!"

ballads of the day—"Till the End of Time," "It's Been a Long, Long Time," "It's Only a Paper Moon," "He's Funny That Way," "Symphony," "You Won't Be Satisfied," "Day by Day," "September Song," "Try a Little Tenderness," "A Ghost Of a Chance"

covers of hits by other artists—Goodman's "Gotta Be This or That," James's "I'll Buy That Dream," Kenton's "Shoo-Fly Pie," Bing Crosby's "White Christmas," Sinatra's "Why Was I Born?" Como's "I'm Always Chasing Rainbows," Les Brown's "There's Good Blues Tonight"

"Virtually every time we went into a recording studio in 1945 we came out with at least one hit," Herman recalled. "Almost all our records were selling the maximum number in wartime. A number of bands were doing as well, but we were causing more excitement with the Columbia promotion and the popularity of our presentation."[17]

According to Leonard Feather, the late-1945 Herd's "sense of euphoric exhilaration lost little time in communicating itself to the public." Feather had "vivid recollections of that period, having been on the Wildroot programs for a while, introducing a different member of the band each week for a featured number—a policy hitherto unheard of in commercial radio."[18] On one show Feather sat in at the piano when Herman sang "Long, Long Journey."

For the Wildroot series debut, the band performed—now with Shorty Rogers on trumpet—"Put That Ring on My Finger," complete with Bill Harris's "Volga Boatmen" quotation. But there was an extra "wow!" shouted by Jackson. A stunning trumpet solo by Berman perked up "On the Atchison, Topeka and Santa Fe," on which Herman sang and Phillips soloed. In the fast-paced "Wild Root," Phillips and Harris soloed, the brass played rolling unison passages, Herman played the clarinet, Jackson shouted a well-timed "yeahhh!" and Berman blew high in a brassy finish. "Neal Hefti wrote this melody line based on 'Flyin' Home,'" Herman commented. "We had played it for months before we ever got the Wildroot radio show."[19]

"Friends, this is where we cut out," Herman said at the close of the premiere. "It's our first show, and we hope you liked it. Be back with us next Saturday, same time, and latch on to some more songs by Frances Wayne." But Wayne's stint was ending with the band, and so was Hefti's. The two left for marriage and new career directions, respectively—he in late 1945, she in the spring of 1946—further diluting the First Herd.

Shorty Rogers and then Conrad Gozzo did strengthen the band in some ways. The twenty-three-year-old Gozzo, from New Britain, Connecticut, had played with Isham Jones, Norvo, Chester, Thornhill, Shaw's navy band, and Goodman and was a top lead trumpeter, an unsung skill in jazz bands. Rogers, from Great Barrington, Massachusetts, brought many talents. He could play section and solo parts, on trumpet or flugelhorn, and in the full band or Woodchoppers and could compose and arrange. He had studied at the High School of Music and Arts in New York City, then with Wesley LaViolette, then at the Los Angeles Conservatory. He worked six months in Bradley's band in 1942 and with Norvo's during part of 1942–43. He joined Herman just after receiving his army discharge in September 1945. Rogers played section trumpet, wrote charts, and helped revive the Woodchoppers. He recalled his time with the band with pleasure: "Everyone [in the band] was influenced by Bird and Dizzy and was trying to bring their way of playing into the band. Neal Hefti and Ralph Burns and the other arrangers were marvellous to me, and it was like going to school, a graduate course, a real luxury. Pete Candoli took me in and watched over me like another brother."[20]

Shorty Rogers after he had left Herman's band, in the 1970s. (Courtesy Nick Puopolo)

On November 16, the band recorded "Wild Root" at Columbia; and on November 26, it made "Everybody Knew but Me," starring the singing Herman, but the band flubbed a new piece called "Blowin' Up a Storm." The band sounded strong and crisp on "Wild Root," the brass section dazzling in its power and precision. Berman, Phillips, Bill Harris and Herman on clarinet soloed before the massive full-band ending. Herman sang the slow minor-key lament "Everybody Knew but Me" with Bauer's warm guitar in solo and in duet passages with Phillips. On December 10, the band returned to Columbia to nail "Blowin' Up a Storm" and also recorded the pop songs "Atlanta G.A." and "Let It Snow, Let It Snow, Let It Snow."

A group effort (with certain brass parts recycled from "Is You Is or Is You Ain't My Baby?"), "Blowin' Up a Storm" was a study in dynamic variation. Opening with the piano leading the rhythm section, it built to a fury in the brass before the finish, with Jackson, Herman on clarinet, Phillips, Bill Harris, Bauer, and Berman all soloing. As Herman told it, the song's origin was unusual: "As a gimmick on the Wildroot show we asked people to submit titles. This is one that won."[21]

Burns's "Atlanta G.A." chart contained dissonant brass fills and solos from Bauer and Aless, with Berman's horn soaring madly. "Let It Snow" featured full-band chords, with Berman and Harris soloing. Four varied ensemble chords ended the piece. Herman kidded that Hefti's chart "ruined our chances of getting a hit record. The intro must have run about 198 bars [fourteen, actually], and that's too much for a pop record; but it was just so good I couldn't bear to leave it out. It was a case of letting our musical honesty carry us away. So Vaughn Monroe wound up with the hit record."[22]

*b*y the end of 1945, the First Herd reigned as America's top swing band. It grossed twenty thousand dollars a week from radio, records, and stage shows and often set records for theater, hotel, and ballroom crowds. It won the best-band polls in *Down Beat* and *Metronome.* Fans voted Phillips, Bill Harris, and Tough as jazz's top tenor sax player, trombonist, and drummer of the year, respectively. Herman pointed out that Jackson should have won an award for yelling, an estimation that Jackson did not contradict: "My bit was always screaming 'Woody Hoimannn,' and 'yowww.' I knew just when to yell, and the band would respond. We were all geared up to beat the Chicago Bears every night. [Herman] taught me that non-metronomical time was where it should be, as against the format all other bandleaders demanded, which was that whatever tempo the band started with, it should end there. He also wanted his band to have a grin on its face . . . we were not only jazz musicians, but entertainers as well." Jackson's nightly shouting and mugging, and the five trumpet players' parading on the top riser, swinging back and forth, prompted Herman to call the band's shows a "three-ring circus." Tommy Dorsey needled: "I don't know how they play, but they're sure as hell great dancers!" During "Apple Honey," Pete Candoli would sneak off, put on a red-and-blue Superman suit, and jump back in time to play his walloping solo. "It brought down the house" the first time, Herman said, "and it remained part of our act."[23] This caused Burns to dash off "Superman with a Horn," a short, searing showpiece for Candoli echoing Chick Webb's 1937 "Harlem Congo."

*I*n December 1945, Igor Stravinsky, the Russian-born classical composer, tossed the band a bouquet. Apparently Stravinsky was taken with "Bijou" and Hefti's unison brass writing in "Apple Honey," "Caldonia," and "Northwest Passage." Famous for his daring ballets *The Firebird, Petrouchka,* and *The Rite of Spring,* Stravinsky wired Herman: "I wish to write a piece for you as a Christmas gift." Herman regarded the telegram as "one of the wildest moments I ever had—having one of the world's great composers write for me was beyond imagination."[24] He named the resulting nine-minute, three-movement work "Ebony Concerto," though it was technically a sinfonietta. Although himself unaware of it in detail, Stravinsky was short of money at the time. His accountant murmured the situation and asked Herman to treat "Ebony Concerto" as a commission. Herman gladly paid.

Stravinsky towered as "sort of a hero to guys like me and Candoli—sort of an 'in' classical composer," Hefti said.[25] Herman found Stravinsky a likable man with an easy sense of humor, and the composer liked Herman's clarinet playing and called him "Wood-he" in his strongly accented English. When Stravinsky arrived to oversee rehearsals, the band was playing six shows a day in the Paramount and using an upstairs rehearsal hall. The band would practice, then have about eighty minutes off while a movie played. At the first practice with Stravinsky, the bandsmen were wearing their band uniforms—dark suits, white shirts, and ties. Herman noted with amusement that "the maestro arrived with a towel around his neck, in an old sweatshirt, gray slacks and tennis shoes."[26]

Band members huffed and puffed, sight-reading the piece's snarled rhythms and unusual voicings, but pressed on bravely. "I looked at my bass part and there was a quarter note, then another bar and another quarter note on the third beat, and so forth down the line for maybe twenty bars," Jackson said. "After all the bass I had been playing, I thought this was easy. Then we started rehearsing it, and in the second bar I got totally lost. Each of us had a separate part to play, and unless you counted strenuously, you got messed up."[27] Herman recalled the composer's patience with affection: "Stravinsky hummed and whistled and tapped his foot while he dragged us through it. After that first rehearsal, at which we were all so embarrassed we were nearly crying because nobody could read, he walked over and put his arm around me and said, 'Ah, what a beautiful family you have.'"[28]

*f*urther evidence of the Herd's resounding success is found in a *Newsweek* article from the end of the year: "Herman and his outfit have put almost nine years of hard work into building a band which is commercial and at the same time sticks to Woody's concept of jazz and swing."[29] And *Metronome* put Herman on both its December 1945 and January 1946 covers, calling the former a Special Woody Herman Issue. It contained photo-profiles of every band member, with extended coverage of Herman, Burns, Bill Harris, Jackson, Phillips, and Wayne; it even included stories about the Goldfarb, Mirenburg, and Vallon firm, road manager Abe Turchen, press agent Marvin Kohn, and band boy Nat Wexler. How had such success come about? Much of it is due to Herman's steady, patient, quiet ways, his honesty, decency, and modesty. Quick to place credit—upon Burns, Hefti, Jackson, Tough, and Harris—Herman had, however, earned his success. Lamond found Herman's "an easy band to play with. He never would strain you up, like Benny Goodman would. He gave me a free hand. He was a good guy to work for. A lot of the time I didn't even look at the music; I just felt my way through it."[30] And Tough recalled of his fifteen months in the band that "Goodman was fine, by anybody's stan-dards; he was a precisionist. Dorsey was fine, but he played a lot of tunes that made you want to smoke while you were playing. [But] Woody led by nods toward us. You met him, and when he said a few sentences, you knew what he expected. It was all old blues, but it had to be *new* blues. I never had another musical experience like it. Without seeming to rehearse him-self, he brought so much *knowledge* to any band he had, you were turned on before you got to the hall. There was excitement such as I never knew before."[31]

The First Herd roared on in 1946, taking changes in stride. Norvo and Shorty Rogers formed the core of the new Woodchoppers. The entire band added three long concert pieces to its repertoire: "Ebony Concerto," Burns's lovely "Summer Sequence" (three parts, running eight minutes), and "Lady McGowan's Dream" at six minutes. And Herman hired two vocal quintets—the Blue Flames early in 1946, the Blue Moods later in the year. Tommy Dorsey (with the Sentimentalists) and Monroe (with the Norton Sisters and the Moon Maids) also featured vocal groups in 1946.

The times called for change. The swing era was ending. Some name bands playing prewar books and routines already sold fewer records and drew smaller crowds. For jazz players, bebop was the latest trend. In Herman's band Burns, Bauer, Jackson, Lamond, Hefti, and Berman were already experimenting with bop. Norvo and Shorty Rogers joined them and adapted the style for the big band.

Of course, the Herd did not totally reject more traditional mate-rial. On January 3, Columbia recorded two dance-tempo ballads on which Herman played alto sax: "Welcome to My Dream," with Wayne; and "It's Anybody's Spring," on which Herman sang the carefree lyrics. But in the Ritz Theater on January 19, with Orson Welles emceeing, the "new stuff" had its turn. Herman's and Duke Ellington's bands played in a concert sponsored by *Esquire* magazine at which winners of the 1945 *Esquire* Jazz Poll soloed, and some tunes became V discs. The Herd's familiar favor-ites were complemented by Burns's new chart of "Mean to Me" for Bill Harris; "Jackson Fiddles While Ralph Burns," which Burns played with

Jackson; and Shorty Rogers's "Nero's Conception," written for the new-look Woodchoppers manned by Berman, Bill Harris, Herman, Phillips, Norvo, Bauer, Jackson, Lamond, and Rowles, who was on army leave. Already thrilled about his collaboration with Stravinsky, Herman ranked starring with Ellington "one of the highlights of my life. . . . the joy, the abandon, the madness in our own band—that was Duke's influence."[32]

Throughout the rest of January, between theater dates, dances, concerts, and Wildroot shows, Herman's band kept struggling to learn "Ebony Concerto." Stravinsky rehearsed the men for up to four hours one day. "We stayed pretty befuddled until he sang the piece to us," Herman confessed. He chose to premiere "Ebony Concerto" at a concert booked for March 25 in Carnegie Hall. Since Stravinsky was already committed to a European tour, he urged Herman to hire Walter Hendl, assistant conductor of the New York Philharmonic, to rehearse and conduct at Carnegie so that Herman could focus on his clarinet part. And that part was by no means easy, Herman announced: "I was never a serious clarinetist. Everybody's part was hard, but I had this so-called 'solo' part. . . . I went to fine clarinetists and asked if there was anything I could do to play this thing a little better, and they all looked at it and said, 'Why that's the hardest goddam thing in the world.'"[33]

The Wildroot broadcasts held the band's legions of fans and wooed new ones. Radio-script hype added to the crazy spirit. In one show, Herman read: "We've booked a very bouncing *ballade* called 'Red Top,'" whereupon an announcer read: "Hold on to your hat, Aunt Hannah, we're heading for the hollow!" "The writer of the Wildroot shows tried making a ridiculous personality out of Woody," Simon observed. "Woody couldn't have liked it."[34]

On February 6, the band recorded and Herman sang the new ballad "You've Got Me Cryin' Again" with the Blue Flames. The next day he sang "No, Don't, Stop!" at Columbia with solos from Bauer and Bill Harris. Columbia rejected "You Haven't Changed At All" with the Blue Flames and Wayne's stand-in, Lucille Linwood.

The band played one Wildroot show with Bailey guesting on "Can't Help Lovin' That Man" and Herman receiving a "King of Swing" award. After nine days in Detroit and Ontario, Herman led the Herd back to the Columbia studio in New York City on February 17. The session produced a hit blues tune—"Panacea"—and two ballads, "Heaven Knows," which faded quickly, and "A Jug of Wine," which was only released in 1989. Herman, who sang all three, said that "Panacea" came from Feather, "who wrote some amusing lyrics to the blues. Ralph Burns put in some interesting bits with the trumpet and trombone playing against the ensemble."[35] It began as a slow blues with Herman singing. Then came shifts into double and quadruple tempo, a ripping solo by Bill Harris, frantic bass by Jackson, and short blasts from Pete Candoli. "Heaven Knows" gave solo time to Norvo and Herman on alto sax and paired Herman with the Blue Flames vocally. "A Jug of Wine," the earliest known Lerner-and-Loewe song, written for a Broadway show, gained flavor later.

Lynne Stevens was soon subbing for Wayne, and Jo Stafford guested on the March 8 Wildroot show. Stafford sang "Walking My Baby Back Home," "Sometimes I'm Happy," and "Day by Day." The band played Paul Weston's staid charts of the tunes, which were making Stafford a bigger star than Tommy Dorsey, for whom she had sung. Wayne returned on March 15, singing "It Might As Well Be Spring" and "Till the End of Time."

On a March 22 show from Philadelphia, Herman introduced "a sort of battle royal in the brass section called 'Ee-Ba-Ba-Lee-Ba.'" It cashed in on the "bebop" craze, which Hampton and Beneke's Glenn Miller band had tapped in on with the release of Hampton's "Hey Ba-Ba-Re-Bop" record. Like "Superman with a Horn," "Ee-Ba-Ba-Lee-Ba" became a wild showstopper. It started with Herman's fast, sunny vocal—"Oh well, oh well, I feel so good to-dayyy"—before shifting to an ear-shattering round of solos by Pete Candoli, Berman, Shorty Rogers, and Gozzo. Although "Superman with a Horn," "Ee-Ba-Ba-Lee-Ba," and Burns's "Great Northern" all were short enough to record, Herman passed them by. His reasoning appears to be that they relied on visual action and might not be anything special as records. He was glutting the market with his records, anyway, and had other numbers for recordings that he liked better.

A medium-tempo "Rose Room" from a March Wildroot broadcast featured Herman on clarinet, Bill Harris, and Phillips, with strong drumming by Lamond. A broadcast of "Black Orchid" from about the same time starred Phillips, Harris, and Herman on clarinet, and one of "Let It Snow" plugged the Columbia record. A short "Get Happy" showcased Harris and Aless, with duets starring Berman and Pete Candoli on trumpets and Norvo and Bauer on vibes and guitar. Berman's "They Went That-a-Way" featured Berman quoting the "William Tell Overture" and other themes, and Norvo, Phillips, and Herman on alto soloed after Jackson shouted "Woody Hoimann!" Still another gem from the Wildroot shows was a rendering of "I Surrender, Dear" starring Norvo with full band. In the radio script Herman referred to Norvo as "old Mr. Vibes himself" playing the "beat bars." A Wildroot show that spring also presented a stunning "Woodchopper's Ball," played seven years after the original record. The Herd took a fast, light approach, with new section voicings, vigorous solos by Phillips over the rhythm and by Harris and Candoli over piano chord changes, a shout or two from Jackson, and a couple of Hefti's brass section runs approaching mayhem. The band also invented an ending filled with key changes, which were drowned in applause. These splashes of new color kept the song alive. "Am I sick of 'Woodchoppers' Ball'? Sure I am," Herman would say, "but it was great the first one thousand times."[36]

When Rowles left the army for good in March, Herman was ready: "We've got to do a Carnegie Hall concert, and we're going to play Stravinsky. Someone will be in touch with you, get your ticket, come to New York." "I regretted one thing," Rowles said. "I had to take Tony Aless' job. Tony was happy. It was a helluva band. All of a sudden he was through because I was coming out."[37]

It was indeed a "helluva band." But Simon said the success had begun to boomerang: "Wherever the band played, the same selections were requested and the young, eager, but bored musicians began to find fewer opportunities to play new numbers. One they did get to play was 'Ebony Concerto.'"[38] Herman programmed it just before the intermission of the two-hour concert presenting twenty-one pieces. But the piece, for which Herman had to rent a French hornist and a harpist, received mixed reviews. Barry Ulanov of *Metronome* rated it "more like a French imitation of Igor [Stravinsky] than the great man himself. Rhythmically, tonally and melodically it is as dry as dehydrated eggs, and far less palatable."[39] The *New Yorker* wrote: "It would be fun to hear what Mr. Stravinsky might do with an arrangement for the Herman ensemble of the 'St. Louis Blues' or 'On the Atchison, Topeka, and Santa Fe.'"[40] *Time*'s April 6 issue hailed the concert, but not the "Ebony Concerto," enthusiastically:

> Stoop-shouldered, skinny Woody Herman, an earnest jazz veteran at thirty-two, is the top U.S. jazz favorite, having outdistanced Duke Ellington and Benny Goodman in polls conducted by *Down Beat* and *Metronome. . . .* He started to rise when he started imitating. His five trumpets now sound like Harry James, only louder, and his tricky tonal effects like Duke Ellington. He also borrowed from Ravel and Stravinsky. When he acknowledged his debt to Stravinsky, the composer replied: "We all steal. But never steal from yourself. Then you're not being progressive." Says Herman: "I think that sums up jazz."
>
> The audience in Carnegie Hall was filled mostly with bobby-soxers who came to hear Woody, not Stravinsky. [They gave "Ebony Concerto"] a polite hearing for a minute or two, then coughed restlessly. They came to life again on "Panacea" and "Your Father's Mustache." Stravinsky didn't send them. Woody did.

"Ebony Concerto" fared better in the long run. Herman summed up the work's pluses and minuses cogently: "I think it was a complete gem, a work of art, but we had no more right to play it than the man in the moon. Stravinsky had no desire to write jazz or anything like it, and the work should never have been judged a jazz piece."[41] Herman kept "Ebony Concerto" in his band book with the idea of recording it and building a concert tour around it in the fall.

Aside from the "Ebony Concerto," the rest of the Carnegie Hall concert deserves mention. When the lights dimmed and the curtain rose, the band played "Blue Flame" in midnight blue zoot suits. Berman handled all of the trumpet solos, except for Pete Candoli's on "Superman with a Horn" and at the end of "Your Father's Mustache." Burns wrote most of the full-band charts, but Hefti did "Everywhere," "Wild Root," and "The Good Earth." Norvo, Shorty Rogers, Jackson, and Bauer wrote the Woodchoppers' numbers. "Sweet and Lovely," taken at a slow tempo, presented Phillips's whisper-soft tenor sax tones blown over a gentle rhythm. "Four Men on a Horse" was a tight, intense, complex piece for rhythm section with speeding, then slowing, tempos.

Norvo emerged as one of the concert stars. He joined the rhythm section in "Red Top," the rousing opener, sharing solo time with Herman on clarinet, Phillips, Bill Harris, and Berman. He also soloed on "Your Father's Mustache," "Wild Root," "Hallelujah," and the Woodchoppers' pieces. Another star was emerging in Bill Harris, who had become the most admired trombonist in jazz. His heart-and-soul playing in "Everywhere" and "Mean to Me" was a triumph. Norvo commented: "Harris wasn't playing, he was praying."[42]

Feather's report of the entire concert was glowing: "It was hard to say which factor was most important—the team spirit, the superb ensemble work in which fourteen horns could work as one; the brilliant orchestrations by Burns and Hefti; or the head arrangements. The band was swinging as no band before it. The rhythm section was experimenting with cross-rhythms, suspensions, tempo change, doing everything to drive beyond the limits of monotonous four-to-the-bar sound."[43]

The recording industry was ill equipped to exploit live events at that time. Bands had played Carnegie Hall before—Goodman in 1938 and 1939, Glenn Miller and others in the 1939 Cavalcade of Bands, and Duke Ellington from time to time—but left no commercial recordings for posterity, largely because so many numbers ran past three minutes. So Columbia left it to others with less equipment or savvy to record Herman's concert. Not until 1951, with both the three-year-old long-playing ($33\frac{1}{2}$ rpm) and new extended-play (45 rpm) microgroove records technology in place, did much concert music reach the marketplace. Then Columbia marketed an album from Goodman's 1938 concert acetate tapes, RCA issued Miller at Carnegie, and Metro-Goldwyn-Mayer acquired and sold private recordings of the 1946 Herman concert. For its album MGM passed up "Caldonia," "Ebony Concerto," "Summer Sequence," "I'll Get

By," "1-2-3-4 Jump," and "I Surrender, Dear," but still offered buyers fifteen tracks.

After Carnegie Hall, Herman and the Herd continued with their radio performances and recording. Stevens joined the band when Wayne left, and Herman kept the Blue Flames for pop tunes, such as "Oh, What It Seemed to Be" and "I'm Always Chasing Rainbows," which was based on Chopin's "Fantasie Impromptu." Columbia next recorded Herman's band on April 14 and 15 in New York City. The first date produced a slow, bluesy "Linger in My Arms a Little Longer Baby," starring Stevens, Herman on alto sax, and Phillips. "Surrender" featured Herman and the Blue Flames, Norvo, and Bill Harris. The fast "Mabel! Mabel!" which was based on Dvořák's "Humoresque," had pleasingly whimsical lyrics: "Mabel, Mabel, sweet and able, get your elbows off the table, go on out and get yourself a guy."

The band played its way west to Chicago and Minneapolis that spring. In Chicago, during a Wildroot show from the Sherman, Herman introduced "Non-Alcoholic," a feature of Wildroot Cream Oil emphasized in its ads. And the Pioneer Musical Instrument Company, maker of the Sweetwind plastic horn, paid Herman, Phillips, Burns, Bauer, Jackson, and Lamond to record four promo pieces. Phillips played a Sweetwind on "Mighty like a Rose," "Sweet Wind Stomp," "Blue Flame," and a medley of folk songs.

On May 16 and 20 in Chicago, the Woodchoppers recorded with Swiss-clock precision "Steps," "Four Men on a Horse," "Fan It," "Igor," "Nero's Conception," "I Surrender, Dear," "Lost Weekend," and "Pam." Shorty Rogers sat in for "Fan It" and "Steps." "Steps," by Norvo and Rogers, was a slow, Ellingtonian blues piece with solos for Herman, Norvo, Phillips, and Rowles and a duet for Harris and Phillips. The title honored Bigard, who was known to his friends as "Steps." Rogers and Norvo also wrote "Igor," an homage to Stravinsky; according to Herman, "Shorty, like just about everyone in the band, was a Stravinsky fan. The guys were always listening to his early things, and then throwing in parts in their solos or charts."[44] "Igor" was fast and lively, with several full-combo stretches, a feature picked up from bop. Bauer, Norvo, Berman, Harris, and Phillips soloed. "Nero's Conception," also by Norvo and Rogers, was a slow, loping blues number featuring Herman's clarinet, Harris playing muted trombone over Phillips's soft tenor, then Phillips over Norvo's vibes. "I should have called it 'Hi Noone,'" Herman said. "I did try to play like Jimmy Noone on this one. I listened to him a lot when I was a kid. I always considered myself a sax player, but it always seemed that whatever kind of band I had, the clarinet fit more." "Four Men on a Horse" featured Rowles, Bauer, Jackson, and Lamond in Jackson's daring brainstorm of mixed rhythms. The recording omitted the full-band finish used in Carnegie Hall. Phillips wrote "Lost Weekend," the nearest the Wood-choppers came to the wild swing of the big bands, spiced with Rowles's piano playing and two false endings. The song reminded Herman of the movie *Lost Weekend,* "so that's what we called it."[45] The pretty ballad "Pam" (called "Billy Bauer's Tune" in 1945) was another example of Duke Ellington's influence, enhanced by Herman's warm alto sax and by Phillips and Norvo playing behind solos by Berman and Harris. Columbia with-held release of a version of "I Surrender, Dear" made May 20 until a 1988 album of 1940s combos. Norvo and Rowles starred in the boppish piece.

Hard-core jazz fans raved about the Woodchoppers, so tonally and rhythmically different from, yet akin to, Shaw's Gramercy Five. The groups were alike in their leadership by a clarinetist and their bold use of electric guitar, although Shaw's group had six players, Herman's ten. In sessions in 1940 and 1945, Shaw's group made just fourteen recordings, twelve of them original jazz numbers and two of them standards: "My Blue Heaven" and "Smoke Gets in Your Eyes." Herman's group made nine records, all in 1946, based on seven jazz originals and two standards: "I Surrender, Dear" and "Fan It" (the latter went back to Herman's days with Isham Jones). But while the Gramercy Five was playing cleanly har-monic chamber music that fit the heyday of swing, the Woodchoppers had ventured into the newer uses of dissonance, counterpoint, and polyrhythms that accompanied the bebop movement. In recording "Fan It," Herman sang and introduced a charming, chiming Norvo solo with "Fan it, Red!" while Bill Harris reeled off a mind-blowing solo spanning nearly two octaves. Only musicians, perhaps, could appreciate the complex finish, which combined a ritard and a descending figure with key changes. Columbia issued an alternate "Fan It"—played with gusto but less daring—in its 1988 album. On the 1946 issue of "Fan It," Columbia's label credited "Woody Herman and His Woodchoppers, featuring Red Norvo."

For Herman's Herd and his fans, the summer of 1946 brought irrepressible creative excitement, which John McDonough has admirably captured :

> The band is playing to a full house—about 2,700 people, mostly young. . . . As the group blares its way full-throttle through one of its wildest routines, suddenly a violent, stabbing trumpet break seems to come ripping through the theater from nowhere. A musician literally comes flying through the air from the upper balcony down toward the stage on a support wire. He is dressed in a Superman outfit and hits the stage running before blasting out a few more slashing high-note spires between echoing drum breaks. The crowd cheers madly. . . . just another show for the Woody Herman band. The high-flying trumpet player in the Superman outfit playing "Apple Honey" was Pete Candoli.[46]

Herman recalled, forty years later: "It was madness, but my background was show business. And we indulged in show business that would make Kiss [the fiery 1980s rock group] look like a string quartet."[47]

But the troublesome talent drain went on. When the band left Chicago for a month in Detroit, Troy, New York, and Lincoln, Nebraska, trumpeter Marky Markowitz departed and was replaced by alumnus Cappy Lewis; guitarist Charles Jagelka, who performed as Chuck Wayne, succeeded Bauer; and Joe Mondragon took over for bassist Jackson. As before, sidemen left for varying reasons: better-paying jobs with other bands, studio work that required less travel, or the chance to lead a band or small combo or cash in on their experience with a notable bandleader and find stardom of their own. And some simply left so as to get some rest. By June 21, the Blue Flames had gone, and Herman replaced them with the Blue Moods. The Moods debuted on radio, joining Herman on "Surrender" and "When We Meet Again" and starring on "Who Do You Love, I Hope?"

Chuck Wayne, a twenty-three-year-old New Yorker, typified Herman bandsmen in that he was young and launching a career. A guitarist with only five years' experience, Wayne had logged mostly combo time in the New York area. After Herman he would play backup for such megastars as Tony Bennett. Mondragon, a twenty-six-year-old Californian, had played in Los Angeles and military units and had recorded with Rey's band. Like Wayne, he became a fixture in West Coast combos and studios.

For the final Wildroot show, broadcast from Fort Worth on July 5, Herman played "Crazy Rhythm," "Surrender," "Night and Day" (for the Blue Moods), "Liza," "Linger in My Arms" (with Stevens), "Heaven Knows" (Herman and the Blue Moods), and "Wild Root." Minor record companies issued "air shots"—that is, recordings made by copying radio broadcasts off the air—decades after the Wildroot broadcasts, sometimes with weak audio quality and skimpy program notes. Few fans complained, though, about the opportunity to collect some of the band's rare radio music. Meanwhile, with the radio series finished, Herman pointed the band west toward California.

The First Herd, with Joe Mondragon on bass, poses for a formal portrait in late 1946. (Courtesy Duncan P. Schiedt)

To jobs at the Palladium, the Avadon, and Casino Gardens, the First Herd added movie and recording work in August and September 1946. At United Artists the band made the sound track with Billie Holiday for *New Orleans,* which was released in 1947. Holiday sang "Do You Know What It Means to Miss New Orleans?" and Herman performed in "The Blues Are Brewin'." On August 18, Stravinsky led a run-through of "Ebony Concerto" on a CBS broadcast from Casino Gardens. "Summer Sequence," "Bijou," and "Caldonia" also made the program, as did Burns's new chart of "Sidewalks of Cuba"—a Mitchell Parish–Irving Mills tune— and Shorty Rogers's version of "I've Got News for You," a witty new blues number sung by Herman.

When the band recorded "Ebony Concerto" the next day, Herman added John Cave on French horn and Stanley Chaloupka on harp, and Norvo sat out. In the Hollywood studio, when all was ready, Stravinsky wanted vodka. Gozzo crossed a street and returned with a glassful. According to Rowles, "Stravinsky downed it like a real Russian. And his old lady came up and toweled him and changed his shirt, and we did the record." "When we finally recorded it," Herman said, "Stravinsky made cuts. He didn't make cuts for just anybody; but he did for us, and was pleased at the end. I got to know him socially because we lived not far from each other. I had some beautiful moments with the man."[48] Herman often told an anecdote that showed his self-deprecating sense of humor. At dinner Stravinsky was discussing clarinetists: "German clarinetists, they have the full, rich tone. French clarinetists have a light and dainty sound. But you, Woody . . ."[49]

"Ebony Concerto" reached stores as a Columbia Masterworks classical item on a twelve-inch disc. The moderato and half of the second, andante movement filled the first side, and the rest of the andante and all of the final, moderato movement covered the flip side. The split personality of the piece created marketing problems for Columbia. Herman fans were put off by the green and gold Masterworks label, which was reserved for more traditional classical music. In turn, Masterworks Series fans rather sniffed at "the Woody Herman Orchestra Conducted by Igor

Stravinsky." Moreover, the recording sounded thin and strained. But Herman kept his plans to play the piece in an autumn tour of the Midwest and East.

With Cave and Chaloupka out, with alumnus Reid in to make up a trombone quartet, and with Norvo back at the vibes, the First Herd next made a sound track for *Rhapsody in Wood,* a George Pal puppet-cartoon, or Puppetoon. This introduced "Rhapsody in Wood," another of Burns's concert-length pieces. Pal had made an eight-minute Puppetoon with Duke Ellington—*Date with Duke*—about a month before. Later that summer, the Herman band played "High and Happy" at Republic for a segment in the movie short *Hit Parade of 1947.*

Herman, Sonny Berman, Chuck Wayne, Flip Philips, and Neal Reid pose, perhaps as a publicity shot for Rhapsody in Wood, *about August 1946. (Courtesy Ingrid Herman Reese)*

The alumni Cappy Lewis and Reid were joined in September by McCall, who replaced Stevens. "'Juggy' Gayle, a songplugger, heard Mary Ann in a club in San Diego, and told us she was singing better than ever," Herman said. "He was right."[50] Her talents were demonstrated in the two songs she sang for the Herd's recording sessions of September 17–20. In "Romance in the Dark," she sang the slow, torchy lyrics to Rowles's accompaniment, while the bouncing "Wrap Your Troubles in Dreams," recorded on September 20, proved her versatility. "Wrap Your Troubles in Dreams" also featured a vibes-guitar intro by Norvo and Chuck Wayne, a solo by Herman on clarinet, and Phillips's comments on tenor sax.

The nine other records made during this four-day rush did produce two memorable solos by Berman, on "Sidewalks of Cuba" and "Uncle Remus Said" and Bill Harris's stunning solo feat on "Everywhere." The sessions also promoted the writing and rising importance of trumpet player

Shorty Rogers on "Back Talk." The most ambitious pieces recorded at this time were "Summer Sequence " and "Lady McGowan's Dream." On September 19, Burns played on the three-part "Summer Sequence," which contained bits by Chuck Wayne over the saxes, Rowles, Bill Harris, Rubinwitch in a rare baritone sax solo, Norvo, Phillips, and Herman on alto, with the full band tiptoeing in just before the coda. Fifteen months later, a fourth section was added to "Summer Sequence," and it was released for sale to the public with "Lady McGowan's Dream." In his *New Yorker* review, Balliett dismissed "Summer Sequence" as largely trivial, impressionistic in places, and mimicking the work of Duke Ellington's ace arranger Billy Strayhorn. Nor did Burns's five-minute, two-part "Lady McGowan's Dream" impress the world. Yet with its easy Caribbean feel, it was a good vehicle for Herman's alto sax, with solo time for Norvo, Bauer, and Phillips, an intricate reed-section passage, and a full-band coda. Herman said Burns wrote the piece "in honor of a woman, supposedly a 'literary celebrity,' who entertained the band lavishly in her suite at the Ambassador East in Chicago. But it turned out to be a hoax. I don't think she had a quarter to her name."[51]

On October 12, the Woodchoppers recorded "Some Day, Sweetheart" and a version of "I Surrender, Dear" with Chuck Wayne on guitar, which set it apart from the May 20 version. The men played "Some Day Sweetheart" in a medium-fast tempo with lively solos by Herman on clarinet, Norvo, Wayne, Rowles, Phillips, and Berman. Columbia marketed a four-record Woodchoppers album with "Igor," "Steps," "Four Men on a Horse," "Nero's Conception," "Lost Weekend," "Pam," "Someday, Sweetheart," and the October recording of "I Surrender, Dear." Clearly, Columbia had joined others in sensing the terminal illness of the swing bands. The bop sound and the voicings of the mid-size "cool" bands of Miles Davis and Gerry Mulligan in 1948-50 evident in the Woodchoppers' music, on the other hand, did not fade in popularity. Schuller explains that "with Rogers' writing, the Woodchoppers were progressive in outlook, aware of advances in both recent jazz and contemporary classical music without fawning over it, capable of superior and—in the case of Bill Harris—outrageously inventive solo work, all in a true chamber ensemble conception."[52]

$d$uring October and November, the Herd took "Ebony Concerto" on tour. Bookers expected more cultured fans to accept Stravinsky, but they were wrong. Among the good receptions were big disappointments, mainly because the tour was ineptly promoted. The first stop was Baltimore, where a Stravinsky protégé conducted the piece. As Herman recalled, "When the band started playing it, the audience booed. They didn't want to hear it." But "of all the schools we played, Purdue University gave us the worst reception." Purdue's 6,200-seat Hall of Music was packed for 7 P.M. and 9:30 P.M. shows on November 22. "Ebony Concerto," as Herman saw it, "thoroughly confused the audience. . . . Many decided that the music wasn't me, that we were insulting their intelligence."[53]

Critical acclaim for the band, too, began to fade with the player turnover. Balliett was moved to write dourly that the band's repertoire consisted only of fast and slow pieces. He considered Bill Harris's trombone style suitable for a circus band; regarded Phillips merely as a copier of Ben Webster and Lester Young; and opined that both of Herman's solo stars had almost nothing to say beneath all their staged emotionalism. He noted, without really praising, Herman's more humorous vocals, the band's tendency to shout and scream, and the catchy endings. Like the Shriners, he reckoned, the Herd had harmless fun.

Critics, managers, radio sponsors, and booking and press agents all drenched Herman in advice that he did not seek for widening his band's appeal. Maybe because constant conflicts were starting to wear him down, Herman accepted too much advice—programming more pop tunes, adding the vocal groups, forcing "Ebony Concerto" on fans. Simon concluded that "he probably was unaware of it, but the strain of keeping a band on top was beginning to tell on Woody. The men were showing signs of discontent with having to share the spotlight with some rather mediocre singers." Simon recalled that

> Outsiders tried to horn in. Recording men and personal managers, according to Herman, "would steam up some of the men and try to get them to go out on their own with new bands." The result—uncertainty, mistrust, dissension and unhappy prima donnas. "Everything would have been all right if they had left us alone," Herman said.[54]

In fact, since the First Herd took shape in 1944, various band members had made outside recordings.

Berman commandeered Bill Harris, Phillips, Burns, Chuck Wayne, and Lamond and—adding baritone saxophonist Serge Chaloff and bassist Artie Bernstein—called the group Sonny Berman's Big Eight and produced "Curbstone Scuffle," "Nocturne," and "Bird Lore" for Dial Records on September 21, 1946.

At the same session, Burns borrowed Chuck Wayne and Lamond from the Herman band, plus Chaloff and Bernstein, to record "Dial-ogue" as the Ralph Burns Quintet.

Harris had led moonlighting groups in 1945–46 for Keystone and Dial.

Hefti combined Herdsmen Aless, Bauer, and Jackson with trombonist Kai Winding, tenor saxophonist Charlie Ventura, and drummer Alvin Stoller to record "I Woke Up Dizzy" and "Sloppy Joe's" for Keystone in 1946.

Jackson led combos at recording sessions in 1944–45 for Queen and Keystone.

Phillips organized a combo composed of Hefti, Bill Harris, Burns, Bauer, Jackson, Tough, Hyams, and clarinetist Aaron Sachs in October 1944, recording "Pappiloma" and "Skyscraper" at the first of several sessions for Signature.

Herman gave his blessings to anyone who wanted out, and even offered them some charts. "Only one thing," he would say. "Don't ask me for any money!"[55] Generally at that point the men would decide to stay.

But for a Columbia session in Chicago on December 10, new hires replaced trumpet stars Berman, Shorty Rogers, and Pete Candoli, while Norvo and two others were simply gone. This watered-down crew, barely a shadow of what the band had been, made the last of the First Herd's recordings. "Woodchoppers' Ball" reflected Burns's and Hefti's modern voicings in brass and reeds, solos by Herman on clarinet, Bill Harris, Phillips, Cappy Lewis, and Rowles. By now, though, "Woodchoppers' Ball" had gathered mold. "I've been sick of it for years," Herman said. "But it's been such a big number for us that I really shouldn't knock it."[56] In another obviously commercial move, the band reworked "Blue Flame." Herman's clarinet painted indigo hues in a nod to Duke Ellington, Rowles played lovely modern piano fills, and Harris's muted and open trombone solos preceded guitar-strumming by Chuck Wayne. The band next recorded "The Blues Are Brewin'," to plug *New Orleans.* Herman sang Burns's chart, and Harris soloed over the saxes. The First Herd played blues tunes sparingly, but beginning with "I Ain't Got Nothin' but the Blues," played them well. Finally it recorded alto player John LaPorta's "Non-Alcoholic." Herman said LaPorta "had a pretty wild concept even then; this one was based on the whole tone scale, and in those days it could have passed for some Russian piece."[57] Phillips, Harris, and Herman on clarinet soloed.

These recordings were made in a small studio suited for the Woodchoppers. "The big band in there was like a subway at rush hour," Herman said. "Yet the sound was fine . . . this band could record in the men's room and still sound the way it should, because these guys listened to themselves and adjusted to whatever conditions there were. The test of when a band is really making it is when it is in balance with itself. . . . I'd look up at any section and the men would already be moving around, busy making the sound of the band balance."[58]

*f*or eight years, Goldfarb, Mirenburg, and Vallon had managed most of the Herman band's financial affairs. But now in 1946, as many bands fought postwar inflation, Herman entrusted the responsibilities to Turchen. The two had met in the summer of 1945 when the First Herd was playing in Sioux City, Iowa. A local war veteran and band groupie, Turchen amazed Herman as a fixer; when no one else could get a car during those years of rationing and shortages, Turchen had a new one, plus all the gasoline he could use. If transportation was needed, Turchen jumped in as chauffeur. Later Turchen followed the band to California. Barnet characterized him as "a charmer. And everyone thought he was good for Woody as a manager, because he always found bookings when there weren't any around."[59]

The band grossed more than a million dollars again in 1946, and the Hermans were eager to buy a home. After 1945, they had left the Garden of Allah apartment complex for a leased house in Laurel Canyon. By the end of 1946, they paid $60,000 in cash for a three-level house high on Hollywood Boulevard that was being vacated by Humphrey Bogart and Lauren Bacall. It offered a sweeping valley view from a rear terrace that jutted out from a mountainside.

Beneath the surface, however, a personal problem was developing. While living in the Garden of Allah with little Ingrid, Charlotte Herman had begun drinking too much alcohol and taking powerful pills. "Start mixing Nembutals and booze, and you're on your way home," Herman said. Her habits had been influenced by the fast-living movie crowd all around her and by the loneliness and boredom of raising a child while Herman was away for up to forty weeks a year. Herman decided that the "only way I could help was to go home."[60]

After a dance at Indiana University, he announced his plan to break up the skeletal First Herd, in which he, Bill Harris, Lamond, and Phillips were the only original stars remaining. The band's last job was in Castle Farms Ballroom, Cincinnati, on Christmas Eve. Economics provided a reason to quit. Postwar costs for salaries and travel kept rising, fees had to be higher, and bookings became scarcer, even for an aggressive agent such as Turchen. When bands led by Goodman, Tommy Dorsey, James, Les Brown, Teagarden, Carter, and Ina Ray Hutton also dissolved, December 1946 marked in the minds of many the end of the Big Band Era. The big bands yielded to small combos, bop bands, pop singers, plenty of postwar records, drive-in movies, midget auto racing, and television, which gave cheaper thrills.

A *Metronome* editorial written for the January 1947 issue—"Obituary in Rhythm"—mourned that "only once before was a band of such unequivocal standards and evenness of musicianship organized. That was the Ellington band. It still is, but the Herman band is not. Woody Herman's magnificent band is dead. *Requiescat in pace.*" "It was a hard decision, breaking up the First Herd," Herman said. "We were making lots of money that year. . . . Some of the best things we did never got on record. But that's what everybody says, isn't it? I wouldn't have missed it for the world."[61]

After hustling as a leader for ten years, the Hermans could afford to take their first real vacation—nine days in Bermuda. But memories of their achievements remained for fans:

> There were many qualities worth noting about the First Herd, but three things stood out. The cohesiveness and power of the brass section, and the muscular, distinctive, solo voices of Flip Phillips on tenor saxophone and Bill Harris on trombone. The trumpet section featured the lead and high-note work of Pete Candoli and Sonny Berman. Herman was mightily impressed by that section's power, saying, "When those guys blew, I ducked! [And] Harris was so powerful he used to pull the whole trombone section with him."[62]

Herman also looked back on the First Herd with affection: "It was a tremendously exciting band. Ideas and whole tunes sprang out of that group like sparks. Flip would blow something. Pete would grab it and first thing you knew we had a new number. Chubby liked to recall how the guys would come off the stand set after set, congratulating each other on how well they sounded. Almost every night I felt like saying 'Thank you.'"[63]

And well he might: Since the summer of 1944, the First Herd had made eighty-some Decca and Columbia recordings, plus transcriptions and V discs, and fifty Old Gold or Wild Root radio shows and numerous others for the AFRS, local stations, and the networks. It had played in three movies and several shorts, in top theaters, clubs, hotel ballrooms, and in Carnegie Hall and had grossed more than two million dollars.

The band gave record sellers a mixture of short-term hits, long-time classics, and innovations in "Laura," "Apple Honey," "Northwest Passage," "Goosey Gander," "Caldonia," "Happiness Is Just a Thing Called Joe," "The Good Earth," "Bijou," "Wild Root," "Ah, Your Father's Mustache," "Blowin' Up a Storm," "Panacea," "Everywhere," and several Woodchoppers pieces, plus music in extended forms—"Ebony Concerto,"

"Rhapsody in Wood," "Summer Sequence," and "Lady McGowan's Dream." It introduced Burns, Hefti, and Shorty Rogers as writers, and added other names to the honor roll of jazz stars: Pete and Conte Candoli, Berman, Gozzo, Bill Harris, Phillips, Rowles, Jackson, Bauer, Chuck Wayne, Lamond, Frances Wayne, and McCall.

And as Duke Ellington's band had done, the First Herd inspired others. Bobby Sherwood's lively "Cotton Tail" used Tough's tumbling drum coda, Hefti's unison brass, and a clarinet solo reminiscent of "Apple Honey." Raeburn recorded a number entitled "Boyd Meets Stravinsky." So at the end of 1946, Herman could bask in the Bermuda sun, his place in jazz's hall of fame already won. There was but one problem: he was only thirty-three! What would he do for the rest of his life?

chapter five

the
FOUR BROTHERS
band

$\int$or a while in 1947, Herman stayed home, played golf, dined with his
wife, played with Ingie, subbed for KLAC disk jockey Al Jarvis, and loafed
around Los Angeles. Although "clean" himself, he took Charlotte Herman
to Alcoholics Anonymous meetings (and was aghast to see certain friends
and former sidemen working to kick their habits.) Since boyhood Herman
seldom had rested for so long. Now he enjoyed family times and getting
about to hear other music. But he remained a show-biz name. At the
southwest corner of Hollywood and Highland Boulevards, the chamber
of commerce cemented a gold star bearing his name as part of its Walk of
Fame for tourists.

Recording, radio, and business reached Herman's attention, as
did the stabbing message from New York City: Sonny Berman, a heroin
addict, had died of a heart attack at twenty-two. Herman summed up his
career: "Sonny was one of the warmest soloists I ever had. For his youth
he was so mature in his playing. He was just scratching the surface of
what he was about to do."[1]

Herman's other stars still sparkled, however. Phillips and Bill
Harris led a combo on the Fifty-second Street jazz strip in New York
City. Pete Candoli joined Beneke's "Glenn Miller Band." Jackson performed
with Ventura's combo, then led a bop sextet in Europe. Burns and Hefti
wrote music in Los Angeles, and Hefti toured with James. Lamond and
Rowles worked Hollywood studio and club jobs.

Herman formed Continental Artists, a booking office in the
Wilshire district, and staffed it with three former road managers, Jack
Archer, Milton Deutsch, and Turchen. Among the clients was Spade

Cooley's "western swing" band modeled after Wills's Texas Playboys. When Herman's booking contract with General Artists Corporation expired, he became Continental's client, too. Herman also guested on a radio show with singer Peggy Lee and her husband, guitarist Dave Barbour. He did not appear to miss his past life: "I had fun without any urge to get back in front of a band."[2]

Meanwhile Columbia stayed in touch. From February through August 1947, Herman sang on twenty-five records, with clarinet and alto sax cameos thrown in. Sometimes large bands, marshaled and rehearsed by Burns, backed him; other times he played with small combos with some of his former sidemen. A Four Chips quartet helped on February 4 and 5 to produce "Across the Alley from the Alamo," "Baby, Baby, All the Time," and "There Is No Greater Love." Herman went on to do "Ivy" and "Can You Look Me in the Eyes (And Say We're Through)?" on March 10, "That's My Desire" on March 19, and "Pancho Maximillian Hernandez (the Best President We Ever Had)" and "Somebody Loves Me" on March 31. Each Four Chips roster changed. The last two sessions took place in New York City, where Herman's breakups with Goldfarb, Mirenburg, and Vallon and with GAC were being contested.

Back in Los Angeles on April 21, after Burns rounded up a violin section, a harpist, a French horn player, five sax players, and a rhythm quartet, Herman sang "In the Blue of Evening," "Am I Blue?" and "Blue Moon." The next day Herman and Shore sang the duets "Tallahassee" and "Natch" with Sonny Burke's crisp studio band. On May 7, with a seventeen-piece band coached by Burns, Herman recorded "Between the Devil and the Deep Blue Sea," "Blues in the Night," "Under a Blanket of Blue," "I Got a Right to Sing the Blues," and "Blue Prelude."

On May 27, Herman sang "Baby, Come Home," "Bloop Bleep," and "My Blue Heaven" backed by eleven musicians. Columbia packaged eight tunes from this run of "blue" and blues numbers and sold them as an album called *Eight Shades of Blue*. (It added four in 1956 to create *Twelve Shades of Blue*.) In Los Angeles on August 15, Herman sang "Boulevard of Memories" and "Civilization (Bongo, Bongo, Bongo)" with a band of seventeen. With a similar band on August 26, he recorded "A Tune for Humming" and "Baby, Have You Got a Little Love to Spare?"

Although Columbia may have been tempted to credit these efforts to Woody Herman and His Orchestra, it stayed honest. The bands on these recordings were not working, touring bands led nightly by Herman. Nor did the big bands playing Burns's charts mimic Herman's. Burns stocked the pickup bands with strong players, and at two sessions Herman shook hands with twenty-year-old Stan Getz, then a tenor-sax unknown.

These 1947 records were sales-oriented pop or novelty fare. Herman's talent for the latter boosted "Civilization" to good sales, but all twenty-five were light on jazz content. Making them was easy money, however, and they kept Herman in the public eye, ear, and memory. So did the movies *New Orleans* and *Rhapsody in Wood*. An added feature of *Rhapsody in Wood* was Herman playing "Blue Flame" on, and explaining the origin of, the clarinet and singing Carmichael's new tune "Ivy."

*I*t was not family crisis and the need to rest that kept Herman off bandstands. Across the land, business kept sinking. *Billboard*'s story "Band Biz One-Niter Blues" told of major bands taking cuts in pay for one-nighters. Tommy Dorsey had gone from $3,000 to $1,750 before quitting. Barnet was down to $750. Kenton took a cut from $1,750 to $1,500. While Shaw retired quietly, Dorsey shelved trombone and baton loudly, grousing that "bop stinks!" Goodman, Krupa, and Barnet hung on to bop-oriented bands, with gaps between bookings.

Duke Ellington, James, Les Brown, and Basie made it playing old things. Hines, Gillespie, and Billy Eckstine started "modern" bands that they could barely sustain. Kenton, Thornhill, and Raeburn led bands blowing daring new music, too, but scarcely survived. An embittered Eckstine gave up his money-losing crew in 1947, saying: "Woody Herman—get a load of his things—'Northwest Passage.' All those things were nothing but a little *bit* of the music that we were trying to play. They got the *Down Beat* Number One Band, yap, yap, yap, but Woody better not have lit nowhere near where *my* band was."[3]

Still Herman kept his admirers. The June 1947 issue of *Metronome* quoted Dick Haymes: "We have so few real *leaders* in the [jazz] field. Outside of Woody Herman and Duke Ellington, what bands have really tried to improve music? The others are just trying to keep a dead art alive. It's the same old tenor and trumpet chorus routine, always playing the same stale old riffs."[4]

Bebop had developed gradually since the early 1940s. Elements could be heard here and there, by assorted pioneering artists, and slowly some of the more established bandleaders used them. By 1947 bop had "arrived" commercially and continued to be developed musically. It appealed especially to those bored with swing and looking for an antiswing— a protest of, and rebellion against, the smug, tuxedoed "name" bands. And for a time, bop did woo players and fans across the land. Informal, intense, sloppily attired small groups of players, using seemingly "wrong" chords, abrupt stop-and-start and rhythmic staccato lunges, and linear themes, were all playing bop. A sense of humor colored this music, as in such titles as "Bop, Look and Listen," and "To Be or Not to Bop." So did the wearing of tightly tailored zoot suits, dark glasses, berets, and goatees. And so did misuse of hard drugs and booze for certain of the front-line stars.

Bop's future hall-of-famers included Monk, Tadd Dameron, Parker, Don Byas, Dexter Gordon, Roach, Curly Russell, and Davis. Gillespie, Eckstine, and others tried big bands, but quintets or sextets were the norm. Lucky Thompson, John Lewis, Manne, Wardell Gray, Howard McGhee, Bud Powell, Oscar Pettiford, Fats Navarro, Terry Gibbs, Chano Pozo, Tiny Kahn, Ray Brown, and George Russell won loyal fans. So did scat singers Gillespie, Leo Watson, Dave Lambert, Buddy Stewart, Roy Kral, Jackie Cain, and Kenny Hagood.

Hole-in-the-wall recording firms—hawking such labels as Asch, Bel-Tone, Blue Note, Clef, Continental, Dial, Guild, Keynote, Lenox, Majestic, Manor, Musicraft, Regis, Savoy, and Stinson—promoted bop. First Herd alumni, always musically advanced, were not behind the times, either: Pete Candoli, Hefti, Bill Harris, Phillips, Lamond, Jackson, Bauer, Shorty Rogers, Burns, and Rowles all led or played on any number of bop recordings.

From something as bland as "Back Home Again in Indiana," the great musicianship, lightning minds, composing and soloing ingenuity of the boppers could create "Donna Lee" (Parker), "Ice Freezes Red" (Navarro), "Trumpet at Tempo" (Howard McGhee), and "Tiny's Con" (Aaron Sachs). "How High the Moon," recorded by Goodman at ballad tempo in 1939, became bop's breakneck anthem under many names: "Bean at the Met" (Coleman Hawkins), "Bird Lore" and "Ornithology" (Parker), "Hopscotch" (Vivien Garry), "Indiana Winter" (Esquire All Stars), "Low Ceiling" (Beryl Booker), and "Slightly Dizzy" (Joe Marsala.) Bop stars sat in with other leaders' combos, dodging possible contract or booking disputes with fake names. For example, Gillespie recorded as "Gabriel," "Izzy Goldberg," "B. Bopstein," and "John Birks." Shorty Rogers moonlighted as "Roger Short," alto player Art Pepper was sometimes "Art Salt," and Parker became "Charlie Chan."

There were many differences between combo bop and big-band swing. In *Inside Bebop,* Feather discusses such differences—having to do with scales, harmonies, beat, phrasing, construction, intervals, and passing notes—exhaustively. The big change was that repeated riffs, so common in swing, all but vanished. In bop, a theme, instead of repeating itself, wove its way through a twelve-bar format with a continuous, often baffling line that was hard to remember or hum. And some old themes played in quarter or eighth notes were speeded up to sixteenths, thirty-secondths, even sixty-fourths! For musicians, it was graduation from coloring books to Double-Crostics; for fans, it was a leap from ABCs to Sanskrit.

Ernie Royal, a twenty-six-year-old high-note trumpeter playing bop with a combo on Sunset near Vine, inspired Herman to reenter the business. As Herman told it, "Trying to make something different happen was always in the back of my mind. Then you hear a great player or two, and the idea is replanted."[5] The ability to make something different happen, in fact, constitutes one of Herman's main virtues as a jazz artist. Instead of screaming "Caldonia" the rest of his life, he spread word that he would invest money, talent, and energy in a bop-oriented band. "I had gotten to know my family at last. And the [First] Herd had been making good money," he explained. "But I guess the most important thing was I felt I had to do something productive that I really liked."[6]

Respect for Herman made it easy for him to recruit talent. Hanging around Hollywood that summer, for instance, was the twenty-six-year-old Dallas native Jimmy Giuffre. A composer and clarinet and sax player, Giuffre heard of Herman's plans and offered a new sax-section idea. Giuffre had been writing for four tenors. So had his college roommate and Air Force Band comrade Gene Roland, also twenty-six and from Dallas. A brass player with Kenton from 1944 to 1946, Roland had come from the east and was connected with a band consisting of trumpet, piano, bass, drums, and four tenors. Getz; John Haley "Zoot" Sims, twenty-one, from Inglewood, California; Herbert "Herbie" Steward, twenty-one, from Los Angeles; and Giuffre played the saxes. A trumpeter named Tommy DiCarlo led it, while Roland and Giuffre wrote its book.

This obscure combo worked jobs in the summer of 1947 in the Spanish section of Los Angeles. When Herman scouted it with Burns, he was so smitten by the sax sound that he soon hired Sims, Steward, and Getz for his new band. But Herman wisely picked talent that could also play his old hits. Steward could double on alto, allowing the band to blow equally well with three tenors and one alto or with two tenors and two altos, the First Herd's alignment. He kept a baritone sax for variety and range, giving the job to the twenty-three-year-old Bostonian Serge Chaloff. A devotee of Parker's, Chaloff had played in Raeburn's, Auld's, and Jimmy Dorsey's big bands. Although Herman assigned most writing to Burns, he also encouraged Giuffre, Shorty Rogers, and free-lancers. From the start, this band's numbers for three tenors and one baritone produced the most unique reed voicing since Glenn Miller's. To some it became the most influential in modern jazz. Herman, deciding to focus more upon jazz than upon pleasing dancers and selling records, "knew right away this was an important sound that belonged to us. One of my strongest convictions—aside from the belief that it is basically music to have a ball with—is that jazz has to swing. When you stop swinging, you're competing with [classical composer Dmitri] Mitropoulos, and man, that cat cuts you!"[7] Still, his basic goal—to "create a mood and hope somebody digs it"—remained firm.

Shorty Rogers and his wife bought their dream house in Burbank, California, but, he said, "nothing was happening. Eventually I got a little work with a band led by Butch Stone that had Stan Getz and Herbie Steward in it, [but] as soon as they let me know that Woody was re-forming, I was back!"[8] Herman had a firm and in some ways risky game plan: "As we put together a roster, I didn't want to repeat what I had already done. When that happens the music just becomes repetition, which is what most bands were about. . . . I never wanted to sell nostalgia. Where there are certain tunes associated with a band, it would be unfair not to play a few to recapture memories for people. But I never considered it our big job, or our future, to delve into the past."[9] So just five First Herd veterans joined the 1947 band: Lamond, alto Sam Marowitz, Rogers, Markowitz, and Burns. The new sax team contained Marowitz, Sims, Steward, Getz, and Chaloff. Notable in the brass section were Royal and Earl Swope, a power trombonist. Joining Rogers, Royal, and Markowitz as trumpeters were Stan Fishelson and Bernie Glow. Ollie Wilson, a ballad soloist, and Bob Swift formed a trombone trio with Swope. Freddie "Frazier" Otis started an eight-month stint as pianist. Two former bassists staffed the rhythm section: Yoder, who played bass and served as road manager, and Sargent, who returned to play guitar this time. Jerri Ney, who could double on vibes, landed the job of female vocalist.

The Four Brothers Band's trombone trio of Ollie Wilson, Bill Harris, and Earl Swope. (Courtesy Duncan P. Schiedt)

Royal had apprenticed with the Hampton and Basie big bands and had done a three-year musical hitch in the navy. Getz starting at fifteen had played for Teagarden, Chester, Kenton, Jimmy Dorsey, and Goodman. Steward had performed with Chester's band at sixteen, and then with Bigard, Freddie Slack, Shaw, and Rey. Sims apprenticed with Bob Astor, Sid Catlett, Sherwood, Dunham, Goodman, and, in early 1947, Bill Harris's

Sextet. To untutored ears, Sims, Getz, Steward, Al Cohn, and Giuffre—all Lester Young disciples—sounded alike.

Herman said that when he started that band, he "definitely made a pitch to get people who were enthused about the music."[10] "Back Talk" and "Non-Alcoholic," two of the First Herd's last numbers, had pointed to the future with their bop chording and phrasing, short drum fills and accented "bombs," baritone sax solos, linear structures, faster tempi, tighter voicings, more written music, and fewer head arrangements. In September 1947, Herman began rehearsing new charts written by Burns, Shorty Rogers, Giuffre, and twenty-one-year-old Brooklynite Cohn, who was then with Rich's band.

The band debuted on October 16, 1947, in the Municipal Auditorium in San Bernardino. One-nighters in San Diego and Long Beach followed. Just three days after opening, the band set up to record for Columbia in Hollywood. Two novelty ballads resulted: "If Anybody Can Steal My Baby" and "I Told Ya I Love Ya, Now Get Out." The band played Burns's charts with wind-up-toy control. It relied more on written ensemble parts than on solos (Swope, Getz, and Royal played only short solos), sounding tinny, yet playing with gusto and purpose.

But California one-nighters in Bakersfield, Watsonville, the Edgewater Beach Ballroom in San Francisco, and The Havana in Oakland, fell flat. Small, cool crowds, it seemed, had come more to watch than to listen or react. Then there was a five-day gap of no work between Watsonville and San Francisco. The Bay Area shows put off *Down Beat*'s West Coast writer, Ralph Gleason. Clearly this band suffered in comparison to the First Herd and to Kenton's big, loud jazz ensemble. As James A. Treichel sees it, "The real challenge to the new band was to find its own personality by combining new music with old. . . . [But] Ollie Wilson playing 'Bijou' was no substitute for the original."[11] Gleason did praise Royal and Shorty Rogers and liked Ney singing "It's Been So Long," "Lover Come Back to Me," and "There'll Be Some Changes Made."

Ever since the success of "Woodchoppers' Ball" in 1939, Herman's bands had worked when he wished. But by 1947, the picture had changed. Name bands performed more in spurts. The few full-time big bands really into jazz—Herman, Duke Ellington, Kenton, Gillespie, Basie, and Barnet—sometimes had to travel farther for shorter gigs and lay idle in midweek. The Herman band limped on to Reno, took a jaunt through the Northwest in early November, then played three weeks at the Coconut Grove in Salt Lake City and eight nights in the Tune Town Ballroom in St. Louis. The longer stays did give the band time to prepare to make enough records to ride out another of Petrillo's bans, which started on January 1, 1948. One-nighters in Chicago on December 18 and at George Devine's Million Dollar Ballroom in Milwaukee on December 19 earned a better review by *Down Beat's* Midwest writer, Ted Hallock. Royal's and Lamond's duets in the tried-and-true "Golden Wedding" and in "Berled in Earl," Shorty Rogers's punchy new chart for Swope, pleased Hallock most.

As in 1942, leaders and record companies raced to beat the musician's union ban, and Herman and his band recorded ten tunes in one week. The December 24 session in Hollywood included a strange mix: Burns's version of Aram Khachaturian's "Sabre Dance"; a pop tune, "Cherokee Canyon"; Shorty Rogers's "Keen and Peachy"; Cohn's "The Goof and I"; the amusing blues "I've Got News for You," arranged by Rogers; and a filler, "Lazy Lullaby." The fast, folk song–based "Sabre Dance" stayed true to the original in the ballet *Gayne* for a while, then roared into big-band bop. But, in Treichel's opinion, "Sabre Dance" sounded "like a stock [arrangement] suitable for playing behind stage acts, not much for listening."[12] "Cherokee Canyon" featured Herman singing lonesome-cowboy lyrics, the subdued band playing backup. Jazz fans found ecstasy in a sax-section passage in "I've Got News for You" and its two-timed lover's lament wailed out by Herman. Shorty Rogers had transcribed the segment for five saxes note-for-note from Parker's twisty-turny alto solo in "Dark Shadows," a blues sung by Earl Coleman the previous February for Dial Records. Rogers's widely analyzed interlude in turn stirred Med Flory to form the Supersax group decades later. Rogers played muted trumpet behind Herman's voice in the recording, while Swope and Royal punched out solos. "Keen and Peachy" (based on "Fine and Dandy") was a tight brass, sax-section, and full-ensemble piece, with a rapid succession of short solos by Getz, Sims, Swope, Chaloff, and Royal.

Herman explained that "Shorty Rogers wrote the first chorus and the rest we put together with the guys as a head arrangement." Chaloff's solo in this number was the first he recorded with Herman. "The Goof and I" (a play on the best-selling book and movie *The Egg and I*), reminded Herman of "Moonlight Bay." Chaloff, Swope, and Herman on clarinet soloed, but Cohn's chart leaned on section and full-ensemble passages and Lamond's trip-hammer fills. Herman pointed out that "this was one of the first uses of the expression 'to goof.'"[13] "Lazy Lullaby" (written in 1942 by Herman and George) stayed unissued by Columbia until 1963. By then, it packed more historical than musical interest. Treichel notes that "the saxes were voiced so closely at the opening they gave the effect of the 'Four Brothers' sound but with an alto lead. All the sax players doubled on clarinet [Chaloff played a bass clarinet] on this and other ballads."[14]

What was this about a "Four Brothers" sound? On December 27, the band recorded Giuffre's fast-moving "Four Brothers" and a three-minute part 4 for Burns's "Summer Sequence." The landmark "Four Broth-

The full Four Brothers Band. (Courtesy Duncan P. Schiedt)

ers" showcased the sax section and included a merry-go-round of short solos by Getz, Sims, Steward, and Chaloff. Herman played the clarinet, and the crisp band was spurred by the chord changes for "Jeepers Creepers." Herman kept this number in his repertoire for the next forty years, playing it everywhere and anywhere, with countless sax lineups. "Four Brothers" at first surprised even some sophisticated jazz people unable to identify the instruments. *Metronome* printed the three tenor solos for awed fans, players, and students. In due time, jazz singer Jon Hendricks wrote mile-a-minute lyrics, even fitting words to the recorded sax and clarinet solos. In the 1980s, the Manhattan Transfer recorded "Four Brothers" with Hendricks's lyrics; and the National Academy of Recording Arts and Sciences admitted "Four Brothers" into its Hall of Fame. "It was the right timing, the right soloists—a beautiful band with crisp brass sounds," Giuffre reflected. "It was a road map for the future. I was really inspired in combining Lester Young and bebop in that piece."[15] Herman said that he thereafter liked to think of his 1947–49 crew as "the 'Four Brothers' Band. . . . It established our sax section voicing of three tenors and a baritone . . . one of those things you experiment with and it worked."[16]

Burns's piano, Sargent's guitar, Ollie Wilson's only recorded trombone solo in two years with the band, and Getz's silky tenor sax enriched the soft, burnished feel of "Summer Sequence, Part IV." It reached record buyers in 1948, when Columbia put together a *Summer Sequence* album comprised of the four sections of "Summer Sequence" and the two of "Lady McGowan's Dream."

Ney had moved on before December 30, 1947, when the band recorded "Swing Low, Sweet Clarinet," "My Pal, Gonzales," and "P.S., I Love You." Herman readily hired McCall for the third time, starting December 22. Now twenty-eight, McCall had been kneading Holiday, O'Day, and June Christy into a tasty style of her own and had been working as a soloist in Los Angeles. The slow-tempo, sultry "Swing Low, Sweet Clarinet" combined McCall with full band, the creamy reeds, and Herman's clarinet. Lamond's accents in a brief double-time segment reflected modern drummers' subtle ways of time keeping. Herman's amusing "My Pal,

Gonzales," in Shorty Rogers's swinging chart with bop undertones, featured Herman singing George's lyrics of a wife stealer. Chaloff, Sims, and Lamond soloed and filled. "P.S., I Love You" inspired one critic to gush that the much-improved McCall seemed to have been "that rare band canary of any color who had a genuine feel for the blues."[17] Another rated McCall every bit as good as Frances Wayne, "a true talent [possessing] a musicianly concept which [fit in with] Woody's top soloists."[18] The band also recorded, but Columbia never issued, Rogers's arrangement of "Baby, I Need You," on which Herman and McCall sang and Sims soloed. The timely lyrics asserted that just as a bed needs a pillow "we all need *Petrillo!*"

*I*t seemed to Treichel that while the new band "echoed" the First Herd because of Burns's presence, a lighter, bop feel was achieved by Cohn, Giuffre, and Shorty Rogers:

> Their writing was fresh but not far out. It struck a balance between inventiveness and economy, and showed concern for swinging and solo space, important because this was a band that *had players*. Chaloff, Lamond and Royal were the driving spirits. . . . Chaloff was the band's most featured soloist [who] never seemed to sound bad. Chaloff in time won both *Down Beat* and *Metronome* polls. . . . [Lamond's] style did not rely on flashiness but on the understanding that as a unit the rhythm section was *felt* as much as heard. Herman's arrangers left openings in their scores for him, so his one-, two-, and four-bar fills became as much part of this band as the "Four Brothers" sound or Herman's clarinet.[19]

But Balliett, never more than lukewarm about Herman bands, found little to praise in the sax-section sound, in the imitators of Lester Young among Herman's tenor saxophonists, in the repertoire, and in Herman's singing, which, he said, made listeners want to clear their throats.

Petrillo's second ban made it hard to promote and for many fans to judge the Four Brothers Band in 1948. But it pushed on. After the band's January 1–4 gig at the Edgewater Beach Ballroom, Jimmy Raney replaced Sargent on guitar. Then Steward left, and Cohn, twenty-two, came in to play tenor sax and write for Herman.

In late January, Herman teamed up again with Pal on a Puppetoon based on *Tom Thumb*. A sound track, written by Burns, is said to have been recorded, but the project collapsed. On February 2, Universal-International filmed a short called *Woody Herman and His Orchestra* costarring the Modernaires and a dance team. The band played "Blue Flame," "Sabre Dance," and "Caldonia." Then Getz, Cohn, Sims, Chaloff, Swope, Herman, and Royal all soloed on a high-voltage "Northwest Passage" finale.

From February 3 through March 15, the band broadcast seventeen *One Night Stand* programs from the Hollywood Palladium for the AFRS. Airchecks—that is, copies—of these and other shows became valuable records of the 1948 band, however technically flawed they are. They show that the new band still played successful older charts—"I've Got the World on a String," "Non-Alcoholic," "Sidewalks of Cuba," "Northwest Passage," "Apple Honey," "Half Past Jumpin' Time," "The Good Earth," and "Laura"—in addition to plugging the newest Columbia recordings. Although less so than before, Herman still included pop vocal hits: "We'll Be Together Again," "Golden Earrings," "How Soon?" "It's Been So Long," and "Ballerina" with McCall; "Toolie Ooolie Doolie" with McCall and Herman; and "But Beautiful" with Herman. The band also worked up a version of "Ballerina" that spoofed Monroe's runaway hit. Other numbers for McCall included "Just for Laughs," "There'll Be Some Changes Made," "I Got It Bad (And That Ain't Good)," "The Best Things in Life Are Free," "You Go to My Head," "You Turned the Tables on Me," and "Bill." Herman, while better with fun songs, such as "Caldonia," sang straight on the ballads "Let's Fall in Love" and "I Cover the Waterfront." Burns provided new charts for "Lullaby in Rhythm," "What'll I Do?" and "Stardust" to be played as instrumentals.

While most big bands battled money and booking woes, record collecting evolved as a serious hobby, which gave older bands second waves of popularity. Fans started the *Record Changer* magazine as a trading medium.

This mail-order magazine listed classifieds for new or used discs. Subscribers dealt in recordings of such artists as the Original Dixieland Jazz Band, Armstrong's Hot Fives and Hot Sevens from the 1920s, Bix Beiderbecke, Whiteman, and early Duke Ellington, and anyone's music on such rare labels as Gennett, Black Swan, and Odeon. Some Gerun and Isham Jones discs from the 1930s now resold because of Herman's singing or clarinet playing on them, as did the 1936–37 recordings by "the Band That Plays the Blues." That band's first blue-and-gold Deccas had by 1948 been long out of print. Because often only a few thousand fragile copies had been pressed, "blue Deccas" by Herman, Basie, and Bob Crosby had become collector's items. Herman himself refused to look back. He could spin stories of vaudeville but chose never to sell nostalgia.

*i*n the spring of 1948, Herman took bookings in the east again. The Four Brothers Band opened on April 20 for four weeks in the Century Room of the Hotel Commodore in New York City. *Down Beat* said that Herman "returned to Gotham in a blaze of glory."[20] *One Night Stands* broadcast some of these shows, with Herman singing Burns's chart of "My Fair Lady"; McCall singing Shorty Rogers's chart of "When You're Smiling"; Burns's lively number "This Is New"; Herman singing "Nature Boy"; McCall singing "I May Be Wrong," "Trouble Is a Man," and "Dream Peddler"; and Herman reviving the 1930s "Blue Prelude." But modern jazz pieces also made the programs: "Tiny's Blues" by Kahn; Gerry Mulligan's fast, linear "Elevation"; and Burns's "The Happy Song."

Solos in most of the Century Room broadcasts continued to be assigned to Swope, Herman, Shorty Rogers, Chaloff, Royal, Sims, and Getz. The band moved on to the Capitol Theater on May 20. Herman had often played the bigger Paramount, but in leaving General Artists for his own booking agency, he had to settle for the Capitol. During this job—playing a grueling four shows daily, five on Saturdays—the band welcomed back Burns on piano and Bill Harris as a fourth trombonist. It left June 17, having shared billings with a comedian, a dancer, a bird caller, a female vocalist in cowboy garb, and movies like *The Bride Goes Wild* with Van Johnson and June Allyson.

On June 28 the band opened at the Click in Philadelphia for one week. A *One Night Stand* broadcast from there on July 2 introduced Shorty Rogers's frantic "Berled in Earl" for Swope. It opened with two trumpets, two trombones, and tenor and baritone saxophones. Treichel regarded it as being "close to Shorty's best writing for the Second Herd . . . spiced with powerful trumpet riffs . . . one that should have been recorded."[21]

Herman's deal with his own Continental lasted about a year before he returned to GAC. Then Goldfarb, Mirenburg, and Vallon sued him for breach of their management contract. The suit claimed $18,637 in back fees and damages and briefly froze the band's music library. (A court ruled against Herman in 1949.) Needing personal management again in such choppy waters, Herman retained Hollywood agent Carlos Gastel. Gastel, who once ran a ballroom in Hermosa Beach, California, now managed singers Peggy Lee, Nellie Lutcher, Cole, and Tormé and Kenton's band.

Herman played Eastwood Gardens in Detroit, then opened on July 28 for ten days in Convention Hall in Asbury Park, New Jersey. By then Jackson had killed his Fifth Dimensional Jazz Group—a bankrupt sextet that had played Sweden and the United States—and returned to Herman. Treichel said that Jackson's pep alone was "worth a couple of extra trumpet players," and *Billboard* said the return signaled "a heightened accent on entertainment."[22] It also heightened the band's bop sound. The Four Brothers Band had stalled in a neutral zone of current pops ("Nature Boy"), swing ("Lullaby in Rhythm"), nostalgia ("Northwest Passage"), and bop ("Elevation"). In a review in *Metronome*, Ulanov had characterized the band before Jackson's return as "a cross between Fletcher Henderson and bop."[23]

Jazz ruled, however, when the band opened on August 8 at the Steel Pier in Atlantic City. An AFRS show opened with "Berled in Earl" and closed with a "Northwest Passage" stretched to accommodate eight soloists and presented a Woodchoppers "Fan It" by Royal, Getz, Chaloff, Burns, Raney, Jackson, Lamond, and Herman. In September, Jackson pulled vibes player Terry Gibbs, a twenty-three-year-old Brooklyn native, into Herman's band. Gibbs had played in Jackson's sextet, and then with Rich's big band. In trading guitar for vibes, Herman restored the musical sparkle and visual flash that Hyams and Norvo had given his bands. (Jazz vibists were few, and consequently high-priced. Herman hired if and when he could.)

The refocused Four Brothers Band played three weeks at the Palace Theater in Youngstown, Ohio, and a week at the Orpheum Theater in Omaha, Nebraska, but lost the road-weary Burns. Lou Levy, who had toured with both Bill Harris's and Jackson's groups, took over at the piano. After a week in the Riverside Theater in Milwaukee, the band headed back east to play Buffalo, then opened for a month in the Royal Roost in New York City on October 24. In the second week Herman signed the twenty-one-year-old trumpeter Bob Chudnick from Philadelphia, known as Red Rodney because of his red hair. The Roost was a fried chicken place in the 4700 block of Broadway and a late-night mecca for jazz aficionados. In September 1948, Parker and Davis combos had performed there, then Gillespie. Dameron led a house band with bop stars Navarro, Allen Eager, and Clarke. Herman's walloping, solo-heavy big band wowed customers with something different. Roost headliners broadcast radio shows, some on the CBS network, others locally on WMCA, emceed by disc jockey "Symphony Sid" Torin. In the style of radio hypemeisters, Torin called the Roost "the Metropolitan Bopera House" and "the House That Bop Built" on his *Symphony Sid Shows*. Each show opened with the featured band hacking out the notes of "Jumpin' with Symphony Sid" plus its own theme song.

The Herman band had now added Shorty Rogers's chart of "I Can't Get Started," starring Gibbs. Sims wrote "Yucca," and Rogers turned in "Keeper of the Flame." (Based on "I Found a New Baby," "Keeper" contained thirteen solos in one broadcast!) Bill Harris reprised with "Bijou," and the band with "I've Got News for You" and "Four Brothers." In a broadcast on November 6, McCall sang "Romance in the Dark," and Bill Harris soloed on Burns's new version of "Flamingo." Shorty Rogers introduced "That's Right" for Herman, revised from "Boomsie," a bop piece that Jackson's combo had played. Rogers also wrote a new Woodchoppers number, "We the People Bop," for the band's television bit on *We the People*. Royal, Getz, Chaloff, Levy, Jackson, Lamond, and Herman made up the Woodchoppers and sang the lyrics "eel-ya-ah" for laughs. Johnny Mandel, a twenty-two-year-old music school grad from New York City, chipped in with a fast "John Had the Number" for Gibbs in a sextet from the band dubbed the Pirates (as in the comic strip *Terry and the Pirates*). Modeled after Jackson's Fifth Dimensional Jazz Group, the Pirates featured Getz, Rogers, Lamond, Gibbs, Levy, and Jackson. On one radio show, McCall sang Burns's smoldering chart of "My Last Affair," on which Herman played alto. Later shows contained bop (Gil Fuller's "O'Henry"), ballads (Rogers's "Out of Nowhere," with Gibbs soloing), and a talking-singing yarn ("I Got a Way with Women," with the vocal by Herman).

Don Lamond at drums and Herman pose with George Way, a drum manufacturer's representative, about 1948. (Courtesy Duncan P. Schiedt)

After the Roost, the band opened on December 7, 1948, for four weeks in the Empire Room in Los Angeles and a Shrine Auditorium concert. The Empire Room held six hundred fans, and about five hundred were turned away on opening night. After that, business faded. There the band broadcast several shows a week for a new AFRS series called *Just Jazz*. These aired still more fresh material: "I Only Have Eyes for You," a Burns chart for Bill Harris; "Early Autumn," Burns's "Summer Sequence Part IV" revised for Getz; George Wallington's "Lemon Drop," arranged by Shorty Rogers with a string of solos and scat singing by Gibbs, Jackson, and Rogers; "Someone to Watch over Me," a Burns chart on which Herman sang and Gibbs soloed; and Kahn's version of Wallington's "Godchild."

Then around Christmas, Herman left Columbia Records. His contract was up, his 1947 Columbia recordings had sold poorly, and the company drifted mainstream, pushing the James and Les Brown bands. Gastel felt that he could help Herman most at Capitol Records, where his clients Peggy Lee, Cole, Lutcher, and Kenton all were ready to record again. Capitol also had signed Gillespie, Barnet, and Goodman. The Four Brothers Band on Capitol excited all concerned. All through 1948, although he lost money in the weakened band market, Herman stayed intent upon making something different happen. His band's late-1948 music was high-powered, its book well mixed with jazz treasures. Its roster was strong and its spirit high, and it could create many moods. Getz told *Down Beat* that it was "the best bunch of readers I ever saw. The arrangers could put anything in front of them and they would play it."[24] Lamond considered it Herman's best band. Gibbs called it "the best in the world at that time, with guys like Zoot, Stan, Serge and Don Lamond. They wailed! . . . It was scary!"[25] Herman labeled the band "spectacular," even though in many respects "the public wasn't ready for it; unlike the previous Herd, it wasn't playing the popular music of the day."[26] The band had found good enough receptions in its travels, but not enough jobs. There was hope, then, that the Capitol deal could help.

The band eagerly recorded "That's Right," "Lemon Drop," "I Got It Bad," "Keeper of the Flame," "I Ain't Gonna Wait Too Long," and "Early Autumn" on December 29 and 30. "That's Right" had to be cut in half and solos stunted to run three minutes. Jackson, Shorty Rogers, and Gibbs, with high falsetto and Popeye growls, scat-sang "Lemon Drop." On "I Got It Bad," lush reeds and Herman's alto sax backed McCall. "Keeper of the Flame" flashed solos by Chaloff, Levy, Herman on clarinet, Sims, Gibbs, Bill Harris, Getz, and Royal. Herman sang Rogers's bluesy chart for "I Ain't Gonna Wait Too Long," backed by full-ensemble blasts, Royal's trumpet darts, Jackson's walking-speed bass, and Lamond's drum fills. Harris and the full band exchanged roars toward the end.

"Early Autumn," which Burns had distilled into a pastoral for Herman on alto sax, Gibbs, and Getz, is the most memorable recording from these sessions. "We did several takes of 'Early Autumn,'" Gibbs recalled. "After Stan Getz and I found out which one Woody selected for issue, we went to him and complained. We said we had played better solos on another take. 'That might be,' Herman said, 'but these are beautiful solos, too, and the band plays best on this take.' That shows you how he thought, and how right he was. Stan and I both won the *Down Beat* poll because of that record."[27] "Seldom in the history of music has one record established the reputation of a player as this did for Stan Getz," Herman said. And the piece endured, in his opinion, "because it was so right in the first place."[28] To others, the piece also showed that the Four Brothers sax scheme could express a wide range of moods.

Chaloff, Rodney, Cohn, and Sims were the best boppers, and Shorty Rogers the writer-trumpeter star, but Getz shone the brightest when the band charged into 1949. The band was, however, a group effort; Cohn said that Herman "let the guys play around with a new chart, run it down themselves, get their own feeling going on it. After that he stepped in and cleaned it up. For that reason the guys got a lot of themselves and a lot of feeling into what they did."[29] One could hear their combined voltage in those first Capitol recordings.

The band closed at the Empire Room on January 3, having made two New Year's broadcasts for CBS radio, then played Salt Lake City's Cocoanut Grove. A snowstorm trapped Herman's band in Salt Lake City after the job. It also left Gillespie in Salt Lake City with his band stranded in Denver. Herman ingeniously played Gillespie's Cocoanut Grove job with Gillespie soloing from the trumpet section.

Herman took such crises in stride. "He could tap-dance like the wind, a skill he used only once in his bandleading career," Nels Nelson wrote in the *Philadelphia Daily News*. "He arrived for a job to find the band bus delayed by a snowstorm, so he entertained the customers with a one-man song-and-dance show until the band stumbled in. 'Who needs Fred Astaire?'" he said.[30] Jackson said Herman's sense of humor and quick wit "knitted everything together. . . . When some disaster would appear he'd go into his Mister Shrug posture. He knew that one of his subjects would handle the problem expertly. . . . He handled critics, jealous bandleaders, personal problems, bad management, money distractions as if they didn't even exist."[31]

Although labeled great by some, Herman's band lost money and talent in 1949. The slide began when Jackson, with a new wife and his own band-leading dreams, quit as Herman left Los Angeles for Chicago.

Herman then went after top bassist Eddie Safranski, who had been with Kenton, only to be outbid by Barnet. From January 10 to 23, Jimmy Stutz, a radio studio man, filled in for Jackson as Herman played at the Blue Note. And in the trumpet section, Ed Badgley replaced Fishelson. *Down Beat* reported that "hordes of musicians and tradespeople" attended the opening anyway, and the band put them "in a daze."[32] The band hit the Paramount Theater in Toledo for four days, then the Music Bowl in Chicago. There Sims left for Rich's band, and Herman summoned Giuffre from Jimmy Dorsey. Sims left happy: "That band's music held up. A lot of great musicians in it. Woody didn't know what to make of us, we were all so young. It was a wild band in a non-musical way, too."[33] Next Swift and his bass trombone moved on. Herman hired Bart Varsalona from the band that Kenton had dissolved, and he signed Pettiford—formerly with Gillespie, Barnet, Duke Ellington, and other bands and New York combos—to play bass.

Herman played the Showboat in Milwaukee on February 6–12 and began a two-week concert tour with Cole in Champaign, Illinois. Gastel's tour, which reached college campuses in Iowa, Indiana, and Michigan; Carnegie Hall; the Syria Mosque in Pittsburgh; Uline Arena in Washington, D.C.; and Town Hall in Philadelphia, made money.

On February 26, in New York City for a TV show hosted by jazz guitarist Eddie Condon, Herman scheduled "Keen and Peachy," "I Ain't Gonna Wait Too Long," "Four Brothers," "I Got It Bad," "Bijou," and "Lemon Drop." Never a bop fan, Condon announced: "We're boppin' ourselves silly tonight!"

Before a date in Symphony Hall, Boston, Glow left the band. "Wild in a non-musical way,"[34] as Sims had put it, Glow accepted treatment for drug addiction. A doctor said that he had the body of a sixty-year-old. Another blow fell on March 4 at the Blue Note when Lamond left for James's band. For about a month, Herman filled with Rossiere "Shadow" Wilson, the twenty-nine-year-old star of many bands, among them Basie's. Red Rodney jumped next. In his view, Herman's band had been "just a tremendous orchestra, section by section, the soloists and spirit-wise. One great guy would leave, and another great guy would take his place and add something."[35] But perhaps his assessment is too optimistic: Herman fans grimaced at the talent drain.

The band played the Click in Philadelphia on March 14–16, the Hippodrome Theater in Baltimore on March 17–23, then headed to Hartford, Connecticut, for three days in the State Theater. For these jobs Herman toured with Tormé, also a Gastel client, and Tormé's bride, actress Candy Toxton. The newlyweds had what Tormé described as "our first major fight" in Herman's station wagon. Herman had insisted they drive it to New York City for their honeymoon. The Tormés agreed, only to face Herman in Hartford after someone had broken into the car and stolen luggage belonging to all three. "Woody took it like the champ he was," Tormé recalled, "laughing it off and assuring me it happened before. Some people have class."[36]

In April, spurred by his "Early Autumn" fame, Getz left to lead a quartet. Then Cohn departed to write for Jackson's new band. Cohn had become odd man out. "I never had anything to play in the band, so it wasn't one of my great memories," he said. "Big bands are fine, but small bands is the only way you can develop as a soloist." Gibbs had detected "a bit of jealousy" within the sax section "because Stan Getz got to the audience more, and Stan was a giant player, even though Al Cohn could play rings around everybody at the right tempo. [But] Woody was a smart man. . . . When a record hits like 'Early Autumn,' you gotta give the solos to the guy who's gonna get the attention."[37] Herman hired twenty-three-year-old Gene Ammons, who had played with Eckstine's defunct band, and the less experienced Buddy Savitt.

The band worked week-long theater jobs in Indianapolis (Circle), Louisville (National), Washington, D.C. (Capitol), and New York City (Apollo). At the Apollo (April 23–27) and for the next six months, Manne, a Kenton alumnus, replaced "Shadow" Wilson. Manne picked up the Herman book so quickly that some sidemen "hugged him, and told him how great he was."[38]

On May 26, the band recorded "The Crickets" and "More Moon" in New York City. "The Crickets" featured Manne's lunging rhythms (sounding at times like seven beats to a measure) while lush reeds, dissonant ensemble chords, and Gibbs on vibraphone accompanied Herman's and McCall's singing. "More Moon," Shorty Rogers's chart of "How High the Moon"—which also provided the basis for Parker's 1947 "Ornithology"—provided solo time for Ammons, Gibbs, Bill Harris, and Herman on clarinet.

While the band toured theaters, problems arose. Because the Loew's Capitol—a downtown "white" theater in Washington, D.C.—had contracted for an all-white band, Royal, Ammons, and Pettiford had to sit out with pay from April 15 through 21. Herman sent them on to New York City to wait to play the Apollo on April 23–27. It was, in Herman's judgment, "weird. Here we were, a white band except for those three, greeted wonderfully in black theaters across the country. But in the seat of democracy, in the capital's largest theater, black players weren't welcome."[39] Also, business lagged. And while Herman seethed over racism and lost sleep over money, the band faded for other reasons, too.

Fans did not appreciate the Four Brothers sax sound or the new book. Those who cheered "Woodchoppers' Ball" or "Apple Honey" were baffled by "Lemon Drop." As an artistic decision, changing to bop was "magnificent," Herman said. But as a business move, it was "the dumbest thing I ever did."[40] The music succeeded only with a small percentage of listeners. For him the band had become an albatross losing $175,000 the first year. To keep financing it he used the "side-door method—take out a sextet to keep my feet on the ground with a little profit."[41] For example, on February 13, with the full band idle, Herman had taken Royal, Getz, Chaloff, Gibbs, Levy, Pettiford, and Lamond to the University of Chicago for a Woodchoppers show.

Even more threatening to the band's health was heroin. Glow's addiction had been the tip-off. Gibbs once guessed that "out of the eighteen guys about eleven [were] really strung out. We started one show with six. [Herman] had every right to fire the rest, but he knew the band was good. I don't think there were any bands around—even Basie's—that were better."[42] "I was so naive that I kept trying to figure out why my band was always falling asleep," Herman said, but "somehow it didn't affect the music. Sure, some of the guys might be late; but then, Duke Ellington put up with late-showing sidemen all his life, and it didn't bother him. It was [my] first real introduction to people who were involved in the heavy drug scene. Up until then it was pretty mild. The heavy thing builds a 'second society.' Every time we would make a replacement we would watch which group the new guy would go walking with. Once it got heavy it almost became cancerous. At times my biggest [job] was to keep everybody awake enough to blow. They'd be nodding halfway through anything. I'd plead with them because I didn't want them to wind up in jail [or] a hospital."[43] Even on the band's bus trips, the "druggies" sat as a section. Chaloff would hang a blanket around them. "He was getting farther and farther out," Herman said. The ugliness reached an onstage shouting match in Washington, D. C. Chaloff kept saying, "Hey, Woody, baby, I'm straight, man. I'm clean." Herman muttered, "Just play your goddamn part and shut up!" An after-show run-in erupted between them in a bar.[44]

After closing at the Regal on June 23, Herman led his troubled band to California, where they worked weekends in the Rendezvous Ballroom in Balboa Beach. The Rendezvous hosted Saturday afternoon radio broadcasts called *Excursions in Modern Music* on Mutual System stations, and Herman's band played five *Excursions* in July. Some weekdays it recorded, either at Capitol or for a Universal-International short called *Jazz Cocktail: The Herman Herd* with the Mellolarks, a vocal group. The band performed "Jamaica Rhumba," "Tap Boogie," "I've Got News for You," a "Lemon Drop" clone called "Lollypop," and "Keen and Peachy." But racism recurred. "Apparently the full band played the sound track," Treichel reported, "but the non-white members [Royal, Ammons, Pettiford] were replaced by white actors on film."[45]

Herman fans who tuned to the *Excursions* shows heard exciting new things. "Terry and the Pirates," by Shorty Rogers, showcased Gibbs. Johnny Mandel produced "Not Really the Blues" and a chart of "What's New?" starring Gibbs, and Rogers penned a "Pennies from Heaven" for Ammons. McCall sang "I Only Have Eyes for You," and Herman was the vocalist on "You've Got a Date with the Blues." He and Cole, plugging a summer tour, broadcast "Yes Sir, That's My Baby" and "I've Got News for You." Bill Harris performed "Everywhere," which was recorded in 1946 but only now released by Columbia.

Since 1948, record companies had been issuing vinyl long-playing (33⅓ rpm) albums based on both new and old material. Columbia released "Summer Sequence," "Lady McGowan's Dream," "Everywhere," and Shorty Rogers's "Back Talk"—all recorded in 1946 and 1947—on a ten-inch LP, *Sequence in Jazz*. For its Coral label, Decca packaged *Woody Herman's Souvenirs*, which included a garage-sale pile of band and Woodchoppers tunes from 1939, 1941, and 1944: "Sheik of Araby," "I'm Comin', Virginia," "Fan It," "South," "Fort Worth Jail," "Too Late," "It Must Be Jelly," and "I Ain't Got Nothin' but the Blues."

On July 14, Herman's band recorded Giuffre's chart of "Detour Ahead," Shorty Rogers's treatment of "Jamaica Rhumba," Mandel's "Not Really the Blues," Hefti's rewrite of "The Great Lie" by Barnet's Andy Gibson, and McCall singing a sultry "More Than You Know." "Detour Ahead," a slow blues, and "Jamaica Rhumba" also starred McCall. Outstanding reeds backed her, and in the latter, both Gibbs and Ammons soloed. (In an article for *Metronome*, Holiday rated "Detour Ahead" as one of her ten favorite records.) Trombones stated the fast, happy theme of "Not Really the Blues," pushed by fine ensemble playing, which set the stage for solos from Ammons, Swope, Herman on clarinet, and Royal. A thoughtful trombone solo by Bill Harris at a slow dance tempo seemed almost magical on "More than You Know."

For a July 20 recording session, Mondragon filled in for Pettiford, who had broken his arm in a softball game. The band recorded "Tenderly," the Shorty Rogers–Gibbs "Lollypop," a novelty, "You Rascal You," and Burns's semisymphonic "Rhapsody in Wood." Herman on alto sax, Bill Harris, and Buddy Savitt soloed in Hefti's delicate waltz-time chart of "Tenderly." "Lollypop" contained scat vocals with solo time for Gibbs and Chaloff and featured a Harris-Swope trombone exchange. Herman sang and Chaloff and Levy soloed in the swinging "(I'll Be Glad When You're Dead) You Rascal You," into which Rogers wrote lip-busting runs for the brass players. Herman also sang two ballads, which were only issued in 1992 for their historical interest: "You've Got a Date with the Blues" and "In the Beginning."

Cole and Herman launched their second tour on July 29 in the Shrine Auditorium, and the AFRS broadcast that show for its *Just Jazz* series. Mert Oliver now took over the bass from Mondragon. Oliver, thirty-two, had worked in Raeburn's and Rich's bands. (Herman had tapped nine other musicians from Raeburn's bands of 1944–47.)

On Saturday afternoon, July 30, the Rendezvous Ballroom housed an *Excursions* show starring both Barnet's and Herman's eighteen-piece bands. Kenton, inactive since late 1948, helped emcee. Herman filled his twenty minutes with "Lollypop," "I Got It Bad," "Four Brothers," "Early Autumn," and "That's Right." Barnet was Herman's match. Music by his writers—Kahn, Matthews, Pete Rugolo, Dennis Farnon, Manny Albam, Gibson, and Paul Villepigue—featured solos by Safranski on bass, Kahn on drums, trumpeter Maynard Ferguson, pianist Claude Williamson, trombonist Dick Kenney, conga drummer Carlos Vidal, vocalist Trudy Richards, and scat singers Ray Wetzel and Buddy Stewart. This talented band played "Be-Bop Spoken Here," "Ill Wind," "Claude Reigns," and a spirited piece known as both "Balboa" and "Bop City." Both bands blasted a "More Moon" finale. "Woody had reorganized along bop lines, and it seemed that that was the way things were going," Barnet recalled. "I held out against bop until '49, but went along with it then because none of the younger musicians knew how to approach big-band playing except in that idiom. When we did that broadcast in the late afternoon [in California] for listeners in the East, no charge was made for admission. People could come in off the beach just as they were, for free. [But] scarcely anyone showed up. I got a message loud and clear. Here we were, Kenton, Herman and Barnet, and we couldn't get a crowd to come in even for free."[46] That night Herman and Cole played Oceanside. Their tour touched San Diego, Los Angeles, San Francisco, Oakland, and Portland, Oregon. For an August 7 show in San Francisco's War Memorial Opera House, they were joined by Christy (who performed with Kenton's band from 1945 to 1947), Tormé, Hampton, and a local octet led by the then unknown pianist Dave Brubeck.

*b*urns and other writers kept turning in new charts for the band to consider, but the effects of drug use among several sidemen created a sometimes heartbreaking scene, as described by Herman: "We tried rehearsing, but had to call it off. The guys would sit around and talk about it, but just didn't have enough energy to play."[47] So in the summer of 1949, the Four Brothers Band started to fall apart. Feather's eulogy is right on target: "something happened to help take bop out of the small nightclubs and record companies into big theaters and ballrooms and on a major [recording company] label. For the first time, a great modern jazz orchestra crashed the jukeboxes and commercial radio—the band of Woody Herman. There had never been a band like this."[48]

But kind words were not enough. Clearly one problem was that the band's Capitol records had barely caught on. In August, lamenting the weak sales with Capitol execs, Herman offered to "make a couple of sides without the band." As he exaggerated it: "I went to the Hangover Bar and Grill, on Sunset Boulevard, and picked up a few guys who weren't too loaded to speak."[49] They recorded one of Herman's vaudeville novelties— "Oh Gee, Say Gee, You Ought to See My Gee Gee from the Fiji Isles"—and "Rose of the Rio Grande." Herman let Capitol use his middle names— Charles and Thomas—to create Chuck Thomas's Dixieland Band. Herman confessed that he "didn't have the courage to come out in the open with it [his identity]. We speeded the tape up so that it put me a tone or two higher. Capitol did a campaign on it in certain areas of the country and it sold a fantastic amount in those places. But then they suddenly decided the ["Gee Gee from the Fiji"] lyric was too risqué, and it got banned on a couple of networks. It hadn't seemed like that when I was eight. It was just a little boy singing a hot tune. Little Woodrow was swinging."[50]

Hit-and-miss bookings took up August. In Portland, Royal said good-bye. The band played Denver's Lakeside Park Ballroom, then moved east for a September 5 opening of a two-week stint at the Blue Note in Chicago. There the crumbling continued. Treichel explains that "times were getting rough. Gibbs balked at a salary cut Herman levied on the band. It reflected the dollar problems for black musicians when Herman could get Milt Jackson [to replace Gibbs] for less money."[51] Milton "Bags"

Jackson, twenty-six, had studied music at Michigan State University, then played for Gillespie, Howard McGhee, Dameron, and Monk.

Soon Herman had to hire twenty-two-year-old Billy Mitchell to replace Ammons. Then Varsalona left, and Herman saved by going with three trombones again. With regrets, Herman faced the bitter truth: "We kept trying to make a go of it, but it appeared that the ballgame was over. Guys who led big dance bands took their umbrellas and ran."[52] Goodman had even started a bop band in January, shelved it for six weeks to take a sextet to England, resumed in August, but disbanded in October, when Barnet also folded and Armstrong shifted down to a sextet. Only Herman, Duke Ellington, and Basie remained in the big-band-jazz field.

Herman closed at the Blue Note on September 18, and the band plodded through one-nighters in Minnesota, Iowa, Nebraska, Missouri, South Dakota, Illinois, Indiana, and Michigan. They were good places in which to hide, and Herman may have wanted to, as is suggested by an anecdote that Treichel tells:

> In May [1949] Woody had commissioned Leonard Bernstein to write a piece the band would premiere in Carnegie Hall in November. A *Down Beat* cover showed them gazing at a sheet of manuscript paper. . . . Bernstein already had written Broadway and popular music and was no stranger to jazz. He was no doubt intrigued by the challenge of writing for a jazz big band. Bernstein completed "Prelude, Fugue and Riffs" in about September, but the band never played it. He apparently attempted to contact Herman about it without success.[53]

Nor did Herman ever perform Burns's 1949 "Red Hills and Green Barns," a suite that resembled "Summer Sequence."

The band opened in late October with Cole in the Paramount in New York City. During that two-week job, Don Lanphere replaced Mitchell on tenor sax, and in a November 4 concert in Carnegie Hall, the band filled its hour with staples before Cole's segment. The Herman-Cole tour did net Herman enough money to keep the band going a little longer. It closed at the Paramount in early November and roved off into the hinterlands again—Iowa, Missouri, and Oklahoma. Herman continued to postpone the breakup by flying to Hollywood to record "Mule Train" and "My Baby Just Cares for Me" with Cole and a trio on November 21. But he finally put the band to rest on December 4 after a show in Oklahoma City. *Down Beat* readers voted it the nation's number-one big band for 1949, but Herman dropped some $200,000 on the Four Brothers Band.

According to Treichel, "the gap between what *was* achieved and what *could have been* done was always there, mocking what *had been* accomplished. Music was written but did not get played, or was played but never recorded. . . . [Still] something should be said about [Herman's] determination which kept the band going longer than any less-stubborn mortal would have. . . . This band was remembered as the 'Four Brothers' Band [but] it might also have been called 'The Band That Paid Its Dues.'"[54]

America's big band era ended. It is easy to explain how and why, but it is debatable when this occurred. Herman fixed the end in 1950, saying that World War II hysteria was over, and emphasis had shifted. People listened to singers rather than bands, and economic reality had reduced the size of bands, which no longer played the pop music of the day. Actually, in Herman's eyes, few of the swing era bands had really played jazz. For each Duke Ellington, he counted a hundred Mickey Mouse bands with blandly smiling leaders. "During the height of the period, we were competing primarily with Duke, Basie, Goodman, Barnet, Chick Webb, Andy Kirk, Jimmie Lunceford and the Dorseys."[55] But little jazz, in Herman's view, came out of other bands, popular as they may have been at times.

As for his own lamented band, he concluded, "my timing wasn't all that good because I blew a lot of money with it. Musically, it was successful. In the long run I felt that what we did was the right thing to do at that point. But I was on shaky ground . . . The public wanted a carbon copy of what they'd heard in 1945–46, and felt I was blowing it. We didn't realize when we started it that the band business was rapidly sliding downhill, and we were doomed before we began. If I were a banker, I wouldn't have invested in a band after 1946. But I was a romantic."[56] Soon after burying the Four Brothers Band, Herman, in an effort to cover some of his losses, organized a Woodchoppers consisting of Bill Harris, Manne, Milt Jackson, Conte Candoli, Barbour, and bassist Keith "Red" Mitchell. They flew to Havana and opened on December 6 for four weeks at the Tropicana as Herman pondered the future of jazz and his role in it.

chapter six

MUSIC *to* DANCE *to*

*f*or big jazz bands, the 1950s were hand-to-mouth years. Leaders quit, came back, quit again. Webb, Lunceford, and the Dorsey brothers were dead. Basie sometimes toured with a sextet. Bop faded. The pop market favored singers, mambo, rhythm-and-blues, then rock-and-roll. Herman bluntly called it a "not important time" for his bands.[1]

After playing in the Tropicana, the Woodchoppers stayed in Cuba to welcome the new year 1950, moving on to the Nacional Hotel. When they returned to the United States, they played Philadelphia, then roamed the Midwest, Texas, and California, which gave Herman a chance to recoup financial losses. Such an extended tour also benefited Herman's family life, since Charlotte Herman accompanied her husband on longer trips. As Herman later remarked, "She's regaining her youth by hitting the road, so to speak. So we have a ball, and we're interested in sports cars and things of that nature. . . . That's one way, if traveling is an important factor, to make it as much fun as you can. My wife and I have both lived this way since we were children, so it's our only way of life."[2]

As the seasons passed, Herman led bands and combos, free-lanced and rested. He played old or safe new charts and left no trail in jazz. (Neither, for that matter, did the grand master, Duke Ellington. His less than memorable records in that period include "You of All People," "Joog, Joog," and "Good Woman Blues." And when he recorded the trifling, highly commercial "Cowboy Rhumba" for Columbia in early 1950, Herman was his guest singer.) Trumpeter Ray Anthony and arranger Ralph Flanagan led pop bands through the early 1950s but stayed away from jazz. Pioneering for big bands seemed to fall to Gillespie and Kenton, who returned with gusto, by default. For six months in 1950, Kenton toured and recorded with his new enormous forty-piece (with strings) Innovations in Modern Music Orchestra. But in late summer, he scaled down to nineteen, with Jay Johnson and Christy as vocalists. Ferguson (from Barnet), Shorty Rogers, and Manne (from Herman) helped Kenton record fine charts by Rogers and Roland: "Round Robin," "Jolly Rogers," "Blues in Riff," "Viva Prado," "In Veradero," "Take the 'A' Train," "Love for Sale," "Dynaflow," "Beehive," and "Jump for Joe."

Herman at the microphone, about 1950. (Courtesy Duncan P. Schiedt)

Wiser from his experiences with drug problems in the Four Brothers Band, in early 1950, Herman decided to form a drug-free big band, assisted by Red Mitchell, a twenty-two-year-old alumnus of Chubby Jackson's 1949 bop band from New York City. Herman hired Burns to rewrite the book, pushing dance tempos, for a low-budget team of three trumpeters, three trombonists, four sax players (three tenors, one baritone), pianist, bassist, and drummer. Only at special times or for records did Herman add horns, guitar, vibraphone, or a female singer.

This smooth new band played the Capitol Theater for a month. From a jazz spot called Bop City, it later broadcast the likes of "More Moon," "Tenderly," "Tiny's Blues," "Lemon Drop," "Golden Wedding," and "Apple Honey." Past stars Conte Candoli, Bill Harris, Cohn, and Milt Jackson sat in at times, as Herman broke in a new rhythm section of Red Mitchell, pianist Dave McKenna, and drummer Sonny Igoe.

Herman's experiment in banning drugs was successful on one level; as he told *Down Beat,* "you can't imagine how good it feels to look at this group and find them all awake, to play a set and not have someone conk out in the middle of a chorus."[3] But the band could neither get steady bookings nor give Capitol much to sell. Free-lancing in Hollywood in March, Herman rounded up studio hands for another Chuck Thomas's Dixieland Band session. The resulting "Calico Sal" and "Jelly Bean" sold poorly.

The big band recorded at Capitol in Hollywood on May 3, with Hefti and Conte Candoli lending their trumpets, Bill Harris and Cohn also in, and Milt Jackson added on vibes. Their labors produced three numbers intended to sell. "Pennies from Heaven," taken at an easy tempo, featured Herman singing with Alyce King's Vokettes. The singers slowed the tempo for "I Want a Little Girl." Burns's livelier "Spain" included solos from Harris, Herman on alto, and Jackson. A light, friendly dance beat, cleanly played section parts, tasteful solos, and new charts of oldies typified "Spain."

Minus vibes and one trumpet, the band recorded Carmichael's "The Nearness of You," with a vocal by Herman, in Nashville on June 25, 1950, along with Berman's "They Went That-a-Way" (retitled "Sonny Speaks" after his death) and Cohn's melodic "Music to Dance To." In Chicago on August 9, a new trombonist in the band, Vernon Friley, soloed on a recording of "Starlight Souvenirs," an "Early Autumn" sound-alike. Friley, twenty-nine, had recorded with Tommy Dorsey and Les Brown. Back to three trumpets, and with Bill Harris gone, the band also backed the singing Herman on a blues novelty, "When It Rains It Pours," and the ballad "Johannesburg."

The "police action" in Korea revived demand for bands overseas and on stateside bases. Herman's played shows for the AFRS, the State Department, the Marine Corps, the National Guard, and network remotes from various venues. Pat Easton worked with the band for a few weeks, singing "Sometimes I'm Happy" and "You're All I Need." Fresh charts based on the old "Perdido" and a new "Celestial Blues" from Rogers made the book. These charts, however sedated they were, did poke some fun: Herman's 1949 clarinet coda in "Rhapsody in Wood" and Cohn's ending for "Sonny Speaks" quoted a radio commercial jingle about Super Suds.

Herman and Capitol, frowning at each other over sales, let their two-year deal expire. So Herman next signed to make twenty-four sides for MGM Records in 1951 and twenty-four in 1952. Record deals were not what they had been, and this one produced good music but little profit.

On January 4, 1951, MGM stood Herman before a good studio band with its star, Eckstine, who was now reaping big dollars with his romantic baritone voice. "The Great Mister B," as he was billed, sang "Life Is Just a Bowl of Cherries," "I Left My Hat in Haiti," the ballad "As Long As I Live," and Rugolo's "Here Come the Blues." Among the guest stars, or "ringers," in the twenty-man "Herman band" sat trumpeters Shorty Rogers, Pete Candoli, and Gozzo, trombonist Si Zentner, sax players Schwartz, Giuffre, Babe Russin, and Chuck Gentry, a French hornist, a tuba player, a bongo man, and front-rank drummer Louis Bellson. Herman and Eckstine sang a duet on Rogers's chart of "Cherries," and Herman played the clarinet on "Here Come the Blues."

Herman then flew back to New York City to lead his regulars in recording four pop tunes for MGM, "Lonesome Gal," "Searching," "Jet," and "Ninety-Nine Guys." The band's numbers were augmented by trombonist Urbie Green, baritone-sax player Sam Staff, and singer Dolly Houston. The twenty-four-year-old Green had left Mobile, Alabama, to work in bands led by Krupa, Carle, and Jan Savitt. Often called to play Bill Harris's solos with Herman's bands, Green in time earned wide acclaim. Houston, a steady performer with a clear, sweet voice, stayed nearly two years. Her MGM "Lonesome Gal" reached millions as the theme for a late-night disc jockey show.

Voice of America shows in early 1951 aired a few new things: "Composition X," which was credited to Burns, a swinging "St. Louis Blues," and Shorty Rogers's new "Business Men's Bounce." On March 14–15, after many sideman changes, Herman's band recorded two vocal numbers, "I Can See You," with Houston, and "It Isn't Easy," with Herman. "By George," Burns's treatment of British pianist George Shearing's "Bop, Look and Listen," had been added to the book previously and was now recorded for the first time. Shearing's gentle, bop-seasoned quintet was selling records for MGM. The fourth number from this session, Kahn's "Leo the Lion," was aptly named for the lion-head logo that MGM stamped on its record labels.

From May 11 through June 9, 1951, the band shared the Hollywood Palladium with the Charlie Teagarden Trio. Herman's program choices for fifteen radio shows for the Marine Corps, CBS, and the AFRS included oldies ("Apple Honey"), new ballads ("I Won't Cry Anymore" and "I Apologize"), and free-lancer Murray Gurlanek's swinging "The Glory of Love" chart. Trumpeter Don Fagerquist and tenor saxophonist Bill Perkins played with the band at the Palladium. A twenty-five-year-old from Massachusetts, Fagerquist played in bands led by Krupa, Shaw, and Les Brown. A year older, the San Franciscan Perkins was just then launching a career. Fagerquist played soft, pure-toned, filigreed solos, while Perkins excelled on ballads and sounded like Getz.

Herman's goal remained to regain lost fans and money—to endure. He dropped both the bop flavor of the Four Brothers Band and the daring of the First Herd. This band, although resembling the Four Brothers Band because of the book and the sax voicing, stayed mainstream, and even catered to broader, less discriminating tastes. The result was a lot of hollow hype: Palladium emcee Bill Baldwin often called it Herman's "greatest band ever" on the air. Herman's frustration with the situation was clear: "We were trying to hit with anything we could. We had [a few] more buyers because our music wasn't as flagrantly 'outside' the mainstream as the 'Four Brothers' Band. We were in there punching, but we weren't doing much better than before."[4]

A Hollywood recording date on June 4 gave MGM marketers "The Glory of Love," Shorty Rogers's "Pass the Basket," Roland's "Hollywood Blues," and "Red" Wooten's "Cuban Holiday." A June 18–19 session again stressed sales. The band remade "Golden Wedding" for Igoe's drums and "Blue Flame" for Urbie Green's trombone, plus "Business Man's Bounce" and Segure's chart of "Prelude to a Kiss." Then a Woodchoppers octet consisting of Herman, trumpeter Doug Mettome, Green, Perkins, Staff, McKenna, Wooten, and Igoe performed the novelties "Brother Fats" and "Three-Handed Woman"; a blues, "My Baby's Gone"; and Staff's "Dandy Lion," another salute to MGM.

On into the late fall of 1951 the band played where it could—Catalina Island, California; Hollywood; Atlantic City; and Averill Park, New York. It produced another film short, *Woody Herman Varieties,* presenting "Ninety-Nine Guys" and "Apple Honey." One August night in St. Louis, Parker, who had come to Kansas City to visit his mother and sat in with Herman's band, guested on "More Moon," "Leo the Lion," "Lemon Drop," and "Laura" and played every solo in "Four Brothers." Urbie Green recorded Parker with a cheap tape recorder, and a bootlegged *Bird with the Herd* tape reached the market in the 1980s. However, Parker's genre was the quintet; with Herman, he sounded unrehearsed, bored, and at times lost.

The band reached New Orleans and played for a month in the Roosevelt Hotel in October 1951. There Herman guested with Leon Kelner's band, singing "I Cried for You" and "Livin' on Love" for MGM. At the hotel job, Herman introduced pianist Nat Pierce to the public; the army had drafted McKenna and sent him to Korea as a cook. Pierce, twenty-six, stayed four years as pianist, arranger, and Herman's alter ego. He had studied briefly at the New England Conservatory of Music but learned arranging mostly on his own and impressed colleagues as a solid jazz musician.

Even in these "not important" years, Herman rated Urbie Green, Perkins, Fagerquist, and Igoe as "winners." And he said Pierce's "playing and arranging became an enormous asset. Just having his spirit and presence around was a treasure."[5] Steve Voce also has high praise for individual players, although his overall assessment comes off as rather subdued:

> The band of 1951 was workman-like rather than star-studded, and epitomized Woody's lifelong desire to bring on and nurture young musicians. McKenna, Green, and Perkins, all to become stars later, [could] be heard at an early point in their careers. . . . Notable too [were] two potent trumpeters, the lyrical Don Fagerquist and the more muscular Doug Mettome [and] another great drummer, Sonny Igoe.[6]

Herman made a number of recordings with other artists, part of his MGM deal. He played alto sax solos on "Harlem Nocturne" and "Nostalgia" with David Rose's studio band, and sang with MGM singer Fran Warren on "One for the Wonder" and "Former Members of the 106th Division."

In the spring his band played the Statler Hotel in New York City and broadcast a Carnegie Hall concert, adding new versions of "Stompin' at the Savoy," "Blue Lou," "Perdido," "Singin' in the Rain," and "Moten Swing" to the book, along with free-lancer Bill Holman's "Prez Conference," named for Lester Young, who bore the odd nickname Prez. After scoring at the Statler, the band earned good reviews, such as *Down Beat's*, which raved about Herman's "Third Herd—his greatest band ever." (Some counted the Four Brothers Band as the Second Herd.)

Business improved, and the band played *Toast of the Town* and *We the People* TV shows. But the pop market continued to block real financial success. Herman grumbled that Columbia executive Mitch Miller, with his run of sing-along albums, "may have set the music business back forty years."[7] And although Herman was willing to change the band's sound somewhat, he would not compromise his basic principles. As Perkins put it, "Woody wanted the band to sound good and swing. He always kept that approach intact."[8]

Burns, who continued to turn in quiet charts that kept the "Four Brothers" sax sound and stressed dynamics, unison trombones, and "cooler" solos, was writing a batch of new dance charts. And with an old friend, Herman was hatching a record-making scheme, sensing that he led the makings of a popular band—if enough people could only hear it. As Pierce saw it, "Woody wasn't happy with MGM. What do you do if a record company won't record what you want to play? You form your own record company."[9]

Herman first offered Columbia dubs of Burns's new "Terrissita," an "Early Autumn" with singing, "Moten Swing," and "Stompin' at the Savoy" at his own expense. Mitch Miller said no thanks. "This was the sort of thing we were up against," Herman moaned. "The music wasn't *exciting* enough for Mitch Miller. Can you believe that? We did things that were completely musical, [but] good music was definitely out. In other words, it was 'Mitch Miller Time' instead, which again proves the disparity of taste in music. We were up against a ridiculous, insensitive opposition in those days. We survived because of good friends like Howie Richmond."[10]

Richmond, once a press agent for Herman, believed that the Third Herd could help his music-publishing firm. So he and Herman formed

Mars Records, renting studios and farming out sales and promo work. Some of the band's fifty-some Mars recordings, made during 1952–54, approached greatness, and a few companies bought rights and reissued the better ones. (Verve Records named such an album *Men from Mars*. As late as 1982, Discovery Records released a three-LP set it called *The Third Herd*, with notes compiled by San Francisco radio jazz jockey Herb Wong, a strong backer of Herman's music.) The Third Herd cut its first Mars records on May 30, 1952, in New York City, with Fagerquist, Urbie Green, Perkins, Igoe, Pierce, trombonist Carl Fontana, tenor-sax player Arno Marsh, and Chubby Jackson the mainstays. The twenty-four-year-old Fontana, from Monroe, Louisiana, proved another winner among the sidemen, and Marsh, also twenty-four, from Grand Rapids, played a strong, honking tenor. Herman sang Neil Drummond's "Blues in Advance" and "Jump in the Line," a novelty. "Terrissita" echoed the rhythmic mood of "Bijou," with Staff soloing on flute—rare in jazz at the time. "Stompin' at the Savoy," fast and brassy, featured Jackson, Marsh, Herman on clarinet, Igoe, Marsh, and Pierce. Perkins soloed whenever the band played tender ballads.

On July 7, the band recorded "Celestial Blues," "Baby Clementine," "Perdido," "Singin' in the Rain," "Moten Swing" (renamed "Moten Stomp"), and "Early Autumn." Mercer's lyrics for "Early Autumn" inspired Herman to rate him as "one of America's greatest poets."[11] "Celestial Blues" carried a double meaning: the name Mars Records itself implied an outer-space theme, and on the record Pierce played the celesta. The gifted Pierce could play jazz on piano, celesta, and organ, dead serious or for laughs. "Baby Clementine" spoofed the ageless song with "in" lyrics for Houston. Urbie Green and Fagerquist solos polished this gem, long lost because of weak marketing. Pierce's straight-ahead "Perdido" chart paraded the strong solo voices of Fontana and Marsh. "Moten Stomp" employed the saxes and unison trombones, with solos by Fontana, Marsh, and Fagerquist. "Singin' in the Rain," Burns's slurring-saxes workover of the motion picture hit song, contained a war-whoop from Chubby Jackson, and Herman fit a quotation from "Stormy Weather" into his alto-sax coda.

From July to mid-October 1952, the Third Herd played the Hollywood Palladium, broadcast for the AFRS, and performed "Our Love Is Here to Stay" and "Almost Like Being in Love" on an NBC telecast. A twenty-nine-year-old Detroiter, Art Mardigan, succeeded Igoe as drummer and stayed until early 1954. Mardigan had been a sideman in combos and in big bands led by Auld and Elliot Lawrence.

Herman finished with MGM on September 30 and October 6 by recording eight tunes for a dance album and approving release of fifteen numbers from the First Herd's Carnegie Hall concert in 1946 for a second album. The dance album, rather a jewel of that type, was based on fresh charts of "Our Love Is Here to Stay," "East of the Sun," "I Would Do Anything for You," "In a Little Spanish Town," "Nice Work If You Can Get It," "I Can't Believe That You're in Love with Me," "This Is New," and "Almost Like Being in Love."

After touring the Pacific Northwest (sometimes with singer Dinah Washington), the Third Herd again hit New York City, where it recorded "Mother Goose Jumps," "I'm Making Up for Lost Time," and "Buck Dance" on December 29. Trumpeters Stu Williamson (for Fagerquist, who left for Les Brown's band) and Mettome, trombonists Fontana and Urbie Green, and saxophonists Marsh and Perkins soloed. Burns's "Mother Goose Jumps," was a round of solos with Herman singing about a Yankee Doodle who went to town playing clarinet "like old man Herman"! It found its inspiration in Gillespie's light-hearted jazz based on "School Days." Wong, with KJAZ-FM in San Francisco, aired the record for twenty years "because it knocks me out!"[12] Pierce's simple "Buck Dance" included solos by Perkins, Pierce, Fontana, Williamson, Green, and Herman on clarinet.

On January 13, 1953, the band recorded again in New York City. Jimmy Logsdon's "No True Love" set the theme for Pierce's bluesy chart, in which Herman sang and Perkins and Fontana soloed. With percussionists Candido Camero and Jose Manguel, the band recorded the novelty "Go down the Wishin' Road," on which Herman sang and Staff played a long flute solo. Pierce's new chart of "Blue Lou" called for cool, quiet power. The first take featured Pierce on celesta, Fontana on muted trombone, Marsh on tenor, and Herman's clarinet. On the second take, played faster, Pierce switched to piano. In a slower, third try, he started on celesta and finished on piano. Chubby Jackson's "Wooftie," which was named for his publishing firm, motored along on bass power, with four solos. The next day, eleven Woodchoppers, including Camero and Manguel, recorded "Never Mind the Noise in the Market," "Run Joe," "Fancy Woman," and "Eight Babies to Mind" to finish the album *Woody Herman Goes Native.*

During March and April, the Third Herd played the Blue Note in Chicago, and radio spots plugged the Mars records. Herman shared billing with singers Mindy Carson and Georgia Gibbs on a show for the *Let's Go to Town* radio series for the National Guard. New charts of "Beale Street Blues," "Sweet Sue," "Muskrat Ramble," and "Boo Hoo" entered the book. In New York City again on May 14, the band backed singer Clark Curtis on "Moody," "I'm Through with Love," and "It Just Isn't Home without You" and recorded "Men from Mars" and "Beau Jazz." Herman put together "Men from Mars," a long-running (five minutes, fifteen seconds) jam session on which Pierce played an electric organ. At first, Mars issued a three-minute trim of it. The full piece turned up in the Discovery album in 1982. Burns's "Beau Jazz" (a play on *Beau Geste*) featured saxes, unison trombones, and solos. Starting with these recordings, twenty-five-year-old bassist Thomas Raymond "Red" Kelly, from Shelby, Montana, replaced Chubby Jackson.

On September 11, in New York City, the band recorded "Four Others," "I Love Paris," "The Moon Is Blue," and "Sorry 'bout the Whole Darned Thing." Veteran Royal sat in the trumpet line. Friley, Frank Rehak, and Winding joined holdover Urbie Green on trombones—a thrown-together quartet that quickly jelled. Giuffre, who was revered for "Four Brothers," had written a sequel for trombones. He called it "A Quart of Bones," although Herman insisted on "Four Others." Rehak, Green, Friley, and Winding nailed it with their precision, harmony, and split-second solos. Herman rated it one of the "cleanest" recordings any of his bands ever made. It was all the grander because the "four others" had played so little as a unit: Winding, a thirty-one-year-old Dane, free-lanced only a few months for Herman, and Rehak, twenty-seven, from Brooklyn, had only worked in lesser bands. Burns's "I Love Paris" chart contained solos by Herman on alto sax and newcomer Jerry Coker on tenor. "The Moon Is Blue" starred Herman on alto and Stu Williamson. In "Sorry 'bout the Whole Darned Thing," Herman, alternating between singing and speaking, told the story of an itinerant musician.

"Marakeesh" and "Love's a Dog," recorded during a Mars session in New York City on October 5, confirmed Herman's opinion about this "not-important" time for his band. Later that month, a wealthy Chicagoan booked the band, clarinet and soprano sax veteran Sidney Bechet, and Eckstine for a few jobs in Illinois schools and colleges.

When Mardigan left in the summer of 1953, Herman hired a fill-in for five months. The constant turnover, a big-band way of life, frustrated Herman, who said it was "like being married and divorced a thousand times."[13] But there was a plus: a road band required the energy found in young people. Some stayed weeks, some a year. Without tryouts, they mostly joined when called. Herman's fame attracted talent scouts from coast to coast. A phone call ("Hey, Woody, you oughta get . . .") from sidemen or alumni often filled his empty chairs.

Sweet-toned Dick Collins, power player Reuben McFall, and Cy Touff now joined the trumpet section, with new trombonists Keith Moon and Kenney (from Barnet's band), baritone sax player Jack Nimitz, and drummer Chuck Flores. McFall, who was twenty-three when he joined the band, had trained at Westlake. Touff's bass trumpet sounded dry, like a trombone that didn't slide. The twenty-seven-year-old Chicagoan had performed with Ventura and Raeburn, and even the New York City Opera Company. Like Staff, Nimitz, twenty-four, from Washington, D.C., doubled on flute. The Californian Flores, who had worked in Ferguson's band, was only nineteen years old.

Private tapes made on jobs in early 1954 showed Herman still pushing dance music. "That Old Feeling," "Stars Fell on Alabama," "What Is There to Say?" and "She's Funny That Way" joined "Moten Stomp," "Blue Lou," "Early Autumn," and "Prez Conference." The band also tried out a version of McFall's "Mambo for Bass Trumpet," "Sentimental Journey" (a head arrangement by the band, which Pierce wrote down later), Burns's new "Strange," and a version of "Lover, Come Back to Me."

The Mars Records venture was struggling financially, with no prospects for improvement. Herman recalled that "the fifties wasn't a good period. Even Count Basie had temporarily cashed in the big band. . . . The pop market was rapidly changing because of people like Mitch Miller, who was running things at Columbia, feeding the nation sing-along recordings."[14] This atmosphere proved deadly for Mars, and at what proved to be his last Mars session in New York City on March 30, Herman recorded three numbers, including the long, fast mambo by McFall in two parts. Of Caribbean rhumba origin, a mambo featured an accented third beat. It was popularized by Cuban-born Perez Prado, the "King of the Mambo," whom Kenton honored with "Viva Prado." Herman on clarinet, McFall, Nimitz, and Touff soloed. When the parts—called "Mambo the Most" and "Mambo the Utmost"—were joined, they ran five and one-half minutes. To woo rhythm-and-blues fans, Herman rented R&B drummer Panama Francis, bassist Lloyd Trottman, guitarist Mickey Baker, and tenor-sax player Sam "The Man" Taylor to record "Mess Around," on which Herman sang, and "Castle Rock." Pierce banged out backroom piano on "Mess Around," a blues by young Ray Charles. "Castle Rock," with solos by Francis, Pierce, Taylor, and McFall, seemed a sellout to Herman fans, who were unaware of his "trying to hit with anything we could."

Herman continued to make guest appearances. Columbia borrowed him for an all-star session headed by Clayton, whose 1953 jam-session album based on "The Hucklebuck" and "Robbins Nest" lifted him to stardom. On March 31, 1954, Clayton led Herman and nine others through "Blue Moon," "Jumpin' at the Woodside," and "How Hi the Fi."

After the U.S. State Department had helped loosen political, legal, and union red tape, Kenton's band toured Western Europe late in 1953. Herman embarked on his first European tour in April 1954, starting in Oslo. Herman played a show in Berlin, performing a number of old favorites, including "Early Autumn," "Apple Honey," "Bijou," "Four Brothers," "Woodchoppers' Ball," and "Golden Wedding," and a medley of "Amen," "Who Dat?" "Laura," and "Caldonia." Germany's famous freeway inspired Burns to name a new piece "Autobahn Blues." England, however, was still off-limits—the British Musicians' Union blocked Americans from playing there. But the London magazine *Melody Maker* backed two Herman concerts in Dublin. A British reviewer, denouncing the union for "simian thinking," reported that "a veritable airlift of jazz fans arrived in Ireland. The band played its heart out for them."[15]

Herman returned in time for the May 1 *Tribute to Woody Herman* radio show on Philadelphia's WKYW, part of a series of big-band tributes. Siefert supplied four hours' worth of records and background data for the show. Jack Pyle told listeners that Herman was a "modest musician in a usually brash field."

While in New York City, where the band was playing in Basin Street in mid-May, Herman and Columbia Records reached a rapprochement. It wanted an album of First Herd hits from 1945–46, Second Herd numbers from 1947, and a 1950s sampler by the Third Herd. Herman agreed to hand over "Four Others" from Mars and record three new Cohn and Holman charts. He also allowed Columbia to pick up a version of "Early Autumn" starring Perkins on tenor sax that was broadcast in Omaha. A studio session on May 21 yielded three recordings. Holman's happy "Blame Boehm"—named for a manufacturer of reed instruments—starred Herman's clarinet. To salute Mulligan's jazz quartet, Holman converted "Prez Conference" into "Mulligan Tawny." Last came "Cohn's Alley," which Columbia renamed "The Third Herd"; the album was sold as *The Three Herds.*

Time magazine's May 31 issue included "That Happy Feeling," an upbeat piece about Herman at Basin Street: "'The most exciting thing in jazz is when a big band can make it,' he says, trying to explain the obsession that returned him so often to the precarious profession. . . . Three years ago, unhappy fronting small combos with his clarinet and sax, Herman was rounding up his Third Herd, and by last week had groomed it to top form. 'This band swings more than anything since the bop era began,' he says without false modesty. 'There's a whole generation that doesn't even know what a big jazz band is.'"[16]

At forty-one, Herman had become a father figure to sidemen in their twenties. His reference to "old man Herman" in "Mother Goose Jumps" supported this image. During June 15–27, Herman's "kids" and the Erroll Garner Trio shared the Basin Street stage. Around midnight, Herman sang sets with Garner, joking about it being "music for tired lovers." This collaboration resulted in *Music for Tired Lovers,* a Columbia album that Herman recorded with Garner in Detroit on July 8. In between Herman managed to sandwich in a quick job at Chicago's Trianon.

Meanwhile, Burns, Pierce, and Cohn worked to counteract the band's drift toward mambo and R&B. Pierce cooked up an "Indian Summer" for Touff's bass trumpet, while Cohn turned in a "Stardust" with a long reed-section passage and solo time for Herman on alto sax, Touff, and Pierce. Vocalist Leah Matthews joined the band for a year, reviving "Happiness Is a Thing Called Joe," "Get Out of Town," "That Old Feeling," "I'm Glad There Is You," "You Stepped Out of a Dream"; she and Herman sang together on "Kiss the Baby." Business lagged, but the band found jobs in Jantzen Beach in Portland, Oregon, and Hollywood.

Capitol Records took over Columbia's late 1930s position of supremacy in the recording industry and recruited James, Les Brown, Duke Ellington, Gillespie, Kenton, May, Anthony, Goodman, Barnet, and Herman between 1949 and 1956. "Back on top of the musical heap,"[17] to quote *Time,* Herman began recording again, now for Capitol, in Hollywood on September 8–9. "Autobahn Blues" featured solos by Richie Kamuca on tenor, Herman on clarinet, Pierce, Flores, and Collins. The twenty-three-year-old Kamuca hailed from Philadelphia and had studied at the Mastbaum School and played for Kenton. "Sleep" gave solo time to Perkins, Pierce, and Nimitz. "Ill Wind" showcased the Four Brothers reeds, Collins, Herman on alto sax, and Perkins. "Strange" featured Pierce, Herman's alto, and Moon's long solo on trombone. "Pomp Stomp" was derived from familiar fanfares and shifted into a happy, moving piece led by the reeds. A tenth-year remake called "Wild Apple Honey"—stretched out to six minutes and kicked off by Herman's "bow! bow!"—offered a brassy "train wreck" coda.

Next the band gave Capitol "Muskrat Ramble" and "Misty Morning." Pierce's light, fast chart of the Dixieland standard starred the saxes, Touff, Herman on clarinet, and trumpeter Bill Castagnino. The reeds also carried Burns's "Misty Morning," with solos from Herman on alto and Perkins. "Boo Hoo," reworked by Pierce from the Lunceford band book of the 1930s, reached Capitol on September 13.

On September 19, Herman recorded Albam's fast and happy "By Play" with a solo by Touff. May's free-lance chart of "Mexican Hat Dance," released as "Mexican Hat Trick," again worked the saxes. On September 20, the band recorded four more. Pierce's "Hittin' the Bottle" chart, based on another 1930s piece played fast, placed Herman's clarinet in front of the trombones and ahead of solos by Touff, Kamuca, and Collins. Burns's "Sleepy Serenade," another clone of "Early Autumn," featured the saxes. The band mamboed again on May's "La Cucuracha Mambo" and "Woodchoppers' Ball Mambo," which was played slowly with bop nuances (and with quotations from "Jumpin' with Symphony Sid" in the closing riff). In Chicago on October 13, the band recorded Burns's "Composition X" as "Gina," and "I'll Never Be the Same" for Herman's alto, Collins's trumpet, and the unison trombones, as well as "Kiss the Baby" and "Long, Long Night." In all, Herman gave Capitol twenty records in a five-week burst of activity.

Business seemed to be picking up, and in addition to the usual recording dates and live performances, another medium—television—was added. After Herman and his band performed in Washington, D.C., and New York City that fall, they appeared on Steve Allen's *Tonight* show for NBC television. The band played "Moten Stomp," Allen sat in at the piano for "Lady Be Good," and Herman sang a medley. To provide Capitol with money-makers, Herman flew to Hollywood in December to record "My Sin Is You" and "Have It Your Way" with the singing Allen Sisters. He then headed east again, to Chicago to front the band at the Blue Note for New Year's, and then to New York City for a four-week Statler job. A second appearance on the *Tonight* show on January 27, 1955, treated viewers to "Muskrat Ramble," "Men from Mars," "Kiss the Baby," and a songs-for-tired-lovers medley.

On June 6 and 7, Herman directed another burst of recording for Capitol. Pierce's chart of Horace Silver's "Opus De-Funk" featured the saxes and six solos. Burns's "Cool Cat on a Hot Tin Roof" referred to Tennessee Williams's brooding drama *Cat on a Hot Tin Roof*. For "Pimlico," Touff and Herman on clarinet played in counterpoint. Pierce soloed and Burns worked in a racetrack "post-time" bugle theme at the finish line. "Captain Ahab," a long flagwaver (the swing bands' designation for a fast, frantic piece) featured three duels: Touff and Moon on bass trumpet and trombone, Kamuca and Art Pirie on tenors, and Collins and McFall on trumpets. A long "Sentimental Journey" provided solo space for five players, including a few chimes from Pierce's celesta. On "Where or When," Holman strung together unison section passages, Herman's alto, Kamuca's tenor, Moon's trombone, and ensemble parts. A long number by free-lancer George "The Fox" Williams, released as "Skinned" on one side of the record and as "Skinned Again" on the other, featured Flores. Judging from its eclectic mix of boogie, hand-claps, and simplistic clarinet toots, Herman still was "trying to hit with anything." He even played alto on "Love Is a Many-Splendored Thing" and, with harpist Ted Sommer and a small, soprano-heavy choir, on three other current pop tunes.

Later the band performed at Basin Street, with a side trip to Washington, D.C., for a *Wide World of TV* show, then it moved on to New-port, Rhode Island, for the newly established outdoor jazz festival. There it played "Four Brothers," and Herman sang with Garner's trio. But Herman lost Pierce, who left to try his own band. Pierce saw Herman as an exemplary bandleader: "I learned a lot from Woody—how to pace the night, what tunes to play in what spot. Woody kind of let things evolve. He made it comfortable, more like you were working *with* him rather than for him. The ship was tight, but it was loose at the same time."[18]

But by early fall, the ship appeared to be sinking because of low bookings. So Herman sank it and put together another combo. Capitol recorded Herman with a big band in Hollywood on November 30, but it was quite a different band. The trumpeters were Collins and John Coppola from the dead band, augmented by Gozzo, Pete Candoli, and Ray Linn. Touff blew his bass trumpet beside two sit-in trombonists. Kamuca found himself teamed with three studio sax players. In the rhythm section, Norm Pockrandt played piano with studio guitarist Al Hendrickson, bassist Monte Budwig, and drummers Flores and Rich. This hastily assembled group taped Shorty Rogers's "Square Circle," free-lancer Dave Cavanaugh's "Hi-Fi Drums," with Rich on drums, and easy dance charts of "I Hadn't Anyone till You" and "Dream" for a Capitol album that also featured the Les Brown, Kenton, May, Anthony, and James bands.

Herman led the Las Vegas Herd, a group composed of Collins, Coppola, Touff, Kamuca, Pockrandt, Budwig, and Flores for a month in Nevada. On December 1, this band recorded the Capitol album *Jackpot!* which featured "Bags' Other Groove," "Wailing Wall," "Bass Face," "Junior," and "The Boot," plus the Basie standards "9:20 Special," "Broadway," and "Jumpin' at the Woodside." The whimsical cover photo showed a bug-eyed Herman catching coins streaming from a slot machine.

The next venture with Capitol was to be a blues album. For the first recording session, the same octet (called the Swingin' Herd for this album) recorded and Herman sang "Every Day (I Have the Blues)" and "Basin Street Blues." In a *Tonight* show aired before Christmas, this combo performed "Every Day" and "As Time Goes By."

For a New Year's Eve job and telecast in Philadelphia, Herman built a big band around Coppola, Collins, Touff, Kamuca, and Budwig, adding Marsh and the future stars Wayne Andre on trombone, pianist Vince Guaraldi, and vibes player and drummer Victor Feldman. In the holiday show broadcast over WCAU-TV, this band performed "Captain Ahab," "Opus De-Funk," "Four Brothers," "Four Others," "Square Circle," "Northwest Passage," "Darn That Dream," and "Woodchoppers' Ball."

Herman bobbed in and out of sight in early 1956. An eighteen-piece band with a mix of new and old (Coppola, Collins, Andre, Bill Harris, Kamuca, Marsh, Guaraldi, Bauer, Budwig, and Feldman), spurred by new drummer Bill Bradley, recorded on March 13 in New York City. Herman sang "To Love Again" and "For All We Know." An altered band, with drummer Gus Gustafson, convened in Chicago on May 15–16 to finish the blues album, recording charts by Pierce, Burns, Albam, and Hefti: "Call It Stormy Monday," "Smack Dab in the Middle," "Pinetop's Blues," "Trouble in Mind," "Blues Groove," "Dupree Blues," and "I Want a Little Girl."

Herman combos and bands wandered the land for the rest of the year, working when and where they could—the Steel Pier in Atlantic City, the Cat and Fiddle Ballroom in New York City, the Lagoon in Salt Lake City. Since burying the Four Brothers Band in 1949, Herman had played music to dance to with nearly empty pockets. Despite financial woes, low bookings, and turnover in musicians, Francis Davis, writing in the *Atlantic,* could rate Herman's 1950s bands as "admirable for ensemble polish and a fine book."[19] The Third Herd left a hundred or so recordings for Mars, MGM, Columbia, and Capitol, foremost among them "Four Others," "Mother Goose Jumps," "Perdido," "Moten Stomp," "Singin' in the Rain," "In a Little Spanish Town," "Autobahn Blues," "I Remember Duke," "Captain Ahab," and "Stompin' at the Savoy." During these years Herman "found" Pierce, Fontana, Marsh, Urbie Green, Perkins, Kamuca, Red Mitchell, Igoe, Mardigan, Flores, Touff, Collins, Fagerquist, Stu Williamson, Andre, Guaraldi, and Feldman. Musical innovations included using solo flute, celesta, organ, and bass trumpet and expanding into mambo and R&B. Such experiments led to any number of jazz musicians performing stylistic "fusions."

Feather noticed that the band's repertoire "became more eclectic" in the mid-1950s. "Herman was no bandwagon-jumper," he said, "but he kept pace with every development in jazz. When the funky trend emerged he had Nat Pierce write arrangements of such Horace Silver hits as 'The Preacher,' 'Opus De-Funk' and 'Sister Sadie.' He even toyed with rock [but] with less success."[20]

Yet there were detractors, including the ever critical Balliett, who saw the Third Herd as little more than a reincarnation of the Second Herd, stampeding in the same musical directions as before. His assessment is true enough; but it was in some ways a dart that could be thrown at big bands in general during this weak period. And at least Herman tried.

On into 1962, Herman led short-lived bands of various sizes and with a shifting lineup of sidemen for concert tours, festivals, and records. Nomadic trumpeters came and went, with Rolf Ericson and Bill Chase the best of the field. Bill Harris and Jimmy Guinn led a pack of trombonists. Lanphere, Jay Migliori, and Joe Romano made names as tenor-sax soloists. John Bunch, Pete Jolly, Russ Freeman, and Guaraldi played the piano at various times, while Feldman and Eddie Costa doubled on piano and vibes. Budwig, Jimmy Gannon, and Chuck Andrus stayed longest among the bass players. Jake Hanna and Jimmy Campbell excelled as drummers.

Musically neutral, however, these bands left few memories and showed no profit. Record sales lagged, and contracts changed. Herman dealt with Norman Granz's Verve Records, then Everest, Roulette, Atlantic, Crown, Philips, and Sesac Transcriptions. Scarcely any royalty money reached him when reissues of music that he had made with his better bands came back onto the market through such record enterprises as Big Band Landmarks, Ember, Forum, Jazz, Jazzland, LaserLight, Metro, Piccadilly, Pickwick, Surrey, Top Rank, Sun, and Vogue.

Granz had produced concert tours and records since the 1940s. The UCLA grad bought Herman's Mars masters and contracted with Herman for a year of new vocal and band music. The deal produced more than forty new cuts for Verve between January 1957 and January 1958. But they offered little of jazz value. In Los Angeles Herman sang with a sextet in January, a ten-piece studio band in March, a septet in April, and woodwinds, strings, accordion, and rhythm section in May.

But also in early 1957, with new charts from Roland, Pierce, Cohn, and Dameron, Herman formed a sixteen-piece band of his own and toured the South and Midwest. On July 2 and 3, this band—composed of Castagnino, Coppola, William Berry, Andrew Peele, and Danny Stiles on trumpet; Bill Harris (by now, a balding forty), Willie Dennis, and Bob Lamb on trombone; Migliori, Jimmy Cooke, and Bob Newman on tenor sax; Roger Pemberton on baritone sax; pianist Bunch; Gannon on bass;

and Don Michaels on drums—recorded for Granz in New York City. The resulting album, *Woody Herman 1958,* was packaged in an austere, black-and-white cover and included Silver's "The Preacher," Bunch's "Why You?" and Roland's "Blue Satin," "Bar Fly Blues," "Gene's Strut," "Roland's Rollin'," "Ready, Get Set, Jump," "Stairway to the Blues," and "Wailin' in the Woodshed." Although there was some flash to the music, it stayed mainstream. The same can be said of Cohn's "Try to Forget," Dameron's "Small Crevice," and Bill Harris's "Downwind." Herman, Pierce, Harris, Pemberton, Cooke, Migliori, Coppola, and Castagnino soloed. Herman continued to play "Ready, Get Set, Jump," a happy ride for ensemble and solos, for about a year, "The Preacher" for two years, and "Wailin' in the Woodshed" through 1964.

While in the New York area, the 1957 band played in Hershey, Pennsylvania, and Atlantic City, then worked, when it could, its way west to the Hollywood Palladium. On September 25 Herman sang a dozen more album songs for Verve with a Herd-sized band led by Frank DeVol.

On New Year's Eve, in New York City again, Herman fronted a band in which Harris, Cohn, Sims, Pierce, Chubby Jackson, Lamond, and assorted help telecast "Apple Honey," "The Preacher," and "Woodchoppers' Ball." Herman then flew home to Hollywood to sing "Caldonia" and three other numbers with a quintet led by Barney Kessel to complete his deal with Granz. In all, Granz issued two albums of Herman singing—*Songs for Hip Lovers* and *Love Is the Sweetest Thing, Sometimes*—plus *Woody Herman 1958,* a few singles, and three Mars collections: *Early Autumn, Men from Mars,* and *Jazz, the Utmost.* But the Herman-Granz partnership stalled over money, and Herman shopped for a new deal.

During mid-January 1958, he led a well-rehearsed sixteen-piece unit at a Los Angeles nightspot called Peacock Lane. Private tapes reached the market from there some thirty years later. Bill Harris, Marsh, Jolly, and Hanna starred in "Opus De-Funk," "Autobahn Blues," and "Ready, Get Set, Jump," and the band backed Harris's wrenching solo on "Gloomy Sunday." Old favorites in the repertoire—"Four Brothers," "Early Autumn," "Captain Ahab," and "Northwest Passage"—still had a place beside new material—Roland's "Natchel Blues," "Park East," "Saxy," "Like

Some Blues, Man, Like," and "Wailing the Blues." The prolific Roland produced sixty-five charts for Herman in fifteen months.

Ever low on money, Herman took what work he could find, even trading nostalgia for a two-year pact with Everest Records in Los Angeles. As hi-fi swept the recording industry, Kenton, Goodman, James, Glen Gray, and others rerecorded old hits. For the Everest hi-fi album *The Herd Rides Again,* Herman recruited trumpeters Royal, Privin, Glow, Markowitz, Al Stewart, Burt Collins, and Nick Travis; trombonists Rehak, Bob Brookmeyer, and Billy Byers; saxophonists Cohn, Marowitz, Sam Donahue, Paul Quinichette, and Danny Bank, with a rhythm section of Pierce, Chubby Jackson, Bauer, and Lamond. On July 30 and August 1, 1958, they revived "Northwest Passage," "Caldonia," "Wild Root," "The Good Earth," "Bijou," "Black Orchid," and "Blowin' Up a Storm" for Everest and recorded new compositions and arrangements: Benny Harris's "It's Coolin' Time," Mandel's "Sinbad the Sailor," Burns's chart based on "Crazy Rhythm," his Latin-flavored "Fire Island," and Cohn's treatment of "I Cover the Waterfront."

Was the effort worth it? This was the Elvis era, when millions hummed Presley's "Blue Suede Shoes" instead of Roland's "Stairway to the Blues." Pop music had veered far from big, riff-playing bands. Herman's Everest discs lacked fire and eschewed flute, vibes, bass trumpet, and flugelhorn as he stubbornly opted for jazz. The days of "two for them, one for me" had become "twelve for me, and to hell with it!" But Herman had to scrape to find new jazz material that would sell to a public whose attention had largely drifted elsewhere.

Major Quincy "Mule" Holley, Jr., from Detroit, played bass on tours and records for a while in 1958–59. An alumnus of combos led by Gordon, Parker, Fitzgerald, Wardell Gray, and Oscar Peterson, the thirty-four-year-old Holley played in a tiptoe-light manner. He also gave Herman the most onstage pep since Chubby Jackson and performed what he called "a little Slam Stewart act"[21] (bowing the bass while humming) on "The Preacher."

Herman made an Everest album in September 1958 with Ernesto "Tito" Puente, a multiple talent on vibes, timbales, piano, and alto sax.

The thirty-four-year-old New Yorker had won acclaim in Latin American music, both with his own units and those of others. The twelve numbers in this album—which Everest sold as *Herman's Heat and Puente's Beat*—blended styles and involved new stereophonic sound processes. Herman led a hand-picked studio dozen plus a rhythm section with string bass, conga drums, and added percussionists, including Puente on the timbales. This ensemble recorded "Latin Flight," "New Cha-Cha," "Mambo Herd," and "Cha-Cha Chick." Puente's rattling rhythms and the band's searing brass dominated the music, with Herman's alto sax featured on "New Cha-Cha" and "Cha-Cha Chick." Herman's working band finished the album, making Cohn's "Blue Station," A. K. Salim's "Pillar to Post" and "Balu," plus "Midnight Sun," "Woodchoppers' Ball," and "Lullaby of Birdland." Puente and his crew joined for "Tito Meets Woody" and "Carioca."

Next Herman took a band to South America, admitting that the three-month goodwill tour, underwritten by the U.S. State Department, "helped us stay afloat."[22] The band survived several white-knuckle flights through the Andes to play in Brazil, Chile, Peru, Ecuador, Bolivia, Venezuela, Colombia, and Jamaica. When they played in Bolivia's airport—the highest in the world—the players could scarcely breathe, and sponsors kept bottled oxygen onstage. Herman's overseas receptions were mostly good. He received generous press and played any location, even, as Holley put it, "in bull rings and next to swimming pools for the elite."[23] But it was a tough life. Audiences became hard to find in the late 1950s, so Herman agreed to these "hardship tours," which kept at least a few bands playing when most had folded.

After South America, Herman worked up an album with the Spanish-guitar star Charlie Byrd. For Everest, Byrd and the Herman band remade Stravinsky's "Ebony Concerto" and a version of "Summer Sequence" that spotlighted the guitar. Byrd composed four other tunes for the project: "Prelude A La Cha-Cha," "Love Song, Ballad," "Original No. 2," and "Bamba Samba." Arranger Sid Feller polished these charts, all recorded on December 26, 1958, in New York City. Herman took second billing on the album, which Everest called *Charlie Byrd—Bamba-Samba Bossa Nova, Featuring the Woody Herman Big Band.*

Soon Herman again resorted to low-overhead small groups. Holley, trumpeter Howard McGhee, tenor-sax player Seldon Powell, and Gus Johnson—a drummer in his mid-forties who had played with Basie and Fitzgerald—played on a few short jobs. Then on January 26 and February 1, 1959, having connected with Roulette Records, Herman recorded *The Woody Herman Sextet at the Roundtable*. But it was studio music, produced by Herman (clarinet and alto), Nat Adderley (trumpet and cornet), Byrd (guitar), Costa (piano and vibes), Bill "Keter" Betts (bass), and Campbell (drums). They taped "Lullaby of Birdland," "Moten Swing," and "Early Autumn," plus the originals "Black Nightgown" and "Just a Child" by Mandel, Bechet's "Petite Fleur," Albam's "Inside Out," Moe Kauffman's "The Swingin' Shepherd Blues," Adderley's "The Deacon and the Elder" and "The Late, Late Show," and Herman's "Pea Soup" and "Princess 'M.'"

In the spring of 1959, the British Musicians' Union at last allowed "controlled exchanges" with American jazz musicians. So with State Department help, Herman took half a band to England and Saudi Arabia, adding nine British musicians to form an "Anglo-American Herd." As the English tenor-sax player Don Rendell recounts it, rehearsals had some initial difficulties: "We thought things were going quite well, and then suddenly Woody really hammered us." Eddie Harvey, an English trombone player, said that the British had not grasped that Herman wanted them to play with about four times their usual volume. "After the peptalk, the effect was electric, just as though Woody had turned a switch," Harvey said. "We never looked back." Voce reported that "the Anglo-American Herd was a triumph, and for the first time a British audience was blown out of its seats by the authentic Herman sound. Bill Harris was a sensation, soloing on 'Playgirl Stroll' and the slow, rambling Gene Roland composition 'Like Some Blues, Man, Like.'" Harvey recalls that he "had trouble playing because the hair on the back of my neck kept standing on end every time Bill Harris blew. He was fantastic."[24] The band played a twelve-minute version of "Like Some Blues, Man, Like," which Harvey called "a hell of a thing to play because it was so slow, and you had to get it right to make it swing." "What a pity," Herman told Rendell, "that we didn't get to record during the tour."[25] On a tape made in Manchester, Americans Reunald Jones and Adderley (trumpets), Bill Harris, Guaraldi, Byrd, Betts, Campbell, and the British performed a program of numbers from the book of past Herman bands.

After his return to New York City, Herman led a sextet with Adderley, Costa, Byrd, Holley, Sims, and Gus Johnson in June 1959. Later Herman assembled a big band for summer work, playing oldies, recent recordings, and new charts, including "Chelsea Bridge," "How about You?" "For All We Know," Roland's "Oo Skoobeedoobee," and Coppola's 1956 "Blues Groove," renamed "Country Cousins." A few sidemen of note filtered through the band. And Nabil Marshall "Knobby" Totah, a bassist from Ramallah, Jordan; Ken Wray, an English trombonist; and baritonist Ronnie Ross, from Calcutta, India, temporarily gave the band an international air.

Herman and a hand-picked band recorded two vocals and ten instrumentals for Sesac Transcriptions during July 31 and August 1, 1959. Jazzland, Vogue, and Surrey Records later reissued some of these tunes in commercial albums. Surrey pushed them as having been performed by "Woody Herman and the Fourth Herd," but the band was nothing of the kind. Its music did, however, contain bright moments and solos by trumpeters Rodney and Royal, trombonists Jimmy Cleveland and Brookmeyer, and saxophonists Cohn and Lanphere in front of a rhythm section made up of Pierce, Bauer, Lamond, Costa on vibes, and bassist Milt Hinton. From this batch of instrumentals, Joseph Mark's "The Magpie" became a regular performance piece for the band for several years.

Some of the same sidemen helped again on October 3, when Herman led a "Festival Herd" taped by Atlantic Records live at the Monterey Jazz Festival in California. Only once before, at Carnegie Hall in 1946, had live Herman music been recorded for sale. Released in 1960 and reissued in 1982, the *Live at Monterey* album—one of Herman's best—included "Four Brothers," the slow, nine-minute "Like Some Blues, Man, Like," "Oo Skoobeedoobee," "The Magpie," and "Skylark." Tired of introducing "Apple Honey" for fifteen years, Herman named the ten-minute festival version of the popular song "Monterey Apple Tree." Festival Herd stars included trumpeters Chase, Conte Candoli, and Al Porcino; trombonist Urbie Green; and tenor-sax players Sims, Perkins, Kamuca, and Lanphere, with Flory on baritone. Feldman on piano and vibes, Byrd on guitar, Budwig on bass, and drummer Mel Lewis formed the rhythm section. Thirteen in the band had performed before with Herman, who said: "I wish I could take this band on the road!"[26]

Not that there would be many jobs. According to Pierce, Turchen repeatedly had to save them: "A lot of times we bombed out money-wise. Sometimes there wasn't enough to meet the payroll. . . . There was a lot of scuffling going on. It wasn't easy." But Herman looked back on the rough times with affection: "the best years of our lives were when we were scuffling. We came to realize what a ball that was, when we were playing what we wanted. Maybe we didn't have a porterhouse, but we had everything else."[27]

Herman did not, however, appear to have the approbation of fans or critics. Jazz poll results for 1959–60 from the United States and foreign press, which Feather summarized in the second edition of his *Encyclopedia of Jazz*, bypassed Herman as leader, singer, or player, and all of his sidemen. The Basie, Kenton, Ferguson, and Duke Ellington big bands and certain of their solo stars swept those polls. Feather's terse summary of Herman was, at best, ambivalent: "He has made his greatest contribution to jazz history by keeping a big band together, often against severe economic odds, and maintaining an uncompromising jazz style, progressing with all the new trends of the 1940s and providing an incubator for innumerable soloists and writers of major importance."[28]

Business worsened so much that Herman began the 1960s fronting a nightclub quintet featuring Chase. Pierce wrote most charts, and the act spotlighted a tap dancer and the singer-pianist Norma Douglas. The troupe played for a month at the Waldorf Astoria in Manhattan, then at Freedomland, which Herman viewed as a "rinky dink version of Disneyland" in the Bronx.[29] When Freedomland wanted a big band, Pierce rounded up New York people, among them Gus Johnson, saxophonist Charlie Mariano, and trumpeter Joe Newman. The enlarged band played some weekends, but at times during 1960–61, Herman and friends worked little.

In late January 1960, Herman started a short-lived band for a January 22 telecast on WGN in Chicago and a few other jobs. Ericson, Chase, Guinn, Lanphere, and Campbell formed the backbone. On March 22, Herman led this sixteen-man band in making a soon forgotten album, *The New Swingin' Herman Herd,* for Crown Records in Chicago. The session produced ten numbers by Burns with Third Herd echoes: "Montmart Bus Ride," "Aruba," "Darn That Dream" (with sterling solos from Lanphere and Guinn), "Crown Royal," "The Grind," "Single O," and "Hermosa Beach." The band also flawlessly recorded Burns's chart of "I Can't Get Started" for the Chase and Ericson trumpets. "Off Shore," a pop ballad, introduced Gus Mas's flute, along with solos by Herman on alto and Chase. Flute and reeds played major roles in "Afterglow," a romantic tune on which Guinn and Herman on alto soloed. Music in this album, which was reissued as recently as 1992, stood the test of time.

Herman's band kept working off and on, with Don Rader and Chase on trumpet, Kent McGarity and Guinn on trombone, and Campbell as steady members. But by April 1961, only a sextet found work: Herman, Chase, Pierce, Campbell, Andrus, and tenor-sax player Gordon Brisker. In June, for the Waldorf Astoria, Herman added Urbie Green and baritone saxophonist Jimmy Mosher.

By this time Herman had rented Turchen an office in Manhattan. Herman believed that Turchen had "good business sense, and lots of friends in the music business. . . . He could convince people that we were saleable. Abe knew how to get things done. I gave him control of everything because I felt he was qualified, despite his penchant for gambling."[30] Composer and author Gene Lees, who was editor of *Down Beat* in 1959–61, describes Turchen's off-beat ways—with an office TV set going all day, playing solitaire, answering phone calls, placing bets, yet finding bookings as obscure as supermarket openings to keep the Herman band solvent. But in November 1961, not even Turchen could book Herman's silver anniversary concert. There simply was no work for Herman after twenty-five years. Nor had he made any commercial recordings since March 1960.

For a job at Freedomland in December 1961, Herman and Pierce fielded yet another big band, giving tenor saxophonist Sal Nistico, twenty-four, a Syracuse product of Chuck and Gap Mangione's band, his first break. Pierce returned to arrange and play piano, also taking on the duties of road manager, and Herman doggedly presided over the "scuffling organization." It was so scuffling, in fact, that he broke it up and, by January 1962, hacked out a living with a quartet in New York. At first his sidemen were the ever loyal Pierce, Andrus, and Gus Johnson. Philips Records of Chicago showed enough interest to record a dozen numbers for an album called *Swing Low, Sweet Clarinet*—the title tune repeating a Four Brothers Band recording of 1947. "Pee Wee Blues," by Pee Wee Russell and Pierce, and "Alexandra," an homage to Woody and Charlotte Herman's second grandchild, by Herman and Pierce, were originals. The other numbers were standards. The album is of value to listeners, as the nuances of Herman's clarinet playing are more easily audible than when he played with larger groups. But his intent was the same with performing groups large or small: "All we did [on the album] was try to create some kind of mood and hope somebody digs it," a modest Herman told Gleason for the album notes. His point really applies to the ambitions of all jazz-makers of all eras while tending to punch holes in the theories of critics who pen weighty analyses of his music. After making the records, Herman added Sims, Adderley, Chase, and Hanna for a few bookings but then junked it all and went home for a month.

*b*ut Pierce stayed in New York assembling a band that, it was agreed, Herman would lead if it clicked. Pierce tapped new young players from the Berklee College of Music in Boston; one recruit, trombonist Phil Wilson, said: "We wanted to succeed so badly we could taste it."[31]

So there ensued another stretch of poor-but-happy years of Herman's Herds. They played concerts, festivals, overseas tours, dances, radio and TV shows, and school clinics. "Just call it The Swingin' Herd," Herman said.[32] Record labels, album covers, press releases, even the silver-spangled "W H" music stands soon called it the Swingin' Herd, too. The Swingin' Herd recorded about 125 tracks for Philips, Columbia, and Verve albums in five years but had no hit songs. Still, the band produced new stars and continued to experiment with unusual instruments, adding soprano sax as well as flute. Engineers recorded some of the music live, in long versions, from the Riverboat Room in the Empire State Building, Basin Street East, Harrah's Club in Lake Tahoe, Basin Street West, and the Monterey Jazz Festival. The Four Brothers sax choir fell into disuse, as such writers as Kenny Ascher, Chase, Holman, Pierce, Rader, Roland, and Phil Wilson wrote what Robert Laber calls "Basie-on-steroids" charts.[33]

Jazz fans in the 1960s applauded Basie, Duke Ellington, and Herman as national treasures, and Herman's music began to win album awards or at least nominations. Philips producer Jack Tracy remarks that "comebacks are funny things—there are those who recall Basie bursting back from limbo, and starting a new career a decade ago. Others remember Ellington, described as finished, roaring back in the early 1950s. Then there's Woody Herman. Up to 1962 knowledgeable persons would say, 'Yeah, what became of him?'"[34] No wonder they did. While his albums began winning him new fans, the night-to-night band business remained a struggle. He and his men played many a nameless one-nighter between stays in the higher-profile New York City, Chicago, and Toronto clubs and concert halls and summer vacation spots in Cedar Point and Chippewa Lake in Ohio and Glens Falls in New York.

The band played assorted new charts mixed with the old successes "Woodchoppers' Ball," "Apple Honey," "Four Brothers," and "Early Autumn," as had earlier Herman groups. Herman added Joe Newman's "Mo-lasses," Pierce's "Tunin' In," Horace Parlan's "Blues for J. P.," standards, and selected pop songs. Marianne Donne joined the band to sing "My Funny Valentine" and "Chicago."

In October 1962, Philips recorded *Woody Herman 1963* in New York City. This album "opened the eyes and ears of a whole new generation of listeners and disc jockeys to a young, hungry, and enthusiastic group of charge-on-straight-ahead musicians," Tracy raved. "Names likes

Nistico, [Phil] Wilson, Hanna, and Chase began appearing in polls and popping up in conversations."[35] The album cover, showing Don Zolan's pencil sketch of Herman blowing his clarinet, called it "the swingin'est big band ever" and indicated that 1963—"Woody's 25th year"—was "his greatest" (whereas Herman was actually starting his twenty-seventh year). Chase, Paul Fontaine, Dave Gale, Ziggy Harrell, and Gerry Lamy played the trumpets, with trombonists Wilson, Eddie Morgan, and Jack Gale and tenor-sax players Larry Cavelli, Nistico, and Brisker. Gene Allen played baritone, with Pierce, Andrus, and Hanna making rhythm. On "Molasses," Herman returned to his big-band sound—missing in his work since early 1960—with a loud, crisp, energetic ensemble and bold soloists. This number, which ran nearly seven minutes, featured solos by Nistico, Herman on clarinet, and Chase. The album continued with "Blues for J.P.," an updated "Don't Get Around Much Anymore," "Tunin' In," "It's a Lonesome Old Town," Silver's "Sister Sadie," Jack Gale's "Sig Ep," and "Camel Walk," Chase's long novelty blues shouted by Herman.

At this time, Feather detected "a new upsurge in the band's reputation as such soloists as Nistico, [Phil] Wilson and Hanna strengthened

The Swingin' Herd, with Jake Hanna on drums, about 1962. (Courtesy Duncan P. Schiedt)

the personnel."[36] He might also have praised Andrus's bass, Chase's high trumpet leads, and the charts from Chase, Brisker, Bob Hammer, and Pierce. Pierce had hooked top Boston talent for the band: Wilson, a composer, teacher, and trombonist, played for Jimmy Dorsey, and led his own band and quartet. Chase had climbed to eminence playing lead in the Ferguson and Kenton powerhouses. He contributed his arranging and solo talent and gave the brass section its most searing, high-pitched power since the First Herd. Andrus had free-lanced in New York City. Hanna, whom Gleason characterized as "the best [drummer] Herman has had in a long time,"[37] had played in an Air Force unit and toured with Ferguson.

Actually, *Woody Herman 1963* showed off only part of the band's new music. A Sesac transcription made in December 1962, for instance, contained Pierce's new "That's Where It Is," "Pretty Little Girl," "Way Up There," and "Woodpecker's Ball"; Phil Wilson's "Draw Night" and "Golden Gate"; Chase's "Y'Know What I Mean" and "Easy Walker"; and Roland's "Reed Blues," "Take the D Train," "Aurora," and "Freud's and Alice's." The Swingin' Herd played on TV often in 1963—on the *Ed Sullivan Show* and San Francisco, New York City, and Toronto stations.

After much travel between New York City and Hollywood, the band lodged in Hollywood's Basin Street West in May, where Philips recorded *Woody Herman 1963: Encore* live May 19, 20, and 21. From hours of tape, Philips selected for the album "That's Where It Is," Pierce's chart of Herbie Hancock's "Watermelon Man," "Body and Soul," Hammer's version of Charlie Mingus's "Better Git It in Your Soul," a Four Brothers sax reprise in "Jazz Me Blues," Chase's Latin-flavored "El Toro Grande," Pierce's treatment of "Days of Wine and Roses," and an eight-minute "Caldonia."

*t*he National Academy of Recording Arts and Sciences awarded *Woody Herman 1963: Encore* a Grammy for being the best big-band jazz record of the year.

While taping the *Encore* tracks, Philips captured two dozen more numbers. Six of these became tracks for the 1965 album *Woody's Big Band Goodies*: "Wailin' in the Woodshed," "The Good Earth," "Sidewalks of Cuba," "I Can't Get Started," "Apple Honey," and "Bijou," on which Phil

Wilson tried to put his stamp, as the piece was written for, and long associated with, Bill Harris. "You can't just superimpose one [trombone] style on the other," Wilson commented. "Still, Bill and I are both lucky in that Woody loved the trombone. It was his favorite instrument."[38]

*M*ore bookings, TV appearances, and a tour in Europe followed the success of *Encore*. Then it was on to clubs in Chicago, New York, Las Vegas, Reno, and San Francisco. The Swingin' Herd had arrived.

Encouraged by the success of *Woody Herman: 1963* and *Encore*, Philips recorded *Woody Herman: 1964* on November 20, 22, and 23, 1963, in a New York studio. Now the bandsmen included trumpeters Chase, Hunt, Fontaine, Lamy, and Danny Nolan; trombonists Phil Wilson, Henry Southall, and Kenny Wenzel; tenor saxophonists Nistico, Carmen Leggio, and John Stevens. Nick Brignola played baritone, and Pierce, Andrus, and Hanna still made the rhythm. Pierce's take on Oscar Peterson's "Hallelujah Time" featured Leggio and Nistico. Pierce's chart of "Deep Purple" allotted solos to Herman on alto, Leggio, and Nistico. Holman's "Jazz Hoot," with Hanna's distinctive clog-dancing rhythm, included solos by Hunt, Wilson, and Nistico. At the time of President John F. Kennedy's death, the band was recording Chase's treatment of "A Taste of Honey." Siefert, watching the session, said that "when news of the assassination came over the air, you can't imagine what effect that had on everyone in the studio. The whole session slumped into a daze, and the recording process just stopped."[39] In somewhat higher spirits the next day, the band made "Satin Doll," with solos by Pierce, Chase, and Andrus. Holman's odd chart of "After You've Gone" contained a celesta intro and changing tempos. Hammer's "The Strut," Pierce's version of Meredith Willson's "My Wish" (from the musical *Here's Love*), and Coppola's "Cousins" concluded the album.

Success followed the Swingin' Herd at appearances in New York City, Hollywood, San Francisco, and Chicago, telecasts, and a tour in England during July 1964. Philips caught up with it September 9 at Harrah's. There it taped nine numbers for release in *The Swingin' Herman*

Herd Recorded Live plus three that filled *Woody's Big Band Goodies* later on. Singer Joe Carroll, from Gillespie's group, shared the Harrah's stage and toured with Herman for parts of 1964 and 1965. His upbeat nature recalled the energy of Sammy Davis, Jr.

Herman's trumpet section was augmented when Dusan Gojkovic, who played under the name Dusko Goykovich, joined the band. Goykovich hailed from Jajce, Yugoslavia, and had played in the International Youth Band at Brussels and Newport in 1958 and with Kurt Edelhagen's booming, Kenton-like crew in Cologne, Germany. Also a talented writer, he studied at Berklee College during 1961–63 and toured with Ferguson.

In late 1964, after three years with Philips, Herman joined Columbia Records again. His nemesis, Mitch Miller, had gone on to other things, and Columbia's jazz artists-and-repertoire man, Teo Macero, a sax player and composer, was working up albums with Duke Ellington, Miles Davis, and Monk. Macero and Herman first produced *My Kind of Broadway,* in which the Swingin' Herd turned show tunes into jazz at four studio sessions with Ronnie Zito at the drums. A twenty-five-year-old from Utica, New York, Zito had backed singers Bobby Darin and Peggy Lee. On November 27, the band recorded "My Favorite Things" and "This Can't Be Love" to start the album. It continued on February 15, 1965, making "I Feel Pretty," "A Lot of Livin' to Do," "Warm All Over," and "Hello, Young Lovers." On February 24 "Who Can I Turn To?" was added. The wrap-up session, on March 13, produced "Get Me to the Church on Time," "I Do Like You," "Never Will I Marry," "The Sound of Music," and "Somewhere," arranged and played by Chase. Sax star Julian "Cannonball" Adderley liked "The Sound of Music" track: "It is not adventurous jazz, but there's room for everything, and I'm happy to know that Woody is still doing that sort of thing—maybe his music will survive as a result of his being able to play music for just ordinary folks. As far as big bands and what it takes for them to survive, *vive le Woody Herman!*"[40] Herman announced that he was "happy to be back—it's like old home week at Columbia."[41]

Herman's successes notwithstanding, it was not easy to keep a band together in the 1960s. Gleason attributed Herman's longevity to his flexibility:

> In order to survive, a big band today—more than at any other time in history—must be prepared to play every possible kind of engagement. High school proms, Elks club dances, jazz concerts followed by two hours of dancing. Anything. To do this and keep the jazz franchise requires dexterity. Herman solved that problem, just as Ellington and Basie solved it. Herman always has a strong ballad book, great songs, great melodies, arranged by jazzmen to function on two levels—jazz and dance music—simultaneously. You simply can't fake this sort of thing.[42]

Keeping a band still meant a revolving door of talent, too. In 1965 Herman used thirteen players for his five trumpet chairs, eight trombonists for three spots, nine tenor saxophonists for three parts, and three bass players. Zito and Pierce stayed put.

Throughout the spring the band toured for one-nighters, hitting Pennsylvania, Maryland, New York, Michigan, Ohio, Indiana, and New Jersey in one twelve-day stretch. The musicians then leaped from Queens to San Francisco in two weeks, by way of Niagara Falls, Rochester, Pittsburgh, St. Paul, Sioux Falls, St. Joseph, Wichita, and Topeka.

By the time Columbia's next Herman album, *Woody's Winners,* was produced, Anthony Leonardi had replaced Andrus. The album, which was recorded live from Basin Street West on June 28, 29, and 30, 1965, contained a few old favorites ("Northwest Passage," "Opus De-Funk") plus charts by newer bandsmen. Chase's "23 Red" featured three trumpet soloists. Goykovich's "Woody's Whistle" ended with Herman tweeting the pocket toy he used to bring order at rehearsal or to call sidemen back onstage after intermission. The album included three charts by Rader: "My Funny Valentine," which presented solos by Herman on clarinet, Rader, and Chase; "Poor Butterfly," featuring Herman's alto sax; and the six and one-half minute "Greasy Sack Blues," which contained solos by Herman on clarinet, Pierce, and Rader. At thirty, Rader was peaking after years playing trumpet and flugelhorn and writing for combos and the big bands of Ferguson, Basie, and James. The eye-catching album cover, more a marketing tool than an art form, pictured Herman grinning, clarinet upright like a pitchfork, surrounded by fifteen female models.

From the Basin Street West appearances, Columbia recorded enough to piece together parts of two other albums. "I Can't Get Started" featured Chase's horn. "Hallelujah Time" sported a brassy new start-stop-start opening with tenor saxophonist Andy McGhee helping Nistico. The Ellingtonian "Satin Doll" sounded smooth, with Pierce, Chase, and Leonardi inserting solos. Holman's "Jazz Hoot"—a play on TV's folk music show *Hootenanny*—featured Chase, Herman on clarinet, Southall, and Nistico. By now the band had tinkered with Pierce's chart of "Watermelon Man" until it ran past six minutes. Goykovich arranged and soloed on Benny Golson's touching elegy for trumpet star Clifford Brown, "I Remember Clifford," then four soloists romped on "The Preacher." Holman's "Waltz for a Hung-Up Ballet Mistress," a number in quick-stepping three-four time that was deeper than its title, featured a solo by Herman, this time on a soprano sax.

Bigger than a clarinet, the soprano sax had old friends in jazz. Sidney Bechet played one in the 1930s, as did Barnet in his 1930s and 1940s bands, Hodges with Duke Ellington, and Les Brown. The soprano gained new respect with John Coltrane (whom "Dear John C" honored) from 1960 on, boosted by his recording of "My Favorite Things." Herman heard Coltrane at a 1964 concert in Chicago and saw the soprano-sax tide rising. Herman remarked that "in the old days when Bechet and Hodges were about the only people who played it, it was a terrible horn to conquer. But now you can buy a good horn that stays in pitch and it's much easier to cope with."[43]

More one-nighters carried Herman and the band to Toronto and through Indiana, Michigan, Ohio, Pennsylvania, and Connecticut. Big-city stops included the Plugged Nickel in Chicago, Northland Shopping Center in Detroit, and a concert in New York City's Shea Stadium on September 19. After an American Legion Hall date in Greensburg, Indiana, on September 24, the men enjoyed two weeks back in the Riverboat

Room. There on October 8 Herman recorded Hammer's simple blues-riff called "The Black Opal" and a Latin march known as "Mardi Gras."

From October through December, the band played nearly seventy one-nighters in Canada, Kansas, Kentucky, and Louisiana. After a five-hour New Year's Eve job at a country club in Fort Worth, it headed west to open 1966 with a week at the Playboy Club in Los Angeles.

Herman had gained one of his most important and loyal bandsmen in late August 1965 in the person of Bill Byrne, who recalls that Herman "needed three trumpet players in a hurry."[44] The South Dakotan, who had played for Larry Elgart, stayed in Herman's bands longer than anyone—as fifth trumpeter and later as road manager. For an appearance at the Playboy in January 1966, the Swingin' Herd was composed of Marv Stamm, Alex Rodriguez, Byrne, Chase, and Fontaine on trumpet; Jerry Collins, Gary Potter, and Southall on trombone; Bob Pierson, Frank Vicari, Andy McGhee, and Tom Anastas on sax; and Pierce, Zito, and new bassist Mike Moore in the rhythm section. Free-lancer Frank Rosolino, once a Kenton star, beefed up the trombones for a while. The band also appeared on CBS-TV's *Danny Kaye Show.*

Then it shot east again for a flurry of recording dates and live appearances in New York City, interspersed with two European tours. On

Herman band onstage, about 1966, probably in Morocco, with Moroccan folk musicians known as gnaoua. *(Courtesy Ingrid Herman Reese)*

February 28, the Swingin' Herd started work on the Columbia album *The Jazz Swinger*, a reference to the 1927 Al Jolson motion picture *The Jazz Singer*, the first U.S. film with a sound track. Each of the album's eleven numbers featured Herman's Jolsonesque singing, an effort that Gehman characterized as "something I would not have thought possible—make Jolson's dreadfully dated songs not just palatable, but pleasurable."[45]

The crew managed to record Burns's charts of "Carolina in the Morning," "Sonny Boy," and "I'm Sittin' on Top of the World" and Pierce's slow "Dinah" before leaving for Europe on March 1. After eleven performances in England, two in Spain, and five in Germany, the band jetted back for a week at New York City's Playboy Club, opening March 21, and an *Ed Sullivan Show* telecast on March 27. Then they were off again, for a two-month tour—Herman's last for the State Department—that touched more than twenty points in Europe and northern Africa. It was a tired herd that touched down at JFK Airport on June 9.

In a long recording session on June 10 (before working the Stratford Inn in Bridgeport that night), the men wrapped up *The Jazz Swinger* with Holman's arrangements of "Swanee," "Toot Toot Tootsie," and "Waitin' for the 'Robert E. Lee'"; Pierce's "There's a Rainbow round My Shoulder" and "Rock-a-bye Your Baby"; and Burns's versions of "San Francisco" and "April Showers." Herman, whose ties to the city reached back to 1931, saved his most heartfelt singing for "San Francisco." Pierson's flute blended prettily with the saxes in "Rock-a-bye Your Baby." "April Showers" contained a flugelhorn solo for Stamm, a North Texas State music major who had played in several bands and had even worked with symphonies. The long-ignored flugelhorn was turning up in bands again; arrangers liked working with it, and some leaders sought trumpeters who could double on it.

In June, Pierce retired from band travel, but he kept sending charts from Los Angeles. Ascher replaced Pierce in the band, and added his fast, rhythmic "Woody's Boogaloo" to the book. Chase then left in August 1966 to start a band that would merge jazz and rock music—as had the groups Chicago and Blood, Sweat, and Tears. His nine-piece band, simply named Chase, contained four trumpets, organ, rhythm section, and vocalist.

During 1966, Herman ultimately had to make six trumpet and three trombone changes and employed five tenor saxophonists, three baritone saxophonists, three drummers, and four bassists over the course of the year.

The Swingin' Herd stayed put briefly, playing the Newport Jazz Festival, where Getz, Sims, Cohn, and Mulligan guested on "Four Brothers" for Voice of America radio. The band had played the Warwick Musical Theatre in Rhode Island for a week with Bennett before the festival, then worked another week with him in the Carousel Theatre in Framingham, Massachusetts. On July 7, Columbia recorded "Sidewinder" before the band left New York City for the West Coast. Herman's vocal about the rattlesnake, with high notes from Chase, appeared in 1974 in an album called *Jazz Hoot,* which was full of oddities made between 1965 and 1967. Between July 22 and August 18, the band costarred with Tormé at the Tropicana in Las Vegas. Tormé enjoyed the laid-back Herman's company after a three-week hassle over cobilling with Duke Ellington.

Herman's band and Tormé reunited at Basin Street East for a September 8–October 1 show. A critic hailed them as an "unbeatable, under-recorded team," reporting that "Tormé spieled on and on about how much Herman meant to him as a friend and inspiration."[46] Bill Byrne recalled: "Mel was easy to work with. He wrote all the arrangements for his show, so he got just what he wanted from the band. We had good crowds that were real music listeners. Miles Davis came to see us in New York."[47]

Such successes notwithstanding, Herman still had to take on long stretches of low-profile one-nighters in Pennsylvania, Missouri, South Carolina, Georgia, and Ohio and a week with singer Johnny Ray. The band also played Milwaukee, Kansas City, St. Louis, Atlanta, Indianapolis, Chicago, and Cleveland, and December in the Tropicana. Yet another European tour took the band to England, Germany, and Italy from January 21 to February 8, 1967. But the grind kept shuffling the roster. Back in the United States, Ascher left, to be succeeded by four other pianists during 1967. Fourteen trumpet players, ten trombonists, eleven saxophonists, three bassists, and no fewer than five drummers also appeared with Herman that year.

Private tapes made February 11 at the Redwood Motor Inn in Pittsburgh reveal that Herman had added new charts of "Gone with the Wind," "The Very Thought of You," "Free Again," and "Tea for Two." More new music arrived from free-lancer Joe Roccisano.

The Swingin' Herd shared the stage with Byrd again at the Riverboat Room in New York City for three weeks in March. During March 23–25, Columbia recorded seven of their numbers. The band then featured trumpeters Lynn Biviano and Dick Ruedebusch and trombonist Bill Watrous, a short-term pickup from the New York talent pool and a widely recorded sideman. Columbia taped Byrd's "The Duck," Frank Foster's nine-minute "Tomorrow's Blues Today," and "Cousins." The reed players reran "Four Brothers," and Herman sang a vacuous novelty about a guy's girlfriend, "Boopsie." Pierson's flute playing and Zito's drumming uplifted "Free Again," while Herman soloed on alto on "Make Someone Happy."

While the band played the Riverboat Room, Turchen persuaded Bill Byrne to take over April 1 as the Swingin' Herd's road manager. For extra pay, Byrne waded through the flood of travel and lodging chores and, as the years passed, big-brothered nervous newcomers. He certainly had his work cut out for him, as the band played almost nonstop one-nighters throughout August. The list is impressive but exhausting: Pushnik's in Lebanon, Pennsylvania; a Waterbury Police Association concert in a Connecticut armory; the officers' club at Bolling Air Force Base; an Elks Lodge at Huntington, Indiana; a supper club in Milan, Illinois; the Southeast Kansas Jazz Festival at Chanute; the Sheraton Boston for a college dance; four concerts in Disneyland; the Advertising Club of Baltimore in the Emerson Hotel; the Big Farmers Warehouse at Fayetteville, North Carolina; the Milwaukee Jazz Festival; Steamboat Days in Burlington, Iowa; the Newport Jazz Festival; Cobo Hall in Detroit; Palais Royal in Toronto; Wisconsin Historyland at Hayward; Cedar Point near Sandusky, Ohio; the Tail of the Fox in Timonium, Maryland.

Gehman traveled with the band to research an article in the *Saturday Review*. He caught the Swingin' Herd in a Susquehanna River town of ten thousand west of Lancaster, Pennsylvania. "What the hell are you doing in Columbia?" he asked, knowing Herman could not have gotten much more than $1,000 for the concert/dance: "Herman tugged at the lapels of his beautifully tailored blazer and gave me that smile. 'A gig is a gig, man. Tomorrow night we play somewhere in Maryland. I forget the name of the town. I think we're getting less than we're getting here. Same old story, man. Every night a new town.'" Gehman ranked his two weeks with the band "one of the most bone-shattering tours I ever experienced":

> We played small Pennsylvania towns night after night and worked our way up into the coal regions and then into lower New York State. It is never the same band. Sometimes the personnel changes from night to night . . . for various reasons—the hardship of playing one-nighters all the time, and loneliness for the company of wives or girlfriends, the low pay—Herman pays most of his men "road scale," or about $200 per week—or the stern demands of the "Iron Chancellor," as one of his men nicknamed him. . . . Mainly they are youngsters who are willing to work for the money they are paid only because they want to be able to say, "I used to be on the Herman band." That statement will guarantee them work anywhere jazz is heard.[48]

By September, the Swingin' Herd that Herman led in a weekend "Festival Herd" for the tenth annual Monterey event was almost unrecognizable due to personnel changes. Trumpeter Bill Byrne and trombonist Mel Wanzo alone had played in the band just six months earlier. Among the new solo stars were trumpet player Luis Gasca, trombonist Fontana (back in the band only briefly), tenor players Joe Romano, Nistico, pianist Albert Dailey, drummer John "Baron" Von Ohlen, and baritone sax players Cecil McKenzie "Zodiac" Payne.

National Educational Television filmed the band's Monterey appearance, and a crew from Wally Heider Studios in San Francisco sold tapes of the concert to Verve, which was by then an adjunct of MGM Records. The resulting album, *Concerto for Herd*, contained

Rader's "Big Sur Echo" (a play on the 1940 number "Little Sir Echo"), a softly swinging seven-minute piece with solos by Daily, Gasca, Romano, and Herman on soprano sax;

Holman's "The Horn of the Fish," which was written for Herman's soprano sax, or "fish horn," and also featured solos by Fontana and Neil Friel, a piano-bass duet with Daily and Carl Pruitt, and Four Brothers reeds;

"Woody's Boogaloo," lasting more than seven minutes, on which Von Ohlen kept the rapid pace going crisply for soloists Romano, Daily, Fontana, Gasca, and Herman on clarinet;

Holman's nineteen-minute "Concerto for Herd," composed in three movements—a brisk contrapuntal opener, a slow section, then a medium-speed finish relying on mood and dynamics. Russell George, Gillespie's electric-bass player, played the intro, followed by solos by Herman on alto, Gasco, Cecil Payne, Romano, Herman on clarinet, Daily, Nistico, and Herman on soprano sax and a duet for George and Pruitt on amplified and acoustic basses.

Herman and his bandsmen had to wonder sometimes if anyone cared. The big bands made few records and rarely crashed the national prints. Fan (and scandal) magazines, movies, and TV specials concentrated on the rising rock groups while the Duke Ellington, Basie, and Herman bands, and a few others, barely made a buck. For years the Beatles and Elvis Presley had been leading the big swarm of young, fast-living guitarists, drummers, singers, backup groups, amplifiers, monster speakers, and light shows onto stages piled high with cash the world over. For fans of the big bands, the Bee Gees—who had nothing to do with Benny Goodman—and Herman's Hermits—no relation to Woody Herman—were painful reminders that times were changing.

What's more, in poll after poll, Herman finished out of the running as leader, singer, or player. So did his sidemen. Herman never lamented. But critic Ed Mulford called him a victim of what he called "Crow-Jimism," arguing that power brokers denied him top rank because he was white: "In 1964, I was doing interviews with both Ellington and Basie, and both told me they felt that Woody had the greatest band in the world that year, but those critics would never admit it."[49] According to Feather, what success the Swingin' Herd did enjoy "had been attributed to Herman's popularity among his men and the resultant team spirit, as well as to the knack shown . . . in selecting musicians. New recordings flowed to keep pace with the new faces in the band."[50]

Music recorded at Basin Street West in 1965 and the Riverboat Room in 1967 was made into the Columbia album *Woody Live East and West*, which lost a Grammy to Duke Ellington in 1967. Herman's band guested with Bennett on the *Ed Sullivan Show* on November 5, 1967, and played "Woody's Boogaloo." One-nighters and stays at the Riverboat Room, at Cobo Hall during the Detroit Auto Show, and the Scotch Mist in Chicago closed the year.

*t*he new year brought the Swingin' Herd the same round of personnel changes and one-nighters—and worse was yet to come. Herman went through twenty men for the band's five trumpet chairs that year, and eleven for three trombone spots, seven tenor saxophonists and five baritone saxophonists for the four seats in the reed section, plus four pianists, three bassists, and five drummers.

One-nighters in the eastern United States and Canada started in January before a two-week visit to Europe. Stops this time included London, Newcastle, Leicester,

The band with the Hermans on tour, about 1966. (Courtesy Ingrid Herman Reese)

Birmingham, Bristol, Portsmouth, Manchester, Bournemouth, Glasgow, Dundee, and Belfast. After returning to New York City February 13, the band resumed one-nighters. Patrons of the Riverboat Room welcomed it back for three weeks until April 17, and promoter George Wein booked concerts at the Mexico City Jazz Festival between May 22 and 28. The band played five dates with singer Johnny Desmond, appeared at Cincinnati's Coney Island, performed with the Pittsburgh Symphony, and made its annual visit on July 5 to Newport. But it was well-worn turf, even with new faces and steady bookings. The band failed to impress poll-takers, record buyers, or concert-goers. Worse, someone was writing sour notes in the band's business records.

Herman had said that he never thought Turchen's gambling would matter. But there were signs that it did, had he but noticed. During one European tour, Turchen had called him to insist Herman sell his music publishing company to make ends meet, but Herman nixed any sale of his legacy to his family. When Turchen, who had power of attorney, sold it anyway, Herman wakened to "a financial stranglehold from which I would never recover."[51] Matters reached a crisis in mid-1968, when the Internal Revenue Service ordered Herman to appear to discuss serious matters. (They had been writing to Herman's office, but Turchen never told him.) The IRS said that Herman had not paid any personal income taxes or withheld taxes on band salaries for 1964, 1965, and 1966; because the band wasn't incorporated, its grosses were figured as Herman's personal income. With interest and penalties, the $1 million Herman owed rose daily. Dazed, he agreed to pay $1,000 a week toward a settlement.

Pierce had grown suspicious in 1967: "Two IRS agents came to my apartment and took me downtown to show them some payroll lists. Yet [after disclosure in 1968] Woody went straight ahead [and went on working]. I never met anyone else who had such an amazing attitude."[52] Herman was "shocked" about Turchen, and "astounded" by the debt. The years in question had been lean ones, he said: "Financially, the band was just hanging on. We were roaming the wilds, scraping the bottom of the barrel just to come up with bookings."[53] Turchen insisted that Uncle Sam had it "all wrong," but when asked for proof, he claimed that ledgers had "disappeared" from his car. Problems snowballed; according to Bill Byrne, "every week a bus company would come with a subpoena, because Abe hadn't paid. And they would try to take the band's music library."[54]

"For some unearthly reason, I had kept Abe on the job," Herman admitted. "But by August, I couldn't take it any more." Herman fired Turchen and tried connecting with other agents, among them Granz and Herman's bookers in the Willard Alexander office. At last Hermie Dressel, a long-time friend, took the job. Dressel handled business and publicity for certain artists for the Paul Kantor Agency in New York City. (Dionne Warwick and Burt Bacharach were among the Kantor clients.) Herman said he and Charlotte were "appalled at how stupid we had been in our judgment of Abe, but I felt as responsible as Abe for the mess. I was depressed, but I knew that I had to get back to the business of music in order to take care of it as best I could." Lees saw Herman as an odd mixture of "shrewd perception and pure naiveté. He could be almost cunningly observant of people. Yet I believe he was unaware of what Abe had done. What Woody was guilty of was not paying attention. That was the nature of his problem."[55]

Meanwhile, Herman could not pay $1,000 a week—some weeks, the band scarcely worked. Lawyer friends labored to keep him out of prison. "I saw what the government had done to Joe Louis, forcing him to wind up as a hand-shaking shill for a Las Vegas hotel," Herman averred. "I would have preferred going to jail than to finish like that." But Herman said he never considered prison a threat so long as he could work and try to pay the debt: "I always figured the IRS would have less to gain with me behind bars." But he had to face a bitter truth: "I'm going to be on the road for the rest of my life."[56]

chapter seven

LIGHTING *their* FIRE

The 1960s saw innovations in Herman's band as he brought in the soprano sax and, encouraged by trumpeters Clark Terry and Art Farmer, revived the long-overlooked flugelhorn. Feather writes that Herman played "a significant role as an instrumentalist" and played "in a style that showed how keenly he had picked up on the newer developments."[1] Writers soon found fresh ways to use the clear, piping sounds of both instruments.

And other changes were in the air. By the late 1960s, Don Ellis, once a trumpeter with Ferguson, pioneered in using odd time signatures, a plug-in string quartet, and singers mimicking horns. He recorded with such guitar attachments as the echoplex, phaser, and ring modulator. These devices, some electronic, some involving tape loops that could be set for different delays and echoing intervals, produced extraordinary new sounds through inverted vibrations and through altered timbres, which slightly changed the harmonic structure of chords. Ellis also wrote jazz based on Indian music, and used the Fender-Rhodes electric piano and clavinet, which further changed the sound of what he recorded. While the grand masters, Duke Ellington and Basie, stuck to basics, Rich, Ferguson, and Herman borrowed from Ellis. What's more, their writers started reworking hits by rock groups and by the jazz-rock combos Blood, Sweat and Tears and Chicago. Jazz stages changed, too. The few surviving big bands toured overseas, played outdoor festivals at Newport and Monterey, at a *Playboy* magazine festival in Chicago, and at clinics in schools.

From fall to spring, bands at times worked several clinic/concert dates a week. They would conduct afternoon workshops and play a two-hour concert at night for, say, $2,500. Parents, booster clubs, and students would hustle to sell out a two-thousand-seat gym at $3 per ticket for the concert. As a result of the exposure, students of jazz kept getting better. Some college bands matched the pros so well that Rich, Herman, Kenton, and Ferguson could recruit from them. Herman advised kids to find steady careers and only rely on music to keep their minds straight. He valued his work with students, as he told Feather: "We may have to work three times as hard, because we spend the day doing classes with students, then play a concert at night, but it still beats the world's swingingest Elks Club. I learn as much playing those dates for kids as they learn from us. We should have done this years ago."[2] At least one such student was profoundly affected in this way. John Fedchock, who joined Herman's band in 1980, recalls that "Woody's was one of the first big bands I ever heard. I was a junior in high school and the band played a clinic and concert at my school on April 18, 1974. That day inspired me to continue on in music, with the hope that some day I might get a chance to play with a band like that."[3]

Herman offered compelling performances to young and old alike. Sweden, about 1975. (Courtesy Gary Anderson)

But by 1968, Herman knew that he wasn't playing or talking the music that most young Americans listened to. Their passion for rock, country and western, and rhythm and blues made it harder to win young fans, no matter how good a jazz band looked or sounded, or what famous name fronted it. According to trumpeter Freddie Hubbard, it had become "difficult to stay out of rock and make a living."[4] Herman wouldn't be bulldozed, but he began to like the idea of swinging with good rock tunes. Drummer Edward Soph explains that "Woody crossed over for a number of factors: The success of horn bands like Blood, Sweat and Tears and of Chicago; similar attempts by Buddy Rich; the influence of Bill Chase; and the [radio] exposure that such music would provide."[5]

And so he made three timely albums for Cadet Records of Chicago: *Light My Fire* in 1968 (put up for a Grammy but losing to one by Quincy Jones), *Heavy Exposure* in 1969, and *Woody* (topped by Duke

Ellington for a 1970 Grammy). According to Soph, "Cadet [agreed to] press some album cuts into singles to help sales."[6] The players, songs, charts, and writers, coupled with synthesizers, echoes, rotating mikes, electric guitar and piano, and fade controls wrought obvious changes. And to reach the young, Herman's band swung to the beat of new drummers, such as arranger Richard Evans, who wrote all the charts, composed two tunes, and handled the studio production of *Light My Fire*. In a first for Herman, studio engineers also "enhanced" the music with their knobs and dials. Cadet executive Dick LaPalm, a friend and fan of Herman's, supervised the project, and Stu Black, recording engineer at Ter Mar Studios in Chicago, received technical/creative credit.

More than ever, it was appropriate that Herman tended to select young sidemen. He led five trumpeters, three trombonists, four reeds, pianist John Hicks, bassist Arthur Harper, and Soph. He added an electric guitarist and a "percussionist," a catch-all term for one who kept time with woodblocks, triangle, bongos, congas, maracas, or timbales. Tenor players Nistico and Vicari and trombonist Bob Burgess, a fortyish veteran from Kenton's band, soloed. The twenty-three-year-old Soph, a North Texas State grad from Houston, helped light fires with his strong, kicking beat.

For the first Cadet album Herman chose ten numbers. "Pontieo," by Edu Lobo-Capinan, resembled a fast bossa nova. Richard Evans's chart used the echoplex for effects. "Here I Am Baby," William "Smokey" Robinson's hit for his group, The Miracles, presented Herman on alto and Vicari over double-time rhythm. "Hard to Keep You on My Mind," by Jake Holmes, opened with sound effects, echoes, and drums, then broke into fast 5/4 time. Soph's drum breaks and the full band's sharp, accented section playing led up to Herman's soprano-sax solo and a first for Herman recordings: the use of fadeout and echo-chamber treatments. Evans wrote an eight and one-half minute version of Jim Webb's "MacArthur Park" ending with a fadeout and echoes. Evans's chart of "Light My Fire," by the Doors' Jim Morrison, gave the rock hit an easy-listening mood. For Bacharach's rhythmic "I Say a Little Prayer," Evans wrote in spaces to be filled by soloists plus echoplex and fadeout. Nistico and Henry Hall soloed in William

Stevenson's "Hush," a driving blues. On Quincy Jones's "For Love of Ivy," Evans built a Latin-flavored mood. Evans honored Strayhorn, who had died in 1967, in "Impression of Strayhorn," which featured sound effects and Herman's alto. Evans's frantic "Keep On Keepin' On" starred Hall and Nistico, and Ammons had high praise for the result: "I've always liked the sound of all the brass and the feeling that five reeds can get in a band of the type that Woody has had. There's nothing bad I can say about it."[7]

Some attempts to use rock in jazz bands failed, Feather claims, because, quoting Herman, arrangers approached it as condescending or tongue-in-cheek work. "But that all changed with *Light My Fire*," Feather wrote. "Evans made pop-rock-soul numbers seem logical and fresh." The Herman band library "expanded into a happy, generation-knitting fusion of then and now sound."[8] Lees also regarded the change in repertoire with approval:

> Only Woody and Buddy Rich seem to be getting to a young audience. Both are using a lot of the "contemporary" rhythmic devices and playing current pop tunes. "We have to play things they know and like if we're going to bring some music to them," Woody said. "It wasn't possible to do this four, five years ago because the tunes were so bad. But they've improved enormously, and now you can find some good things. You can't ignore the young."[9]

Other opinions were less charitable. In 1984, Barnet grumbled:

> Surprising as it may seem today, and after all he has endured on the road, I was always a little suspicious of Woody Herman's sincerity. He began with an out-and-out Dixieland band, turned toward Ellington, then went into bebop. . . . [Now] he is guilty of adopting some of the crossover tactics that involve rock and roll. Whatever way the wind was blowing, he [has] always presented an excellent band. . . . I deplore "crossover" musicians, but I understand their desire to get a piece of the pie.[10]

But as Herman made clear repeatedly throughout his later career, it was not a "piece of the pie" that motivated him; and his piece of the pie was slender indeed.

The band played when it could in late 1968: the Missouri State Fair; the Laurel Race Track Jazz Festival in Maryland; Elitch Gardens in Denver; St. Basil's Seminary in Methuen, Massachusetts. It played junior highs, police dances, Air Force bases, and National Guard armories, finishing the year at the Conrad Hilton in Chicago. Herman dismissed the band on December 22 for vacations until a month of one-nighters resumed in Dearborn, Michigan, on January 11, 1969. The band opened for four weeks in Caesar's Palace in Las Vegas on Valentine's Day—three shows a night, six nights a week. Soph recalls that they "played the Cadet music every night. The younger folks liked it a lot. The majority of bookings were non-jazz venues—Elks lodges, country clubs, service clubs. 'MacArthur Park' was the big number. But those were bleak financial times. Bill Byrne's credit cards saved us many times. The band had a few drug users, too, and that added to the overall bad vibes. The last sets would be the worst because so many guys would be wacked-out of their brains. God, the stories!"[11] Rehak rejoined the band for just four weeks in 1969 to play trombone. "My life was at an all-time low because of the use of large quantities of heroin and alcohol [in New York City]," he said. "I left Woody's band, at his request, weighing 118 pounds and close to death. He strongly suggested I go to Synanon for help. I did, and the years afterward were nothing short of miraculous."[12]

Soph left Herman in early 1969; a conscientious objector, he had to fulfill his service doing social work in New York. In all, sixteen trumpeters, eleven trombonists, eleven saxophonists, two pianists, four bassists, and eight drummers played with the band that year. In contrast, Herman had needed to hire just two players and three female singers in 1939.

Open dates rutted the road in 1969, too. A week at D.J.'s in Seattle and three in the Century Plaza Hotel in Los Angeles did pay the help until the band embarked on a European tour. Harold Davison, Limited, of London booked the band between April 25 and May 18 in ten towns in England, plus France, Italy, Belgium, Germany, Switzerland, and Austria. Tapes made on May 8 in Cologne show that Herman was still calling numbers from *Light My Fire* along with Pierce's new arrangement of

"Hey Jude!"—which featured Herman singing and shouting—and the oldies "Woodchoppers' Ball," "Make Someone Happy," "Greasy Sack Blues," "Early Autumn," "Four Brothers," "Somewhere," and "Free Again." For a BBC radio show from London on May 12, Herman programmed six of his Cadet numbers with "Woodchoppers' Ball."

The grind resumed back in the United States with a performance at the Brick Township High School auditorium in New Jersey, followed by appearances with the rock band The Who in Fillmore East in New York City on May 30–31 and in Fillmore West in San Francisco on June 17–19. The band was, no doubt, thankful to settle down for three weeks in Caesar's Palace starting June 26. Shows at the Lambertville Music Circus in New Jersey and on National Educational Television the night of August 26 included more *Light My Fire* fare plus "Hey Jude!" "Woody's Whistle," "Caldonia," "Laura," "Watermelon Man," "Squeeze Me," and "Cousins."

Herman's second Cadet album, *Heavy Exposure,* was recorded on September 2 and 3, again using Richard Evans's charts. Innovations for Herman included using a synthesizer and Gene Perla, who played both acoustic and amplified bass, with guests on organ and percussion. Organist Donny Hathaway's "Flying Easy," which showed the influence of Herb Alpert's Tijuana Brass, employed a sound-effects intro, plus a voice announcing a flight "departing for Woody's Sound Machine." "I Can't Get Next to You" lacked piano but featured percussion, guitar, drums, Nistico's solo, and electric bass. For the hit "Aquarius," from the musical *Hair,* Evans combined more studio effects with Herman's soprano sax, wood blocks, Alpert-like brass, and a sound-effects coda whooshing like a jet plane. Herbie Mann's "Memphis Underground" came off as mainstream 1960s rhythm-and-blues. Evans's "Lancaster Gate" evoked a military mood, and the combination of saxes hitting a hypnotic series of low notes beneath flaring brass was reminiscent of bagpipes; the number closed in a studio-enhanced fade. For "The Hut," Evans invoked studio clapping, crowd noise, and a fade. Stevie Wonder's "My Cherie Amour" floated along on an easy rock beat. Running for nearly six minutes, "Sex Machine," a blues by Sylvester Stewart, featured complex rhythm and six solos.

In late September, Herman gained an invaluable colleague in Frank Tiberi, a New Jersey native, who replaced Vicari. In addition to the tenor sax, Tiberi could also play the clarinet, flute, piccolo, and bassoon. He had worked big and small bands, such as those of Goodman, Chester, Urbie Green, and Ruby Braff. First a Cohn and Lester Young trainee, Tiberi had now absorbed Coltrane. Like many other bandsmen, Tiberi was already well acquainted with Herman and his band: "I had known Sal Nistico for a long time, and knew Frank Vicari. I had subbed a few times for Frank in the band, and heard about it when Frank was about to leave."[13] Tiberi soon became a solo star and Herman's main musical aide, standing in as leader.

Another lucky addition to the band was Anthony J. "Tony" Klatka, a twenty-three-year-old alumnus of Colorado State University and the Berklee College. For nearly three years, Klatka played trumpet and flugelhorn, composed, and arranged for Herman's band. Herman also obtained "timely help from a young pianist":[14] twenty-two-year-old Alan Broadbent. A Dave Brubeck concert in Broadbent's native New Zealand had turned him to jazz in 1964. He had attended Berklee on a *Down Beat* scholarship and studied composition, arranging, and piano and won a prize for his sonata for cello and piano. Broadbent's early show of talent was borne out in his work with Herman, and he went on to win *Down Beat*'s 1971 International Critics Poll award for the arranger deserving wider recognition.

Broadbent hated the round of performances at Army bases and Elks clubs but loved rewriting and playing rock numbers. Blood, Sweat and Tears had proved that horn bands could woo fans away from guitars, so when Broadbent wrote a big-band chart of that group's "Smiling Phases," it showcased the piano and flugelhorn and included tempo and key changes and full stops. Herman called for it at a prom, where, Broadbent said, "the kids went wild."[15] Herman was so encouraged by this reception that he also took up Klatka's chart of "Proud Mary" from Creedence Clearwater Revival. For a broadcast from Seattle, Herman programmed "It's Your Thing" and "My Cherie Amour" with "Woodchoppers' Ball," "Woody's Whistle," and "Mississippi Line" (Klatka's new idea of what a fellow trumpet player called "Louisiana swamp music"[16]), with shuffle rhythm and Herman's vocal.

For sidemen who doubled as arrangers and composers, such as Broadbent and Klatka, bus travel provided time to work. Synthesizers could be plugged into electrical systems and placed in a lap or empty seat. As new charts arrived, Herman employed a sixth sense as to what audiences wanted and what needed to be added to the book. If a piece looked good, he would have the writer lead a rehearsal while he listened, watched, and judged. Because new sidemen were well schooled and talented, rehearsals were few and short. The men could read and play a new piece a few times, let Herman change this or that, play it again, and then perform it publicly. Herman often reserved new charts for clinics to let interested people see and hear his band rehearse.

One day, Herman hit Broadbent with a challenge: "Why don't you do something with 'Blues in the Night?'" Broadbent spent a month or so sketching it. "I threw in everything I could think of," he said. "I put in baroque things; and I always had this flair for the grandiose; I knew the ending was going to be big. When I had pieced it together, and we rehearsed it [March 12–13 in Paducah, Kentucky] Woody just loved it."[17] The band backed Herman's vocal solo at the ten-minute number's premiere at the International Inn in Tampa on March 17. Herman also programmed "Caldonia," a merger of "Rose Room" and "Don't Get Around Much Anymore," "Mississippi Line," "Smiling Phases," and a new version of "The Very Thought of You."

Between March 27 and April 5, the band worked the Diplomat Hotel in Miami with Warwick and the Constellations, playing "Light My Fire," "Woodchoppers' Ball," "Aquarius," "My Cherie Amour," and "Hey, Jude!" and backing the singers on "San Jose," "What the World Needs Now," and "I'll Never Fall in Love Again." Next came three shows a night for two weeks at Al Hirt's club in New Orleans; and from April 30 to May 13, Warwick rejoined the band at New York City's Copacabana. Dressel arranged the Herman-Warwick jobs, but the team did not jell at first. As Bill Byrne sees it, "The big problem we had was that Dionne didn't have a conductor for her music. Her lead guitar player was the man in charge of getting our band started and stopped. This didn't work out very well, and she blamed the band if there were problems in the shows. Hermie Dressel got her to hire a pro conductor."[18]

On two *Dial M for Music* shows broadcast on CBS-TV in April, the band played its now familiar eclectic mix of rock and classics: "Aquarius," "My Cherie Amour," "Greasy Sack Blues," "Smiling Phases," "Mississippi Line," "Hey, Jude!" "Woodchoppers' Ball," "Laura," and "I Can't Get Next to You." *Time*'s May 11 issue recognized Herman's musical flexibility and staying power:

> Woody is as much the debonair man of the times as ever: "If I had to play the same music in a locked-in style that I played in the 1940s, I would have taken the gas pipe a long time ago." . . .
> What excites Herman these days, as it does almost everyone else, is rock. . . . The style of his current group is a near-symphonic fusion of rock and the toe-tapping, old-gold sound that was the trademark of his early bands. Mixing updated versions of old Herman specialties with ear-blowing arrangements of such contemporary tunes as "Light My Fire" and "MacArthur Park," the latest Herd has a rare ability to bridge pop music's generation gap. . . .
> Woody never speaks of retiring, and there are quiet moments when he is impressed by his own durability. "It does seem," he admits, "that I've been out there forever."[19]

By July 20, for hotel guests in Clearwater, Florida, the band was testing two more Broadbent charts. "A Time for Love" featured Tom Harrell on flugelhorn; and Herman sang the haunting lyrics of "A Stone Called Person," which described a deranged, stone-like character named Maggie Mae. By mid-August, from the Steel Pier in Atlantic City, Herman was airing "Blues in the Night" and singing Klatka's chart of the Beatles' "Let It Be."

After a spring and summer of one-nighters, plus three weeks at Caesar's Palace, the band—with some new faces due to the constant turnover—showed up at the Monterey Jazz Festival on September 19, with Soph back on drums. A couple of Duke Ellington numbers and Pierce's chart of "Body and Soul" made the programs. Wein then booked the band, Monk, Carmen McRae, and other acts for a tour of the Far East from September 29 to October 17. Bill Byrne recalls the band getting "great receptions."[20]

On October 22, warming up for its last Cadet album, *Woody*, Herman led the band in "Greasy Sack Blues," "A Stone Called Person," and Broadbent's treatment of Blood, Sweat and Tears' "25 or 6 to 4" on NBC-TV's *Tonight* show. The actual Cadet sessions took place on October 29 and 30 with Nistico and guitarist Mick Goodrick helping. Richard Evans produced the album, which consisted mostly of Broadbent's work. "A Time for Love," "Smiling Phases," and "A Stone Called Person" were included. The 6/4-time chart of "How Can I Be Sure" featured Herman on soprano sax, Klatka on flugelhorn, and Tiberi. "Blues in the Night" ran nearly fourteen minutes, with two full stops and six tempo changes; the number can be characterized as a big-band sampler, with solos by Broadbent, Nistico, Klatka on flugelhorn, and others; and dazzling work by the sections—soprano sax leading the reeds, tenor solo over piano and guitar, and a free-form passage near the end with flugelhorns scaling up and trombones easing down. Feather called it a "wildly multi-idiomatic renovation."[21] Klatka's novelty about an evil "Saccharine Sally" featured Herman's vocal and a piano solo by Broadbent.

*a*nother European tour, this time to Scandinavia and Eastern Europe, occupied the band from November 24 to December 13. An agent in Malmö, Sweden, Boo Johnson, booked the band in Poland—Martha Herman's homeland—Finland, Norway, Sweden, Denmark, Hungary, and East Germany. Bookings were in the works, too, for a festival in Montreux, the Parade du Jazz in Nice, the North Sea Jazz Festival in The Hague, and Belvedere King Size Jazz Festival concerts in Toronto, Winnipeg, and Vancouver. Herman's band was back stateside to play Caesar's Palace from December 25, 1970, to January 13, 1971. A holiday radio show contained "Woodchoppers' Ball," "Early Autumn," "Woody's Whistle," "My Cherie Amour," and "Greasy Sack Blues." When the band played a Rotary

Club benefit in East Brunswick, New Jersey, on January 23, a fan filmed a videotape of "Woodchoppers' Ball" and "Aquarius." ·

a tempting new recording contract—Herman's eleventh—ended his partnership with Cadet. Gleason had felt that Herman deserved stronger marketing than Cadet could deliver, so he put Herman in touch with the more jazz-oriented Fantasy Records in Berkeley, California. The sixty tracks that Herman made in seven Fantasy albums during 1971–75 tapped many idioms, but mainly stayed a rock-jazz course. Most of Herman's Fantasy tracks ran four to six minutes, but Broadbent's "Variations on a Scene," recorded with the Houston Symphony in 1974, lasted eighteen. For most numbers, Herman retained electric guitars, basses, and pianos and added alto flute and bassoon. This body of early 1970s work, in the opinion of *Down Beat*'s John McDonough, maintained Herman's place as "a force to be reckoned with in music."[22]

The band recorded the debut album for Fantasy, *Brand New*, in March, after a rare ten-day stint in the Claremont Hotel in Berkeley. Michael Bloomfield, a versatile guitarist from Chicago, guested on four of the eight tracks; only when Herman had teamed with Byrd had he assigned the guitar such eminence. The band's lineup still included Klatka, Burgess, Nistico, Tiberi, Broadbent, and Soph as soloists, with the amplified piano, bass, and guitar powering up the rhythm section. And, as Morton had preached, Herman called for slow tempos in which soloists could swim (see chapter 2, note 9).

Broadbent was definitely the star arranger of *Brand New*, with five charts out of the album's eight. His lilting "Sidewalk Stanley" gave Bloomfield long solo time, but the piece was flawed by Herman's muffled, old-man attempt at rock singing. "Since I Fell for You" featured warm solos by Herman on alto, Bloomfield, and Forrest Buchtel and fresh-sounding reed and full-band segments. The slow "Hitch Hike on the Possum Trot Line" starred Bloomfield, with Herman on soprano sax. Lazy brass, Herman's clarinet, and piano supported "Love in Silent Amber," Broadbent's piece for Burgess's trombone. Finally, the six-minute "Adam's

Apple" was a grab bag of novel reed voicings, some led by open trumpet, and cheerful flugelhorns. Pierce's chart of the piano blues "After Hours," which was played more than thirty years earlier by Avery Parrish for Erskine Hawkins's band, featured Broadbent's electric piano solo, an innovation for the Herman band. Pierce also arranged "I Almost Lost My Mind," a 1970s blues by Ivory Joe Hunter. Klatka's trumpet and Broadbent's piano chords elevated Herman's singing, as did Alan Read's walking bass. On Klatka's chart of "Proud Mary," one passage blended flute with trumpets, and Tiberi wedged in a flood of notes on the tenor sax; however Herman's vocal sounded weak. Indeed, as Feather reported later in 1973, "Herman now sings only rarely, saying 'I can't learn lyrics.'"[23]

Even before the release of *Brand New,* Herman played "Proud Mary" and "After Hours" on Merv Griffin's TV show on April 1, and "After Hours" again April 22 for *The Mike Douglas Show.* Subsequent engagements through the spring and summer—most of them one-nighters—continued to mix new material with oldies and boosted the better Cadet and Fantasy tracks. In California on August 15, the band teamed up with Tormé for the Concord Summer Festival and performed "Greasy Sack Blues" for Merv Griffin on August 17. Herman's band costarred with singers Rosemary Clooney and Eckstine on October 24 for an "oldies night" of such past hits as "Woodchoppers' Ball," "Four Brothers," "Early Autumn," "Laura," and "Caldonia." As Bill Byrne remembers it, "the concert was sold out, and we all got the great response that you get only in Carnegie Hall from a New York City audience."[24]

Through it all, Herman fought turnover, gaining and losing fourteen trumpet players, ten trombonists, nine saxmen, five bassists, and five drummers during the year. Bill Byrne, Tiberi, and Broadbent steadied things somewhat, but one has to wonder how Herman stuck with it. He admitted that "it gets harder as you grow older . . . when the band is good, making it musically, then I'm a pretty happy old man. But when we can't get the right drummer, or this or that—then I'm very old and uptight. Then I can't relax or have any fun."[25] Rudi Blesh feels that superb musicianship does not suffice for a band leader: "Benny Goodman with a peerage of the Dorseys, Artie Shaw, Bob Crosby, Woody Herman and Glenn

Miller, each in his own way kept his eyes on success. In our system with its rules they deserved their success. They were artists *and* businessmen or, at least, leaders."[26] Herman was certainly a leader; all his bandsmen refer to his abilities. What else? Stanley Dance, who named Basie, Herman, and Duke Ellington the "enduring triumvirate" of big-band jazz, points out that each of these leaders "is slow to anger, patient, and able to put on a good face when things go wrong. More important, each has an unfailing sense of humor."[27] Herman attributed part of his success to the type of music he played. In a conversation with Lees, he pointed out that the Duke Ellington, Basie, Kenton, and Herman bands outlived the big-band era because they all played jazz, for which there is always a hard-core audience, while in the 1930s and 1940s they played the top pop music.[28] But Herman pointed to another characteristic that is at least as essential as any other: "I still like the music, though. Otherwise, why would I knock myself out trying to find and keep good players? I could save dough by having a lame band, but if that was all that was left to me, I'd throw in the towel. I've never been in this for the money. . . . This is about music. It's about jazz. It's about excitement."[29]

When Nistico left for the last time in the fall of 1971, Herman hired Gregory Herbert, a twenty-four-year-old composer and alto-sax, tenor-sax, clarinet, flute, and piccolo player from Philadelphia. Trained in the Granoff School, then honed in Ellington's band, Herbert recorded and toured as a soloist with Herman until 1975. Soph left, and Herman replaced him with Joe LaBarbera, a native of Dansville, New York, who had played with Gap Mangione's combo.

The Herd closed 1971 and welcomed 1972 in Downsview, Ontario, then played one-nighters through no fewer than fourteen states before landing again at La Bastille in Houston for nine days, opening on February 11. That winter, the band undertook a foray into a new genre: Anshel Brusilow, conductor of the Dallas Symphony, talked to Herman about creating pieces that combined symphony and jazz orchestras could play. Broadbent took up this challenge.

Unfortunately, Broadbent quit the band as pianist in April. He had clearly left his mark on Herman's music, and more was to come.

Broadbent admitted that he was young, and "wasn't taking care of myself too well" during his twenty-eight months as the band's pianist. "I just didn't want to be part of the road anymore," he said. Broadbent credited the easy-going Bill Byrne for being "the saviour for us all, Woody included." Lees at first did not care for Broadbent's work but came to rank him as "one of the greatest pianists in jazz, and a marvelous composer."[30] Herman, meanwhile, kept his ears and mind open; he would hear, for instance, a Stevie Wonder tune and get someone to adapt it. He might ask an established arranger, such as Pierce or Holman, or an unknown or one of his own eager new sidemen to adapt it. Klatka took up pianist Chick Corea's complicated "La Fiesta"; and Pierce, still answering calls, tailored "April in Paris" and Barnet's 1940s hit "Skyliner" for Herman.

When Broadbent left, LaBarbera recommended pianist Harold Danko, who left the army to join Herman and stayed through October. During that stretch, three old-timers formed the band's mainstay: Porcino, Burgess, and Tiberi—from whom, Danko said, "everyone who went through the band learned a lot."[31]

Wein booked Herman and Harry James for a "battle of the bands" in New York City's Roseland as part of the Kool Jazz Festival on April 14. Although the Roseland had nurtured his first band in 1936, Herman ignored the past. "He enjoyed what was going on *today*," Bill Byrne said, "and what the future might bring."[32] That summer the band bused, planed, and one-nighted its way to a July 17–22 engagement at Monticello (New York) Raceway Park, then to the Sheraton St. Regis in New York, the new home city of the Newport Jazz Festival, where it played from August 17 to 30. Wein, who had helped found Newport and other festivals in the United States and abroad, was dismayed when his three-day 1971 Newport Festival had turned ugly, with wild youths setting fences on fire, breaking chairs, and smashing a stage piano. Wein consequently moved the 1972 festival to New York City for ten days on indoor and outdoor stages. Herman's Newport Festival work involved a Philharmonic Hall "reunion concert" of noted alumni, including Porcino, Phillips, Cohn, Sims, Getz, Chubby Jackson, and Norvo. After the band had played "Better Git It in Your Soul," the theme from the movie *Summer of '42*, and

"Variations on a Scene," the alumni handled "Four Brothers," "Early Autumn," and Broadbent's new "Reunion at Newport."

Herman's second Fantasy album, *The Raven Speaks,* was recorded from August 28 to 30 in A&R Studios. It thrilled Danko to make records with Herman—a "piece of history," as he put it.[33] Players included new trumpet/flugelhorn player Bill Stapleton; trombonist Burgess; and sax players Tiberi, Steve Lederer, and Herbert. Danko, bassist Al Johnson, and LaBarbera formed the rhythm section, augmented by guitarist Pat Martino and a free-lance conga player, Al Pacheco. Tiberi doubled on flute, bassoon, and cowbell, and Herbert also played piccolo, flute, and alto flute, which indicates that the charts required more versatility from the bandsmen.

The Raven Speaks included several new touches in orchestration, one of them the twenty-seven-year-old Stapleton's first efforts for Herman, "Bill's Blues." It featured Herbert and Tiberi in flute-piccolo exchanges. Stapleton, a rising star, both as a player and as an arranger, stayed with Herman until early 1974 and along the way was cited in *Down Beat* as talent deserving wider recognition. Flugelhorns colored the ballad "Alone Again (Naturally)." In Klatka's five-minute update of "Watermelon Man," guitar, congas, and rock drums added to solos by Herbert on piccolo. Herbert could be heard on the same instrument backing Herman, on soprano sax, in a version of Carole King's gentle "Too Late." In a six-minute take of Michel Legrand's "Summer of '42," a flugelhorn choir starred along with Tiberi's flute. And the versatile Broadbent, who had already written thoughtful songs, symphonic-level drama, ballads, and blues, showed his feel for happy swing when the band recorded his "Reunion at Newport."

A *New Yorker* reviewer who caught the band live described the band's sound colorfully: he had his "ears pinned to the wall by the bazooka brass section." But it wasn't just sheer volume that made the band distinctive: "Since we've listened to quite a bit of rock for the past few years, we're accustomed to volume and power, but this was power of a different sort. Rock's power is electronic . . . but the power of brass ensembles is human power, and no stereo set can really reproduce it."[34]

The Hermans celebrated their thirty-sixth wedding anniversary while he rehearsed the band on September 27 and led it in concert with the Dallas Symphony on the twenty-eighth and twenty-ninth. Broadbent had finished his music for jazz band and symphony, which evolved from "Variations on a Scene," plus "Children of Lima," a clarinet piece for Herman.

Roster changes continued. In November, when Danko, Al Johnson, and LaBarbera left, Herman formed a rhythm section with Andy LaVerne on piano, Soph back on drums, and Wayne Darling on bass. Jim Pugh, who had studied in Atlanta and Pittsburgh and at the Eastman School, replaced Burgess. Pugh, who was twenty-two when he joined the band, had played trombone and arranged for Chuck Mangione.

One-nighters along the East Coast and a break before Christmas prepared the band for year-end work at Disneyland and New Year's Eve in the Flamingo Hotel in Las Vegas. On January 13, 1973, the band worked a Superbowl eve football party in a tent outside the Rose Bowl in Pasadena. In the halftime show, it played "Blue Flame," "The Raven Speaks," and "Woodchoppers' Ball" from the playing field.

The next recording session for Fantasy, on April 9–12, yielded a dozen numbers, nine of which went into the album *Giant Steps.* Stapleton, Herbert, Lederer, Tiberi, Pugh, LaVerne, Darling, and Soph starred, and the support troops were Larry Pyatt, Gil Rathel, Walt Blanton, and Bill Byrne on trumpets, Geoff Sharp and Harold Garrett on trombones, baritone Harry Kleintank, guitarist Joe Beck, and conga drummer Ray Barretto.

Stapleton was fulfilling his early promise, with five charts in the album based on the compositions of other writers: "Think on Me," "A Song for You," "Freedom Jazz Dance," "The Meaning of the Blues," and "Giant Steps." Broadbent arranged Thad Jones's tender "A Child Is Born" and created a romping original, "Be-Bop and Roses." Richard Evans arranged "The First Thing I Do," and Klatka turned out a sizzling "La Fiesta." These numbers made up *Giant Steps.* For six years Fantasy held three other numbers—"Killing Me Softly with His Song," "Sombrero Sam," and "Don't Let Me Be Lonely Tonight"—which eventually reached the public in the 1981 album *Feelin' So Blue.*

Critical opinion on *Giant Steps* was mixed. Francis Davis, reviewing the album in *Atlantic,* panned it, saying the band "struggled" with the Coltrane, Corea, and Leon Russell music.[35] But it was hard to ignore the judgment of the National Academy of Recording Arts and Sciences, which awarded the album a Grammy, Herman's second. In Herman's words, that recognition helped his band "gather new strength."[36]

Herman made his usual appearance at the Newport Festival, this time in a battle of bands with Rich, on July 2, 1973. NBC broadcast the battle, which included "Woody's Whistle," "Four Brothers," "Satin Doll," "La Fiesta," "Summer of '42," and "Woodchoppers' Ball," on radio. Rich's charts, in the main, featured himself on the drums, just as Ferguson's trumpet playing carried his band. But those bands otherwise closely resembled Herman's in size and horn lineup. The rest of the summer was devoted to one-nighters and appearances with Mike Douglas and Merv Griffin on television. Then the band roamed the land again to take jobs, catching California's Concord Jazz Festival August 5, camping for two weeks at Disneyland, then Mister Kelly's in Chicago through September 2 and Baltimore's Left Bank Jazz Society, where Herman's young men played the band's old charts on September 16.

Bill Harris died on September 19, and Herman programmed a memorial performance, held in Rochester, New York, of "Bijou" starring Pugh. On October 29, the band flew to Frankfurt to begin a tour—again organized by Wein—of Germany, Switzerland, Holland, Belgium, Italy, Spain, and Portugal. It broadcast "Woodchoppers' Ball," "Summer of '42," "Laura," "Where Is the Love?" and "The Meaning of the Blues" from Hilversum, Holland, on November 4, jetting back November 11 to open for a week in New York City's Half Note Club. After a month of one-nighters, the band closed the year in the Los Angeles nightclub Shelly's Man Hole.

In the winter of 1973–74, it became clear that Herman's financial problems had not disappeared. He had paid little to the IRS, and now it struck again, as Bill Byrne explains: "From '69 on we had a certified public accountant in New York City taking care of the books and taxes. But the

IRS man in charge of Woody's case retired, or was moved out. A new man started from scratch and made his own case against Woody with new interest charges for the unpaid tax years."[37] This put Herman in debt for another $400,000. "Every place I went I had to make deals to keep the government off my back," Herman said. "I had to take money off the top of each booking to pay the IRS. But all we were doing was buying time."[38]

It did lift Herman's spirits any time his band made good music, as it did for Fantasy during January 2–5, 1974. Eight new powerhouse numbers went into an album called *Thundering Herd*;[39] four were held for *Feelin' So Blue*. The long-haired, bespectacled sidemen donned Thundering Herd sweatshirts and posed in a field outside the studio for the album cover photo. In keeping with the football motif, some of the men held up a broken goalpost while three others shouldered "the coach." And the coach was clearly on a roll: *Thundering Herd* went on to win Herman's third Grammy, his second in a row.

The roster included Garrett on bass trombone, the instrument's first appearance in a Herman band on record. Broadbent's arrangements of the other writers' work dominated the album. The band played his charts based on Fred Carlin's "Come Saturday Morning," Legrand's "What Are You Doing the Rest of Your Life?" and Frank Zappa's "America Drinks and Goes Home." Klatka composed "Blues for Poland" and arranged Coltrane's "Naima" and Stanley Clarke's "Bass Folk Song." Stapleton contributed charts based on Coltrane's "Lazy Bird" and Carole King's "Corazón." As always, the band changed tempi and volume, and therefore moods, throughout the album. Gary Anderson, Herbert, and Tiberi could be heard in an unusual flute-trio segment in "America Drinks and Goes Home." In "Come Saturday Morning," Tiberi registered another first in Herman recordings with a long bassoon solo. Shelved for the time being were Alf Clausen's "Feelin' So Blue," Vic Caesar's "This Time," and Klatka's "Evergreen" and "Brotherhood of Man"—a dashing, dueling-trumpets chart based on Frank Loesser's number—on which Stapleton and Klatka played.

In February, trumpeter Gary Pack replaced Klatka—who left to continue his studies—and toured with the Thundering Herd until the end of November. It was an exciting time of concerts, clinics, summer festivals, and two overseas tours. After a spell of one-nighters in the Northwest, the band flew to London on January 21 and launched a fourteen-concert jaunt across England the next night in Farnworth. But soon it was back in the States, hunting for small midwestern towns on a bus driver's maps in biting cold February weather.

On July 4, the band was off to Europe again, this time to Switzerland and the Montreux Festival, where Fantasy recorded *The Herd at Montreux.* What happened there "everybody remembers," to quote Bill Byrne.[40] The show began at 8 P.M. on July 6, with the Thundering Herd the last of four acts. Encores and other delays put the band onstage at 3:30 A.M. From about ninety minutes of music, Herman and Fantasy chose "I Can't Get Next to You," Gary Anderson's chart on a theme from *Jesus Christ, Superstar,* Pugh's workup of Billy Cobham's fugal "Crosswind," Broadbent's fast-stepping "Montevideo" and "Tantum Ergo," his homage to Duke Ellington (who had died six weeks earlier), and Anderson's chart of Aaron Copland's "Fanfare for the Common Man." Finishing after 5 A.M., the groggy bandsmen dashed to Geneva for a 9 A.M. flight to Athens. This began a string of concerts in Turkey, Denmark, Sweden, Finland, Italy, and Germany, then a flight to Toronto for a July 20 and 21 job at the Belvedere King Size Jazz Festival, quick stops in Michigan, Manitoba, and North Dakota, and two more Belvedere Festival nights in Vancouver.

The flurry of activity did not slow down, and the band began September rehearsals in Los Angeles for concerts with Sinatra, his son Frank, and daughter Nancy. Bill Byrne recalls that "Frank Sinatra was easy to work with. He knew what he wanted. His musical director, Bill Miller, rehearsed the band and Frank would drop by to see how things were going. He would sing a couple of tunes to get the feel of the band, then have Bill finish rehearsals."[41] They then took the act to Harrah's Club in Lake Tahoe from September 4 to 10, then Caesar's Palace in Las Vegas. The Thundering Herd went off for a stretch of one-nighters before rejoining Sinatra on September 29 in New York City. In the concerts that followed, Miller led the band for the Don Costa and Nelson Riddle charts Sinatra had made famous: "The Lady Is a Tramp," "All the Way," "My Way," and

"My Kind of Town." The Sinatra tour then visited Boston Garden, Buffalo's War Memorial, the Spectrum in Philadelphia, Civic Arena in Pittsburgh, and played October 12 and 13 in Madison Square Garden, where ABC televised *Sinatra—The Main Event.* Then it was on to Kansas City, Cleveland, and Houston, but the Herd bowed out on October 29 after a show in Dallas: "The Herman band got very little billing on the tour," Byrne reports. "We played one feature tune on the front of the show—'Woodchoppers' Ball'—then it was a comedian and then Sinatra for an hour." Still, the tour paid $3,750 a night, according to Byrne,[42] and Sinatra "complimented the band after every show with such warm, felicitous tags as 'You guys are great . . . the swingingest . . . the end!'"[43]

Other projects kept Herman in Texas in October. The University of Houston had started a Woody Herman archive at its school of music, and Aubry Tucker, who had played trombone in the band in 1971 and worked with Houston's jazz band during 1973–74, had induced Robert Briggs, dean of the school, to contact Dressel and Herman about the archives. The university hosted such events as a reception when the band arrived with Sinatra. "We gave all the music we weren't playing, and later sent more," Bill Byrne said,[44] and Herman donated albums, documents, and an alto sax. Siefert, who had collected Herman lore since 1937— much to Herman's bemusement—took thirty-three reels of tape and a bound index of more than two thousand records to Houston: "I took an entire summer including all my vacation to put together the music in chronological order, along with the date of the recording and the matrix number, where known. I stayed about a week, and was impressed," Siefert said. "They had a reception for the band, and Woody presented the tapes I had made plus original arrangements to be transferred to microfilm." The School of Music called Siefert's collecting, indexing and cross-referencing "a work of true dedication . . . a functional library for the Woody Herman Archives . . . which will be invaluable."[45]

After an optimistic start, however, the project turned sour. After personnel changes at the university, the school lost interest in the archive. But Bill Byrne did not give up: "By 1982, I knew the only way to save what was left of the music was to move it to the Berklee School in Boston where they had a Woody Herman ensemble. I contacted Larry Berk who had started the School. He was a good friend of Woody's. In September, 1982, I collected and boxed up all the music and sent it to Berklee. But by then no one knew where Jack Siefert's tapes were stored."[46] "What happened was never clear to me," Siefert admitted. "I heard all kinds of stories, such as some members of the School of Music saw an easy chance to pick up a collection of Woody's work. But one thing I know is that the archives at Houston never developed as promised, and I know it was a disappointment to Woody and me."[47] Berklee's archives contain music in the band's book after about 1960. "All music from 1936–1960 was lost in New York City, during the '60s, according to Nat Pierce," Byrne said. "The Berklee School has done a good job of protecting the rest."[48]

While in Texas for business with the university, Herman had reserved time days for performing and recording with the Houston Symphony. Jim Wright, manager of the Houston Symphony, was a friend of Bill Byrne's and had heard of the band's playing with the Dallas Symphony in 1972. With Dressel's help, they worked out details for two shows and a session during which they recorded part of the album *Children of Lima*, including "Variations on a Scene," which, at more than eighteen minutes, was the longest work ever recorded by a Herman band. Solo parts went to Tiberi on tenor, Pack on flugelhorn, Herman on soprano, LaVerne, and drummer Jeff Brillinger. Broadbent sustained his "flair for the grandiose" and in album notes dedicated the piece to Herman. Broadbent's sedate "Children of Lima" featured Herman on clarinet. The combined orchestras enabled Broadbent to create a wide variety of moods, ranging from tense Sibelius to wham-bam Broadway musical to Thundering Herd.

After a two-week Christmas break and one-nighters in Nevada and Colorado, the band entered Fantasy Studios in Berkeley, recording enough music on January 6, 7, and 8, 1975, to finish *Children of Lima* and start the albums *King Cobra*, issued in 1976, and *Feelin' So Blue*, issued in 1981. To complete *Children of Lima*, Broadbent turned in four more charts, among them "Far In!" in which Tiberi, Herbert, and Anderson swung a roaring, three-tenor round. Broadbent's chart of the love song "Never Let

Me Go" featured Herbert playing tenor sax, while Herbert played alto flute, at times with Tiberi's bassoon, over a light Latin beat in "Where Is the Love?" On "25 or 6 to 4," Herman on soprano, Dennis Dotson on flugelhorn, and Dale Kirkland on trombone soloed.

On January 7 the band recorded Chuck Mangione's "Echano," which contained an opening brass fanfare, a steady Latin rhythm vamp, section and ensemble passages, and solos from Pugh and Herbert on piccolo. It filled the album *Feelin' So Blue.*

Gary Anderson and Frank Tiberi, about 1973. (Courtesy Gary Anderson)

Next the band set to work on *King Cobra,* whose music stretched the definition of "mainstream" for Herman devotees. Gary Anderson, chief arranger on the album, gave the title tune, by Tom Scott, an Eastern touch, with synthesizer and solos from Pugh, Herman on soprano, and LaVerne. Bare of melody or beat—Herman's musical bread-and-butter—the piece still created a mood, starting with a drum rattle suggesting a cobra's flicking tongue. Elsewhere in the album, electric piano, bass trombone, flute, and bassoon solos filled spaces where the more conventional saxophones or trumpets had gone before. Anderson arranged Stevie Wonder's "Don't You Worry 'bout a Thing" into a lilting canvas for Herbert's flute playing. Tiberi stepped forth with his bassoon to solo in Corea's "Spain." LaVerne's playing on the electric piano filled much of "Lake Taco." "Come Rain or Come Shine," a slow study in chording and tasteful warping of a familiar melody, incorporated an unusual choir of two trombones, Vaughn Wiester's bass trombone, and Dotson's flugelhorn. An arrangement of John LaBarbera's "Toothless Grin" called for vibrato brass-playing, another sound rarely heard in Herman's music.

Herman was clearly heartened by his third Grammy, which he accepted on March 1, 1975: "Considering the climate for big bands, even one that was experimenting with electronic piano and some jazz-rock charts, we were getting good receptions, particularly at colleges."[49] But a grueling spring of one week in Disneyland and three months of one-nighters must have made the news of a personal loss particularly painful: Gleason, the author and critic who wrote liner notes for many albums, died in Berkeley on June 3 at age fifty-eight. A Herman backer with clout, Gleason pioneered in writing in depth about rock music and helped found *Rolling Stone* magazine.

One-nighters again carried the band in all directions, with a July 5 landing for a Newport Festival concert in Carnegie Hall,[50] a show in Shea Stadium, and a week at Buddy's Place in New York City. Another week in Disneyland at the end of July preceded a grind of one-nighters that kept the band crossing the United States and Canada. Herman did somehow find the time—and, dodging the IRS, the money—to start a Woody Herman–Sister Fabian Riley Scholarship Fund at his former high school in Milwaukee. The band had played Summerfest shows there on July 3 and 4 and the first of what became annual seminar-shows. Herman donated proceeds to benefit young Milwaukee-area musicians.

Between September 2 and 17, Herman was out of action due to cataract surgery in Detroit,[51] and when Iowa Public Television telecast the band with Tormé on September 24 and 25, others played Herman's solos. He then missed four days for double hernia surgery in Los Angeles before a week playing Disneyland.

The recuperating Herman must have welcomed the new venue that turned up for the Thundering Herd at year's end—a jazz cruise. From December 13 through 20, the band played on the *S.S. Rotterdam* with Getz for a cruise from New York City to the Bahamas and Bermuda. The Hermans took their granddaughter, Alexandra Littlefield, along.[52] On board Feather asked whether Herman planned to mark forty years of bandleading in 1976 with, say, a band/alumni concert. "Typically," Feather said, "Woody's reaction was casual: 'I really hadn't given it any thought; but now that you mention it, that sounds like a great idea.'"[53]

chapter eight

PAINFUL YEARS

As Herman, his friends, and musicians past and present planned the concert to celebrate his forty years as a bandleader, assorted tragedies awaited their cues. The coming decade would bring personal loss, financial distress, physical pain, and the onset of old age. Yet none of these misfortunes would defeat Herman. With his young band, he continued to experiment with adapting rock music to the big-band idiom, bringing his music to the younger generation. And in spite of slim bookings, these years would also bring honors for Herman.

Unaware of the momentous events that were facing him, Herman started his fifth decade of bandleading routinely enough. Three weeks of one-nighters in early 1976 in eight states and Canada preceded seven weeks in Europe. Polskie Nagrania Records recorded the band's concerts in Warsaw on February 25. One album contained old material, and the other featured new numbers: Beck's "Penny Arcade," Copland's "Fanfare for the Common Man," "Spain," "Corazón," "Kilgore Trout," and "MacArthur Park."

Stateside, one-nighters resumed in March at the Fountains in Bellville, New Jersey, and the band crossed the United States and Canada until a vacation in June. Until late August, the band was on the move again for dates with Bennett in Ohio and Michigan and a week in Disneyland. In one broadcast in July, the band aired "Toothless Grin," plugging Fantasy's *King Cobra* album.

For a two-hour concert from the Jai Alai Palace in Dania, Florida, taped on August 28, Herman used "Penny Arcade," "Fanfare for the Common Man," Stevie Wonder's "You Are the Sunshine of My Life," Stephen

Sondheim's "Send in the Clowns," and Gary Anderson's "Pavane," which was based on a classical theme by Gabriel Fauré. Further shows that fall were coappearances with such singers as Anita Bryant, Sarah Vaughan, and Bennett.

For Herman's fortieth anniversary, PBS producers spliced ninety minutes of his old movie clips, TV guest shots, concerts, and interviews for airing on November 2. The anniversary concert would follow on November 20 in Carnegie Hall. Inviting past musicians and creating one program from forty years of charts challenged Herman; so many people and so much music had to be left out.

Anniversary concert logistics took time. Norvo couldn't miss a club job he was working. But Burns left a tour with a show he was writing, Getz flew over from Europe, and Pierce gathered more stars, while others delved into the archives in Houston to find old music. The day before the concert, the "alumni" converged at the New York Sheraton across from Carnegie Hall. Chubby Jackson said: "If this were an old timers' ball game, people would be amazed to see a cat get to first base; but we mean business! We're here for home runs!"[1]

RCA Records' Ken Glancy arranged for the recording of a concert album. "Our company had [recorded] nothing of Woody's," he said. "I wanted to correct that deficiency. The anniversary was the perfect opportunity."[2] Lees predicted in the *Saturday Review* that the album, produced on the Gryphon Records label, would be "an important historic document, for the band has probably produced more major jazz musicians than any other. . . . The scope of Herman's influence on American music is beyond estimation. And it continues: critics and musicians alike agree that his present virtuosic band is the best he has ever led. Such is the band's precision, coherence, exuberance and power that—heard in person—it is almost overwhelming, one of the most exciting experiences available in contemporary music." Bands playing Glenn Miller's and Tommy Dorsey's music still toured, but Herman dismissed them as mere "ghost bands" and vowed there would be none after his death, because his bands' music—and players—never stayed the same. As Herman said, "People say, 'Wow, what young guys in the band!' The musicians have always been in the same age bracket. The band stayed young. The Coach got old, that's all.[3]

Herman and his fifteen regulars, billed as the New Thundering Herd, appeared with eighteen guests. Seated in the trumpet section at the time were Dotson, Alan Vizzutti, Nelson Hatt, John Hoffman, and Bill Byrne. The trombone players were Pugh, Kirkland, and Jim Daniels. Tiberi, Gary Anderson, Joe Lovano, and John Oslawski played the saxes. Pat Coil on keyboard, Rusty Holloway on bass, and Dan D'Imperio on drums formed the rhythm section. The roster of guest performers included Stiles, Pete and Conte Candoli, Phil Wilson, Cohn, Getz, Marowitz, Phillips, Sims, Giuffre, Burns, Rowles, Pierce, Chubby Jackson, Bauer, Hanna, Lamond, and McCall.

Feather, as emcee, welcomed fans to the "celebration of love." The rising curtain revealed the Herd attired in leisure suits, playing "Blue Flame" from behind smart music stands showing the cover of *The Raven Speaks*. A beaming Herman, open-collared, clarinet ready, ambled onstage to a cascade of applause. "Thank you," he said as the theme music faded. "Lovely to be here, and I just want to say, before we go on, from the bottom of my heart, thank you." (Applause) "And I sincerely mean that. Now—I don't want to keep you waiting. I've got some marvelous 'cats' here, and I want them to blow right at ya." With that Herman started five minutes of "Apple Honey," cheering on the soloists: "Say hello to Flip Phillips, yeahhhh!" . . . "That's Jimmy Pugh! Jimmy Pugh!" . . . "Phil Wilson, Phil Wilson!" . . . "Pete Candoli, Don Lamond, Chubby Jackson, Phil Wilson, take a bow!" Recalling how well Phillips, and "Sweet and Lovely," went over in the 1946 Carnegie Hall concert, Herman programmed that number next.

Herman enjoyed announcing "Four Brothers" because he was able to feature Getz, adding "here's the man that wrote it, Jimmy Giuffre!" . . . "Here's Al Cohn, I'd know him anywhere!" . . . and "Zoot Sims, my man!" Purists may have noted that the performance ignored the baritone part; still, Herman exclaimed: "That's some kind of brothers!" Herman then turned the Candoli brothers loose on "Brotherhood of Man." "Beautiful, men!" Herman exclaimed. He introduced Burns as "one of the truly great giants—great composers-arrangers of all time" and rated "Early Autumn" as "one of the loveliest things I've had the pleasure of doing." Then, as Burns played the piano, Herman brought out Getz—"one of the giants of any kind of music, who just happened to show up from Europe"—to play the solo that helped launch his career. McCall, who was free-lancing in Los Angeles, came on next for a kicky "Wrap Your Troubles in Dreams," with solos from Pierce, Phillips, and Herman on clarinet. In a tribute to Bill Harris, Herman called on Pugh for "Everywhere" and Phil Wilson for "Bijou." Herman ended the "alumni" segment with the Coppola-Guaraldi blues number known since 1956 variously as "Blues Groove," "G Blues," "Country Cousins," and now "Cousins." Cohn, Giuffre, Rowles, and Getz soloed; Lamond started on drums, and Hanna finished. So well did "Cousins" go, Herman opted to "stretch it" and forgo "Woodchoppers' Ball."

Zoot Sims and Al Cohn, alumni of the Four Brothers Band, about 1980. (Courtesy Nick Puopolo)

After the intermission, Herman led the young Herd playing its new music: "Penny Arcade," with solos from Coil, Herman on soprano, Gary Anderson, Dotson, Lovano on tenor, and Pugh; Hubbard's "Crisis," starring Dotson, Pugh, and Lovano; and Pugh on Chuck Mangione's "She's Gone." "Fanfare for the Common Man," Herman said, "takes in all of us"; he played soprano sax and soloed with Lovano. For six years Herman also had enjoyed Broadbent's chart ("it shows all sorts of things") of "the ever-lovin' 'Blues in the Night.'" He presented a shortened version that ran just ten minutes, bringing down the house on the last lyrics: "Mama was right, there's blues in the . . . man, that's *somekindablues,* believe me!"

As a four-minute centerpiece for Getz, Herman chose "Blue Serge," a 1941 piece by Duke Ellington's son, Mercer. Gary Anderson arranged its wistful theme. Herman called Getz back for "Blue Getz Blues" and added a clarinet solo. Finally Herman chose "a group thing that takes in all age groups," a mass performance of "that great love song, 'Caldonia.'"

But before counting the tempo to get it going, he again thanked the audience, and "my lovely family, who came from different areas of the country to hang out with the old man"—referring to his wife, their remarried daughter, Ingrid Reese, and her children.

RCA released its two-LP *Fortieth Anniversary Concert* album in 1977. Tormé, who also hooked up with Gryphon Records—which had recorded Legrand, Horne, and Herman within a few month—pronounced: "I thought the Horne and Herman records were among the best things those two artists had ever done."[4] *Down Beat* called the album tracks "mostly spirited if sometimes uncertain reunion pieces. . . . All in all, a not-quite-great concert, but full of warmth and fun."[5] But Herman saw it as a high note for starting his fifth decade as a "coach."

*h*erman recalled all the hectic travel of the 1970s with fondness: "We were still thundering across the country in the '70s, me by car, the band by bus and plane. Driving across the country, from tank town to city to tank town, still gave me the feeling of independence I had enjoyed since I first left Milwaukee. I made practically all the jumps by car, sometimes alone, sometimes with Charlotte."[6] However, seventy-some one-nighters in the first twelve weeks of 1977 wore everyone down: A supper club in Illinois. A theater in Ohio. A high school in Virginia.

The rigors of road travel contributed to high turnover in Herman's bands. Here, trombonist John Fedchock and drummer Jeff Hamilton catch a few moments to relax in an airport, summer 1983. (Courtesy John Fedchock)

A Howard Johnson in Texas. On to Albuquerque, Scottsdale, Los Angeles. North and South Dakota. Manitoba. Minnesota, Illinois, Wisconsin. Atlantic City, Washington. Nova Scotia.

The law of averages caught up with Herman the afternoon of March 27. He left Great Bend, Kansas, at about 10 A.M., driving alone to Manhattan for a three-hour afternoon seminar and two-hour concert at Kansas State University. He fell asleep at the wheel at about 2 P.M. near the army hospital at Ft. Riley, just a few miles from the Kansas State campus. Many motorists and an army ambulance crew saw the head-on crash. It injured no one else seriously, but it crushed Herman's left leg. Surgeons in St. Mary's Hospital in Manhattan implanted steel pins up to his hip. He stayed there about five weeks, then recuperated, with therapy, in his Hollywood home (borrowing a wheelchair from Basie's wife). Tiberi, who could double on clarinet or alto to play Herman's solos, led the band, as did clarinet star Buddy DeFranco for ten shows. But without Herman, some venues canceled or paid the band reduced prices. Gary Anderson recalls that "the band realized how essential [Herman] was when he was absent." While Herman's leg mended, bad news shattered his spirit: Charlotte Herman had developed breast cancer. Five years of chemotherapy and other treatments followed. Herman said that she "handled things well."[7]

As a consequence of the accident, Herman missed a show with James's band on April 27 in Pittsburgh, a week during the Kool Jazz Festival in Honolulu, and an engagement with Super Sax—a five-year-old quintet playing arrangements of Parker's music—at Redlands University. He did roll onto the Redlands stage in a wheelchair to say hello, thereby honoring a contract that called for him to appear. Just before his sixty-fourth birthday, Herman managed a flight to Boston to accept an honorary doctor of music degree from Berklee College. Herman flew to his band's May 21 job with the Syracuse Symphony, but Tiberi played Herman's solos in "Children of Lima," leaving Herman only to greet the crowd, thus keeping sponsors from having to cancel. Using a walker, he rejoined the band in Cleveland, emceeing jobs with Eckstine at a new theater complex from May 27 to June 5. Trading the walker for a cane but still limping, Herman played later in June. His driving days were over; he missed the freedom of making his own schedules but found it less tiring to take buses and planes or have someone else drive.

During June 17–21 in New York City, he played the clarinet and alto and soprano sax ("Body and Soul," "Rose Room," "Early Autumn," and "Mood Indigo") and sang ("Caldonia") in a studio septet for a Lionel Hampton Presents series album. One-nighters went on for the band, then a *Mike Douglas Show* telecast from Philadelphia with Liza Minnelli, and scattered dates with Herbie Mann's combo, Bennett, Bob Hope, Ferguson, Rich, and Corea.

*t*o be sure, McDonough placed Herman in a second tier of musicians, claiming that Goodman "is the only bankable jazz star left who can pack a concert hall by himself."[8] Maybe so. Herman did, of course, draw crowds when costarring, but his band seldom wanted for one-night jobs, either. On September 22, it embarked on a seven-week tour across Europe; Herman led the men to what a promoter called "the world's northern-most jazz festival" in Umea, Sweden, the Jazzjamboree Warszawa in Po-land—where Polskie Nagrania recorded another album from a concert on October 23—and the Berliner Jazztag in Germany. One-nighters in the United States resumed on November 9 in Schenectady, New York, fol-lowed by a Christmas break, five days at Disneyland. Herman must have been thankful to see the end of 1977, a year marked by ill health for his wife and pain and lessened mobility for himself. For the band, it had been another merry-go-round year—Herman had hired thirty-two men for fifteen spots. The turnover would worsen in 1978, when fifteen trumpet-ers, six bassists, six drummers, six trombonists, nine sax players, and two pianists sat in.

Dressel and Century Records in Hollywood worked out a three-album deal, which Herman fulfilled in early 1978. According to Bill Byrne, "Century wanted the bands of Benny Goodman, Buddy Rich and Woody Herman because we all had material we could play without mistakes for [the new process of] direct-to-disc recordings. Each album side was re-corded non-stop. We used six trumpets because Woody wanted to get Vizzutti's 'Fire Dance' recorded. Alan had left the band in New Orleans in November, and moved to Los Angeles [but] knew all the music we were going to record. It helped to have two lead trumpet players [Vizzutti and Jay Sollenberger] to spell each other on the non-stop process."[9] In Holly-wood on January 3 and 4, Herman led the band's first studio recordings in three years. Century named the first album *Road Father*—an endearing reference to Herman. The band, to which Century Records affixed no gimmick name—no Swingin' Herd, no New Thundering Herd, no Young

Thundering Herd—now included five trumpet players, all of whom could double on flugelhorn; three trombonists; and Tiberi, Lovano, Gary Anderson, and Bruce Johnstone on the saxes. Tiberi doubled on flute and bassoon; Anderson, on flute, alto flute, and piccolo; Lovano, on flute; Johnstone, on bass clarinet and flute; and trumpet player Hatt, on piccolo trumpet.

"Fire Dance" starred Vizzutti in a fast, brassy fiesta mood; Herman soloed on soprano sax. In Mingus's "Duke Ellington's Sound of Love," Herman on alto and Tiberi on tenor soloed in the slow number, which Wiester arranged for the band. Herman called for a four-bar piano/bass/drums intro to "Woodchoppers' Ball," but otherwise the piece endured as the ageless blues-riff. In this first commercial recording of the tune since 1958, Herman respected the original in his clarinet solo—there were also solos by Tiberi on tenor sax, Larry Farrell on trombone, Glenn Drewes on trumpet, and Coil—but fresh writing reflected new chording and voicings, with more ensemble dynamics near the finish. Johnstone wrote, arranged, and soloed on his limber baritone sax in "Sunrise Lady," unique in its fast-flamenco feel, and a passage near the end teamed trumpet and electric piano. "Pavane" featured Herman on clarinet and Johnstone on bass clarinet, backed up by Hatt on piccolo trumpet, Tiberi on bassoon, and Lovano and Gary Anderson on flute. For "I've Got News for You," both Herman and Johnstone sang the wry lyrics (". . . you said your life was tame, but I took you to a nightclub and the whole band knew your name!") while Dotson on flugelhorn and Johnstone on baritone soloed. The solo part on Parker's "Dark Shadows," transcribed for reeds by Shorty Rogers in 1947, stayed in this update by Wes Hensel, but Hensel put in a flugelhorn lead for Dotson to replace the alto sax of Rogers's version. Broadbent's "Sugar Loaf Mountain" featured Birch Johnson and Coil. A Stevie Wonder pop tune, "Isn't She Lovely," provided solo time for Marc Johnson on acoustic bass, Johnstone on baritone, Lovano on tenor, and Herman on clarinet.

Two more Century albums quickly followed, between January 5 and 26, presenting wildly contrasting music. The first, *Together/Flip & Woody*, reunited Phillips with the band and contained love songs warmly played but light on jazz. Credits printed with the album reflect how complicated record making had become: Herman and Glen Glancy were listed as "producers," Gary Anderson served as "musical director" and "orchestra conductor," and others received credit as "disc mastering supervisor" and "mixing engineers." One firm provided direct-to-disc process cutting styli, another made the lacquer masters, while Century and a company in West Germany handled "disc processing and pressing."

The Herman-Phillips team recorded "You Will Be My Music," "There Is No Greater Love," "Easy Livin'," "We'll Be Together Again," "The Very Thought of You," "The Nearness of You," "How Deep Is the Ocean?" and "I Won't Last a Day without You." Violinist Harry Bluestone led a small string ensemble in the last four numbers. This album was odd in that Herman had so little to do. Nor was the easy-listening stuff, based upon syrupy love songs with but few brassy bursts from the band, typical Herman.

New, hard-core jazz, however, was the focus of *Chick, Donald, Walter and Woodrow,* recorded on January 25–26 with guest artists Feldman (vibraharp and synthesizers), Tom Scott (saxes and lyricon), Mitch Holder (guitar), Bill Ross (flute), and Biviano (trumpet). Corea's "Suite for a Hot Band" contained three "movements," running nineteen-plus minutes. Herman wrote for the album's notes: "Chick and I got into a thing about maybe having him write something special for the band. He decided the piece would be a suite in three movements. The first would be a lot of fun to play and be impressive musically . . . like 'Stravinsky meets Sousa.'" The first movement was more Stravinsky than Sousa, with solos by Lovano, Coil, and Herman on clarinet, plus flute-and-piccolo episodes. The second movement, in which Herman sang weakly but played the clarinet adroitly, and Tiberi on tenor, Dotson, and Birch Johnson soloed, was more of a stampede. The last section, with its Latin beat, featured spiraling solos by Holder, Feldman on percussion, Coil, Dotson, Lovano, Johnson, Herman on soprano, and Hatt on piccolo trumpet. "Suite for a Hot Band" lacked a Herd sound or lingering melody, perhaps because the men were playing written music instead of cutting loose. The rest of the charts were based on tunes by Donald Fagen and Walter Becker (who performed and recorded as Steely Dan). Roccisano earned a Grammy nomination for his chart of "Green Earrings"; there was a fast, light, sort of swing to it, with Tom Scott murmuring just a bit on the lyricon (which sounds like an amplified flute), Johnstone playing baritone sax, and some pleasant tinklings from Feldman's vibes. But in general, the album was another letdown for Herman fans; it did little swinging and produced "odd" sounds. As in *Together/Flip & Woody,* this album missed the master's touch. Herman played little, deferred to the composers, and farmed out the writing to distant free-lancers.

The band next hit the road, playing those anything-for-a-buck jobs, school clinics, supermarket openings, dances, conventions, Elks Clubs, and Legion Halls. Band members judged six high school bands and played a Milwaukee concert for the Sister Fabian Riley Fund. They spent a week at Disneyland, played with Corea in Avery Fisher Hall, played a show in Chicago with Eckstine, and worked the Harlem Jazz Festival. Another tour opened October 10 in England, and ended on November 6 in Sweden. Back in the United States, six more weeks of one-nighters carried the band to a Christmas break and a week at Knotts Berry Farm near Buena Park, California.

*I*n 1979, a year full of one-nighters and devoid of bookings with other stars, twenty-nine players trooped in and out of the band. The band had a pleasant change of pace aboard the riverboat *Mississippi Queen,* where they gave three nights of concerts in February. And there were the usual venues: a Newport Jazz Festival concert, a European tour, a week in Disneyland, and a concert from the Monterey Jazz Festival.

The three Century albums had sold poorly, and Herman would endure a thirty-month wait to record again. During the hiatus he saw many of his finest oldies pirated, copied, and retailed on the black market. There was no practical way for him or the many other victims to stop it. Still without a record deal, Herman considered it "vital that this band be recorded," so Herman and Dressel hired Wally Heider to bring a recording truck to the concert at Monterey. Getz, trombonist Slide Hampton, and trumpet players Woody Shaw and Gillespie guested at Herman's concert. There one could notice two changes: amplified piano, bass, and guitar, in use since 1968, were gone from the band, and acoustic bass and piano were back; and Herman sang nothing and soloed only on soprano and alto sax.

*h*erman still growled at nostalgia, such as William P. Gottlieb's pictorial *The Golden Age of Jazz*. For Simon's *Best of the Music Makers*, he said, almost defiantly: "If I thought there weren't any more challenges in life, I would have thrown in the towel. But as long as there is a challenge, living is fun!" Herman rated the new generation of musicians capable of creating music more exciting than any of its predecessors ever could. And when Simon asked him which of his many bands was his favorite, Herman fired back: "The band I'm going to have next year."[10]

Herman in blackface with clarinet in the Zulu Parade, New Orleans, 1980. (Photo by Laura de Vincent, courtesy Gary Anderson)

A signal honor was awaiting Herman in New Orleans after vacation and a month of one-nighters early in 1980. Herman and his band had always been able to break racial barriers when society had allowed them to. In the words of Chuck Stone, "For a white boy, Woody Herman kicked some audacious jazz tail."[11] And Duke Ellington once remarked that "Woody Herman is the one bandleader whose beliefs and music follow the true tradition and direction of our people's music."[12] Now Freddy Coleman, a black drummer with the Dukes of Dixieland, had invited Herman's white band to play for the all-black Krewe of Zulu's 1980 Mardi Gras ball and to ride its parade float. On Friday night, February 15, the band played the Zulu Ball at the River Gate. On Saturday and Sunday it worked Al Hirt's club in the French Quarter, and on Monday a junior college in Mississippi. The next morning the men smeared on blackface and played from the Zulu float. Herman considered it an honor, but it was hard work, as Bill Byrne describes it. "We didn't have a sound system, piano, or electric power as we had been promised."[13]

The band's appearance opened doors and minds. Tom Gaskill, a Hyatt Regency executive, felt the band could draw New Orleans tourists, just as Dixielander Pete Fountain's live-in combo pleased crowds at the

Hilton. But Gaskill had nothing to compete with Fountain other than an empty concrete shell next door. Herman liked the idea of a home base, however, so Gaskill approached investors about equipping the shell for a music hall. The band could play there eight or nine months a year, then tour or vacation the other months. Travel would be reduced, cutting overhead and turnover. And when the band did travel, it might be more in demand and get higher fees. (Costs had reached the point that it needed $18,000 a week to break even on the road.)

While deals were being mulled for a "Woody Herman's" nightclub, the band played one-night jobs in fifteen states. Wein set up a Carnegie Hall weekend—"Mel Tormé and Friends"—on March 28–30, with Herman and the band, Shearing, Mulligan, O'Day, Teddy Wilson, and Bill Evans. "What friends!" Tormé exclaimed. During April 14–28, between train and bus rides lasting up to five hours, the band played in Argentina, Uruguay, and Colombia, then jetted to England for shows from May 12 to 24. One-nighters back in the United States carried the band to a week at Disneyland in mid-June and a show with singer Tina Turner at Belmont Park in New York. Such high-profile jobs were rare, though. In July, for example, the Young Thundering Herd played a Lithuanian Club in Pennsylvania and Polish Festival Days in Michigan.

For the balance of 1980, Herman's big band roamed the land with little rest. It played New Year's Eve in the Hyatt Regency in New Orleans, then resumed one-nighters in early 1981, crossing Virginia, South Carolina, Georgia, Tennessee, Alabama, Louisiana, Texas, Maine, New Jersey, Connecticut, New York, and Pennsylvania. On and on the jobs came and went, in ballrooms, country clubs, high school gyms, colleges, lounges, motor lodges, theaters. A dip into Canada in mid-March touched Winnipeg, Regina, Saskatoon, and Vancouver. The band played in the Hollywood Bowl during the Playboy Jazz Festival on June 10. Between June 29 and July 3 it staged workshops and concerts at State University of New York in Binghamton, then moved on to the renamed Kool Newport Jazz Festival, then to Belmont Park with singer Andy Williams on July 19.

Herman had been concerned that the band made no commercial recordings in 1980, and Dressel had not succeeded in selling the 1979

Monterey tapes in New York and Los Angeles. But in early 1980, Hanna had convinced Carl "Jeff" Jefferson of Concord Records to market Herman's music. Jefferson had started a summer festival in Concord, thirty miles northeast of San Francisco, and had founded his record company in 1973. As the festival grew, Jefferson led a drive to build the 8,500-seat Concord Pavilion, which housed his jazz festival every August. Jefferson envisioned a "Woody Herman Presents" album series featuring small jam groups. In August 1980, he produced the first of three, *A Concord Jam*, with trumpeter Warren Vache, tenor saxophonist Dick Johnson, clarinetist Eiji Kitamura, vibes player Cal Tjader, bassist Bob Maize, guitarist Cal Collins, McKenna, Hanna, and Herman. The group recorded generic ten-piece combo music in Concord Pavilion. Herman played clarinet only on "Woodchoppers' Ball" and in a duet with Kitamura, a fiftyish, self-taught musician from Tokyo. Jefferson also agreed to package the 1979 Monterey tapes for a big band album, *Woody Herman and Friends,* in 1981.

Concord then put together *Woody Herman Presents Four Brothers* in July 1981 in New York City with Cohn, Nistico, Perkins, Phillips, Bunch, Lamond, and bassist George Duvivier. Buyers heard the Four Brothers saxes, but not one note from Herman. And still his band made no records.

The big band ended its recording hiatus on August 15 in Concord's *The Woody Herman Big Band Live at the Concord Jazz Festival,* which included guest stars Getz and Cohn. Herman called it "the best sounding big band album that I have been associated with in forty-six years."[14] As always, new names filled the band: trumpeters Stapleton, Brian O'Flaherty, Scott Wagstaff, Marc Lewis (the son of alumnus Cappy Lewis), and George Rabbai; trombonists Fedchock, Gene Smith, and Larry Shunk; and saxophonists Bill Ross (subbing for Tiberi), Paul McGinley, and Randy Russell, plus Mike Brignola on baritone. Mike Hall played acoustic and electric bass, and Dave Ratajczak was the drummer. McGinley doubled on flute, while Rabbai joined Herman in singing novelties and bop-style scats. The album showcased pianist/arranger John Oddo, who joined in late 1980 and stayed till early 1983.

Concord opened the album with Mercer Ellington's "Things Ain't What They Used to Be" (Herman assured audiences that "they sure ain't!").

Unison reeds and brass punched the solos by Cohn and Herman on clarinet. The band swung for six minutes on Holman's contrapuntal "Midnight Run." Rabbai, Bill Ross, Stapleton on flugelhorn, and Herman on clarinet soloed. The drumming and Ross's piccolo playing imparted a jaunty march mood to Oddo's "John Brown's Other Body." Getz soloed on a flowing Holman chart of Luiz Eca's "The Dolphin." The album ended with Oddo's rewrite of "Lemon Drop," in which Rabbai starred both as scat singer and on flugelhorn in a chain of soloists. In a sort of benediction, Herman said: "That's the way bebop was!"

*d*own *Beat* reported plans for the grand opening of Woody Herman's on September 15. The place would hold five hundred in banked, theater-style seats and be managed by the Hyatt Regency. Herman's band would play cavalcade-of-jazz shows for about thirty-six weeks a year. Loyola University had even approached Herman about teaching. While final plans were still being worked out, Herman flew to Japan to solo at the Aurex Jazz Festival with a seventeen-piece band led by Lionel Hampton. He arrived back in mid-September to find Woody Herman's still unfinished.

Woody Herman's finally opened on December 27, and *Newsweek* covered the event. The show, called "From New Orleans to Swing," began with oldies, then shifted to the new with "Theme in Search of a Movie," a calypso-flavored piece by Oddo. The band played "Pavane" and "Fanfare for the Common Man" before a jam session with the Heritage Hall Jazz Band. "Herman, snapping his fingers and smiling broadly, picked up his clarinet and, head thrown back and eyes closed tight, began plucking notes out of the stratosphere," Annalyn Swan reported in *Newsweek*. "He seems genial but rather bland, as if the millions of miles he has traveled have smoothed away his sharper contours. [But] Herman is as musically eclectic and exciting as they come. 'I'm not interested in my generation,' says Herman. 'I want to experiment, to reach the young.'"[15] Gary Giddins's profile of Herman echoes this sense of mission: "Herman Herds . . . have served in the role of a Greek chorus, commenting on, interpreting and reworking the changes in jazz. He's in constant deadlock with his audience, which is forever demanding the old stuff."[16]

Woody Herman's had opened, but it still lacked some fixtures and lighting, causing inconvenience and discomfort for audience and players alike. What's more, although the band played for five months, people would see Herman on Canal Street and ask what he was doing in town. Herman was convinced that "if there had been good publicity everything might have been great."[17]

The band left for Disneyland in mid-May, then turned to one-nighters from California to Florida to Virginia and Ohio, hoping for a finished Woody Herman's in October and a better second season. But then Herman received jolting news from home: Charlotte Herman had stopped taking chemotherapy, and the cancer was spreading. He lived on the telephone.

It was a worried Herman who led the band to Japan for the Aurex Jazz Festival in August. In Yokohama Stadium, Herman's and Jaco Pastorius's big bands, Brubeck's Quartet, and festival all-stars—including Cohn, Flory, Nistico, and Phillips—performed. Toshiba-EMI released selections from Herman's festival concerts in Eastworld albums. Jefferson obtained rights to enough of Herman's Aurex Festival music for a Concord album, *World Class,* which was issued in 1984.

Herman nixed an appearance in Rome to play in "Ebony Concerto" for a Stravinsky centennial at La Scala; he felt that his own style of jazz had evolved over the years and he didn't want to undertake the concerto, which he considered a classical piece. Moreover, he did not entirely trust his false teeth with the difficult part.[18] Stateside one-nighters resumed on September 10, and the band flew to the opening of the Epcot Center in Disneyworld on October 22. The event showcased the bands of Herman, Basie, and James, the Glenn Miller "ghost band," Fountain, Lionel Hampton, Bob Crosby, and singer Joe Williams.

But back in New Orleans, the gloom thickened. Woody Herman's still hadn't quite gotten off the ground. Backers never came up with promised money, and a deal fell through to air three costly shows already taped for TV. Contractors reneged, promo ideas died. A plan to bring tourist busloads to Woody Herman's dissolved. A proposed radio show never came off; Herman taught nothing at Loyola. The money ran out. And in Hollywood, Charlotte Herman lay close to death.

On November 9, Herman told the band that the nightclub would fold, which meant that his men had to face three weeks without work. Herman flew home to Hollywood, where Charlotte Herman died on November 20. Just weeks before, Herman had cited as his greatest record that he had been married and in love with the same woman for forty-six years. November 30 saw Herman back at work already, at Fat Tuesday's in New York City, where he played in a small group with Oddo through December 4. It was therapy for his grief, plus he knew the IRS would frown if it did not get its weekly tribute. He gathered a full band, played eleven one-nighters, then tried to rest and regroup from December 19 to 30.

Despite setbacks, Herman was able to take a big band out again by early 1983. "As long as you're on the road you have musical freedom," he reasoned. "If you stay put long enough you're going to wind up playing music somebody else wants you to play. And I'm too old and stubborn for that."[19] The band roamed Kansas, Iowa, Illinois, Missouri, Indiana, West Virginia, Tennessee, and returned to New Orleans on January 23. Then it was off to Arkansas, Oklahoma, Alabama, and Georgia, up the East Coast, then out to Ohio.

In April, during another three-week band layoff, Herman played in two record projects in California. Concord taped volume 3 in its "Woody Herman Presents" series live from a concert with nine other musicians in the Great American Music Hall in San Francisco. A fair amount of jam-session music filled the album, which was called *A Great American Evening*. But there was little of Herman; he sang and played the clarinet on "I've Got the World on a String" and "Caldonia" and played on "Pennies from Heaven" and one of Ron McCroby's tracks, "Wave." Then on April 20–21, Eastworld recorded nine tunes with a Herman-Kitamura sextet composed of two clarinets with rhythm section.

The one-nighters with the full band resumed on April 22 in Pittsburgh, from which the band tore off to Cleveland for a rehearsal the next afternoon with Clooney. After a week working the likes of a junior high in

Iowa, a high school in Nebraska, and a junior college in Colorado, the band landed at Caesar's Palace in Lake Tahoe for three weekend shows with singer Natalie Cole. Herman's seventieth birthday took place during a twelve-day job at the Fairmount Hotel in San Francisco. In June, the band costarred in a number of festival concerts and toured Europe for much of July, followed by a week at Disneyland.

Significantly, for the band's next venture in recording, *My Buddy*, it was not the band that was featured so much as Clooney, with whom the band played at the Concord Pavilion on August 7. Clooney had made seven albums for Concord Records, among them salutes to Holiday, Porter, Arlen, and Bing Crosby. On August 10 and 11, Concord taped her in Hollywood singing eight tunes backed by Herman's band and soloists. Musically, the album appealed to a wide range of tastes. The cover photo of *My Buddy*, which was issued before the end of the year, pictured the radiant Clooney and the smiling, leisure-suited Herman in a friendly hug. But Herman only briefly played his clarinet (on Duke Ellington's "I'm Beginning to See the Light") and played a few alto sax fills.

Economics dictated that *My Buddy* would be the band's last album in nearly three years. Interest in the music videos that were aired on cable TV stations was soaring, which cut into the market for LP records. Jazz groups entered the video market slowly, so Herman's band played on the road as before, and more often for TV. On September 18, however, when the band performed "Blue Flame," "Peanut Vendor," "Perdido," and "Fanfare for the Common Man" at the Monterey Jazz Festival, the event was captured on video.

Then one-nighters, some with Bennett, kept the band busy until a November fortnight in Europe. High school and college dates, and a six-night stay in Minnesota for shows with Bennett, ended the year. One-nighters resumed on January 7, 1984, in Atlanta and ended after three weeks in Maine. During a one-month layoff for the band, Herman worked the Rainbow Room in New York City with Vache, Rabbai, Hanna, Bunch, Duvivier, and tenor saxophonist Scott Hamilton. A jazz-oriented singer in her early thirties, Polly Podewell, widened this combo's appeal.

Herman re-formed a big band for jobs in late February, then led it to Maine, Massachusetts, Quebec, and Ontario, then Chicago and the Corn Belt. In ensuing months the band appeared with Bennett, Calloway, Clooney, Jack Jones, and the Four Freshmen.

A PBS-TV special, although it involved the appearances of other musicians, definitely reserved the starring role for Herman and the band. For *Woody Herman's Big Band Celebration,* taped October 16–17, the Herd shared the stage in Houston with Pete Barbutti, Terry, Joe Williams, Kay Starr, and the Dukes of Dixieland. In the show's dramatic opening, "Woodchoppers' Ball" was heard through the sound of a helicopter zeroing in on the outdoor theater, with cameras catching Houston at twilight. In the mood-trombone slot, Fedchock played his chart of "What's New?" and the band's majestic "Fanfare for the Common Man" was awe-inspiring.

Herman on alto sax fronting the full band, July 1984. (Courtesy John Fedchock)

With the death of Basie in April, the time was ripe for retrospectives and opinions concerning the dubious future of big bands. But it was also a time to acknowledge accomplishments. The National Academy of Recording

Arts and Sciences enshrined "Four Brothers" in its Hall of Fame in 1984; the same year, the Big Band Hall of Fame inducted Herman. The numeral "1" on his plaque indicated that he was the first inductee (followed by Whiteman and Glenn Miller). Siefert, who stood at Herman's side that day, said "they felt this was the right order because Woody had been out there for nearly fifty years, and did so much for exposing the young talent in America and around the world. They felt Whiteman was due the honor because he was the first to make big band jazz acceptable and commercial. Miller was honored for his great popularity during the World War II years and his service in the army, although as a major bandleader he had only been out there for a five-year period."[20]

Time-Life Music also caught on to the nostalgia mood and produced a boxed set of Herman records in its Big Bands series. The twenty-one recordings—made between 1939 ("Woodchoppers' Ball") and 1947 ("Keen and Peachy")—were acquired from Decca and Columbia, enhanced to meet higher audio standards, and marketed with a pamphlet written by critic John Wilson. Two of the cuts never had been released—a throwaway take of "Apple Honey" and a version of "Yeah Man," both made on February 19, 1945, for Columbia. Herman felt honored by such reissues and was proud that people still wanted to hear his old music. Other reissues also started flowing from the vaults of Decca, Columbia, and Capitol, and in 1981 Trend/Discovery Records of Los Angeles began reviving the Third Herd's better Mars sides from the 1950s.

Meanwhile, there still was a real Herman band in late 1984. While it was playing in Boston, alumni from the area joined it for a Sunday reunion concert, which merited a mention in *Down Beat*. The road band later played a jazz cruise on the *S.S. Norway* for a week in late October and one-nighted its way (with many open dates) to Reno, where it finished three shows at year's end before a long hiatus.

Herman emerged from a month-long break on January 30, 1985, to play the King Cole Room in New York's St. Regis Hotel for ten weeks. The combo included Barbutti, Rabbai, Pierce, Hanna, Frank Wess or Seldon Powell on tenor saxophone, and Duvivier, Ray Drummond, or Lisle Atkinson on bass. Herman also appeared with Tormé, Horne, Joe Williams, Al Jarreau, and Wynton Marsalis on *Night of 100 Stars,* a TV special from Radio City Music Hall

But band leading was clearly in Herman's blood; he formed a full band again in mid-April. Fedchock, who had enrolled in the Eastman School of Music to continue his studies, came back, and Herman relied on "Big John's" trombone playing and new charts. The new band skipped from New York to Indiana to Michigan, then toured the West. There were shows with singer Patti Page in San Jose, but engagements consisted mostly of one-nighters for the band alone through June. No doubt discouraged by the lack of jobs, Herman then disbanded yet again to put together a combo of Hanna, Cohn, Bunch, Buddy Tate, Steve Wallace, and Harry "Sweets" Edison to tour Europe. With Pierce in for Bunch, the group played Japan and Australia. Full-band jobs resumed on August 21 in Kansas City. Among the one-nighters was a reunion with Clooney at the Paul Masson Vineyards in Saratoga in mid-September. The *S.S. Norway* cruise from Miami, starting October 5, this time ran for two weeks, with Tormé aboard.

Stravinsky's "Ebony Concerto," which had lain neglected for lack of adventurous and talented players, enjoyed a revival with Richard Stoltzman, who could face it unafraid. Stoltzman, a clarinetist of renown, had become popular in classical music but was eclectic and fond of jazz. As he recollects his meeting with Herman, he was jamming in New York City with a group led by Simon: "There was Woody at one of the tables, and there I was onstage playing 'Take the "A" Train' or something. George Simon introduced us." There the idea took shape of reviving "Ebony Concerto," which Stoltzman characterizes as "a kind of thunderbolt that wipes out all the petty comments about classical music and jazz, all the petty differences and discrimination. Here's Stravinsky, and here's the indigenous American ensemble, the big band, and the result, in one swoop, says 'valid'! . . . It doesn't really present any special problems, save those that all music presents."[21]

Rehearsals with Stoltzman began on October 20, and the Herman-Stoltzman tour visited Illinois, Ohio, and Indiana, performing on college campuses and at museums and a high school. The band played the first half of the concerts. Stoltzman then came on for Oddo's "American Medley" (blending "Amazing Grace," "America the Beautiful," and "Battle Hymn of the Republic"), three pieces for solo clarinet by Stravinsky, a number by Claude Debussy, a medley from *West Side Story,* and "Ebony Concerto." The closing number was a jam session for all on "Cousins."

However talented Stoltzman was, he felt challenged by Fedchock's chart of Duke Ellington's "Come Sunday." The ending called for Stoltzman to play with force over the band. His manager muttered to Mike Brignola that no one could make a skinny clarinet audible over a full band. "You better talk to Woody," Brignola said, "'cause he does it every night." Fedchock marveled at Herman the player as well: "He really swung. Even when he was playing [past age seventy] with minimum chops [lips, facial muscles, lungs, energy] and ideas, everything felt good. Every other clarinet player was so preoccupied with what notes he was playing and how many he could play. But Woody's main thing was swinging. Even if he just played something simple it would come off because it really felt good. Woody's swing feel was very relaxed, very flowing."[22]

By now a rickety seventy-two-year-old widower, Herman conveyed ownership of the band, library, and contracts to Reese in late 1985 and phased out Dressel as business manager. Reese formed Keep Swinging, Inc., to help cover the IRS and other bills. Her son, an aspiring songwriter, and her daughter, who was still in high school, remained in Nashville. Reese retained the firm of Thomas Cassidy, Inc., to book the band. Reese was happy to be part of it all again, as Herman and the band were part of her life from earliest childhood: "When kids at school used to ask what my dad did, and I told them he was a bandleader, they'd say 'Huh?' It didn't mean much to me either until he took me backstage and I'd meet celebrities like Paul Winchell, the ventriloquist."[23] But as Reese discovered, things weren't what they used to be for bands. Manne, for one, regarded the "big band syndrome" as "virtually finished" and mournfully commented on one aspect of the band's demise: "Big bands gave an individual a chance to be heard nationally and gain a reputation because they had the kind of following the rock bands have now. Nowadays, it's very difficult to gain a reputation in Woody Herman's band, for instance. I know Woody's got a good band, but I can't tell you who's in it."[24]

Herman was virtually finished, too. Age, the rigors of travel, leg pains, touches of emphysema, life without his wife, all wore him down. And then the IRS intervened again, this time with a crushing blow:

> The IRS was getting the lion's share of our earnings, but few were aware of it aside from close friends. I had refused to go public with it while Charlotte was alive. She was fiercely proud, and there was no point in causing embarrassment. I lived well on the road, taking enough expense money to ensure good accommodations and meals; but I was aware that it would end if we missed a payment to the government every week. Then, suddenly, in 1985, the government notified me that the house would have to be auctioned off to help satisfy the tax debt.[25]

The house sold for $99,000, although Herman thought it worth $350,000. Herman, who had been denied any credit—including a personal bank account or credit cards—since 1968, became bitter: "I figured that, with the visits I had made to other parts of the world for the State Department, they might at least leave me something to hang my hat on."[26] He and lawyers worked out a deal whereby he could rent his former home for $1,150 a month. But when the new owner, William Little, decided to sell the place, he pressed Herman to vacate. A judge granted a six-month extension while lawyers fought on for Herman, enabling him to stay.

He could have raised money from legions of friends or from benefit concerts. But he never asked, and no one offered. The IRS, in selling Herman's house, "massacred him," according to Tiberi. "I never saw him in such pain."[27]

chapter nine

FINAL CURTAIN

*a*s Herman looked back over his fifty years of bandleading, he could be proud of his accomplishments: "We haven't merely survived the collapse of the big band era, the crush of rock and roll, and a twenty-year income tax battle which kept me at the brink of poverty. We also have managed to keep the music adventurous, and ensure the requisite energy by keeping the ranks filled with talented young men."[1] The upcoming anniversary offset some of his woes and led to an album, a book, a special concert, and written praise in 1986. But he started the year modestly (to keep the IRS at bay), playing in a quintet with Hanna at the Vine Street Bar and Grill in Hollywood. He re-formed a big band January 17 in Atlanta, and it motored for two months in twenty states and Canada. Tapes made on

January 24 from a job in Florida include five new charts by Fedchock: "It Don't Mean a Thing (If It Ain't Got That Swing)," "What's New?" "Pools," "Central Park West," and "Epistrophy." In 1982, Fedchock had arranged Lou Donaldson's "Fried Buzzard" with baritone sax and trombone solos and later composed "The Great Escape." In all, Fedchock wrote seventeen charts for Herman, a process that came easily to him, as he recounts: "After [my first Herman] concert in '74 I tried to get as many of Woody's recordings as I could find. Familiarizing myself with the sound of the band and all its great arrangements paid off later when I became Woody's chief ar-

John Fedchock and Mike Brignola soloing on "Fried Buzzard" at Disneyland in July 1984. (Courtesy John Fedchock)

ranger. I already had a feel for the kind of chart that would work best for Woody and the band."[2]

On March 20, Concord Records taped a concert in San Francisco's Great American Music Hall for the album *50th Anniversary Tour,* Herman's first full-band album in thirty-one months. Herman had always felt dissatisfied when in a recording slump, and he reported that work on the album made him "feel I'm back in North Beach and I'm sixteen years old!"[3] Herman dedicated *50th Anniversary Tour* "to my dear friend Jack Siefert, who has the patience of Job"; they had been friends for nearly fifty years.

The album's contents reflected the band's current book—a peculiar mix of new jazz numbers borrowed from composers outside the band and Fedchock's arrangements of comparatives oldies, such as the Duke Ellington band's "It Don't Mean a Thing," the 1940 ballad "What's New?" Monk's 1940s "Epistrophy," and Coltrane's "Central Park West." The truly new material was Fedchock's "Blues for Red," which honored Kelly and in which Lynn Seaton voiced amusing grunts and hums over his bass notes; Lou Donaldson's "Fried Buzzard"; Enrique García's "Conga"; and "Pools," an engaging piece by Dan Grolnick, who played in, and wrote the piece for, the jazz group Steps Ahead. Tiberi, Fedchock, Mike Brignola, drummer Jim Rupp, and pianist Brad Williams performed impressive solos in the album.

The flurry of laudatory essays that commemorated the anniversary did not, for the most part, offer new views. McDonough's article in *Down Beat* stressed Herman's astonishing staying power and flexibility, which had impressed other critics as well: "The most remarkable thing is that he's remained a force in music from decade to decade while keeping the brand name intact. Like Tide detergent, Colgate toothpaste and other venerable brand names—he has continually reinvented himself in response to changing markets."[4] *USA Today*'s feature focused on Herman's youthfulness—as indeed articles had since the sixties. In Stoltzman's words, Herman was "a man of the present, not a man of the past. He could just play simple licks and get away with it, but all of a sudden he'll play something really outrageous—without a net!" But Herman's open-mindedness and experimentation caused his own artistic dissatisfaction, a problem he had been grappling with now for five decades: "The youth is changing. They're open to jazz. But general audiences still come in with a hangover and say, 'Entertain me.'"[5]

And even though Herman himself lived in the present, like many anniversaries, this one was the occasion for nostalgia. Francis Davis's article in the *Atlantic,* while full of praise for Herman's indefatigability, expressed longing for the earlier, better days of Herman bands:

> While his new recruits are better educated in music than their predecessors, they are green by comparison in ways that count more. A studied facility in running chord changes is quite different from the ability to tell a meaningful story in a few choruses, and storytellers have been in short supply in recent editions of the Herd. The new arrangements tend toward the formulaic, and the old favorites are tossed off in a perfunctory manner. "That's the way it was," Herman will sometimes say after the band honors a request for "Caldonia," [but] you find yourself thinking, No, it must have been better than that.[6]

Terry Teachout, of the *New York Daily News,* took a different angle by traveling with Herman and his bandsmen from Iowa to Kansas. His description of the band's performance in LeMars, Iowa, departs from the by now rather tired remarks about youth and change and presents a poignant picture of an aging, lonely man whose life is in music:

> LeMars is jumping tonight. It is Founder's Day at Westmar College, a local United Methodist school with an enrollment of 430, and the college is throwing a Saturday night dinner dance in honor of the occasion. Fifteen men are settling themselves on a folding bandstand, leafing through thick folders of music and idly tuning up their instruments. Most of them are in their twenties and early thirties. Their leader, who is waiting for his cue in the hall outside the dining room, is seventy-three.
>
> The drummer strikes a crisp roll on his tom-toms, the trombonists wave plastic mutes in front of their golden bells, and Woody

Herman's Thundering Herd swells confidently into the slow, mournful strains of "Blue Flame." The short, stooped, balding man quietly steps from the wings and begins to make his slow and careful way to the bandstand. He does not smile. He is too tired to smile. . . . Every wrinkle on his deeply lined face seemed to stand for another year of bumpy bus rides and cheap motels. . . . As the room swells with the heartfelt applause of expectant dancers, the last of the big band leaders finally reaches center stage, picks up his clarinet, and begins to play the blues. . . .

At 12:40 the dancers were gone, the albums sold, the autographs signed. The pianist and bassist were jamming together. Woody was standing alone near the bandstand, listening to the music, idly snapping his fingers to the beat. He picked up his clarinet and tossed off a low, breathy chorus of "Willow Weep for Me." Then he put it down, did a stiff little dance step, and slipped out of the room without a word. Homeless and wifeless and futureless, Woody Herman was still taking what little pleasures he could find.[7]

As old age stole over Herman, he realized the importance of capturing his life on paper, and he spoke often with Stuart Troup, then jazz critic for *New York Newsday*. Troup taped many interviews with Herman about his life—during bus and car rides through the Midwest, during automobile rides going to and coming from engagements in and around New York City, at Herman's Hollywood Hills home, and in Manhattan bars. In one interview, Herman told Troup that it had become harder each day to find strength for another trip. As Troup recalls, "Herman was never quite up to par. He was often too tired to do much talking after an engagement, and he often arose late the following day."[8] Onstage the band was swinging, the booking agent found it work, Bill Byrne took care of the business, and Fedchock and Tiberi attended to the music—but often Herman couldn't remember where he had played the night before, and he detested being a "government serf."[9] Herman did manage to keep his sense of humor, however: at one point he quipped to Voce, who was also working on a book in England: "I am too old to retire—however, I am still younger than the President, Ronald Reagan!"[10]

*t*hree more months of travel led to the fiftieth anniversary concert at the Hollywood Bowl on July 16. (Nothing could be booked for the true fifty-year mark in November.) This event—which was advertised as "Celebrating Woody Herman!"—accommodated an outdoor crowd of twelve thousand. The Young Thundering Herd was joined onstage by an alumni band—including Pete and Conte Candoli, Rader, Fontana, Getz, Flory, Nimitz, Rowles, Pierce, Budwig, and Flores—and guest artists. As Herman assembled the program, he doubtless thought of a half-century of friends, players, places, and people—his parents, his wife, and Sister Fabian, who in their own ways all stoked his musical fires.

For the first hour the alumni band, rehearsed by Pierce, performed such oldies as "The Good Earth," "Opus De-Funk," "Blowin' Up a Storm." It grieved Feather, however, to see nonalumni filling in while former stars, such as Giuffre and Phil Wilson, sat out. (It griped him even more when Herman sang nothing and omitted "Woodchoppers' Ball.") The regulars in the Young Thundering Herd played new music, sharing the stage with assorted sit-in guest stars. Burns premiered "The Godmother," which was written in memory of Charlotte Herman. Getz soloed on Tiberi's "Ti-Land," "Easy Living," and "The Peacocks," which he had recorded with Rowles. Clooney sang "My Buddy." Rowles, with his daughter Stacy on flugelhorn, performed Larry Gales's "Loco Motif" and Strayhorn's "Lotus Blossom." The Cuban trumpeter Arturo Sandoval, who had caught Herman's ear in England, soloed on "Conga." Before "Ebony Concerto," Stoltzman warmed up on Debussy's "Maid with the Flaxen Hair," helped the band on "Fanfare for the Common Man," and traded solos with Herman on "Greasy Sack Blues." Stoltzman, Sandoval, a harpist, a French horn player, and an alto clarinetist helped on "Ebony Concerto." Then the massed bands and guests closed with a long blues. A video of the concert was to have been both televised and put on sale; Bill Byrne lamented years later that neither occurred, which he attributed to "suspicious dealings."[11]

*a*fter the concert, Herman led the band back on the road, but the steel pins in his leg made it harder than ever to walk, climb stairs, or pass airport metal detectors. He hired Ed Dye, a musician friend of his daughter's, as an aide, but road fatigue never relented. The nightly music was his only payoff, and he could barely work the two hours. The band traveled by bus from coast to coast and teamed up with Joe Williams for a Cincinnati concert on August 26. Then it hurried to Baltimore, Cleveland, and the Chicago suburb of Schaumburg.

The band drove west for weeks of one-nighters, then moved on to Kentucky, Michigan, Illinois, Wisconsin, and Tennessee. Its regular *S.S. Norway* cruise left Miami on October 11, and music selected from seven evening concerts went into a video titled *Woody Herman and the Ultimate Herd* with guests Cohn, Calloway, and Joe Williams. Later in New York City, Herman's band played a three-hour show in the Hilton with Quincy Jones and Roberta Flack; and Podewell sang with the band for five weeks of bookings.

Herman might have been tired out by his schedule, but the IRS was as energetic as ever. As an article in *People* magazine made clear, Herman stayed on the road for the money, little of which he would ever see. One photo caption read: "'If you can play music every night, nothing can get to you,' says Woody, performing for $4,000 at a Chicago mall."[12] By 1986, that sum didn't go far, especially since the article set Herman's balance due the IRS at $1.5 million. Teachout was blunter than *People:* "I don't doubt that Woody Herman liked applause, but that wasn't why he stayed on the road. He continued to tour because he owed the government money. His options were limited. He could exchange one prison for another."[13] Friends and band members were irate: as Garment mourned, "All he's got left are his clothes, his instruments, his talent and his great contribution to jazz." Garment enlisted Senator Daniel Patrick Moynihan, a jazz buff, and others, hoping that Congress might vote to forgive the debt. And Herman was bitter: "I'd like to have a settlement so that for my last remaining breaths, the heat would be off. Once they have you, they have no pity. I keep paying and paying, and nothing changes, [but] I'll go down swinging."[14]

On November 17, a Thursday afternoon, Herman suddenly gasped for breath in his room in the Sheraton Russell on Park Avenue in New York

City. He called the front desk. An ambulance crew raced him to Bellevue Hospital's emergency room, where medics pumped water from his lungs. Bill Byrne and Tiberi were told that it was a case of congestive heart disease. The two ran the band without Herman for four weeks through eleven states while Troup, Dye, and Podewell stayed with Herman. When Herman was recovered enough to smile and take Troup's hand, he said: "You know, Igor Stravinsky was right. He said that growing old is just a series of humiliations."[15]

Herman rested at the Pennsylvania home of Jack and Mary Siefert until December 6. Siefert recalls how the now failing Herman faced his own father's ill health in the 1960s: "he was sitting in my home trying to reach his father in a convalescent home in Milwaukee. He finally got through and afterwards turned to me in tears and said, 'He didn't even know who I was.' When I started to commiserate he stopped me: 'The important thing is that I remembered who he was.'"[16]

With Siefert doing some of the chauffeuring, Herman was able to lead the band on December 7 at Washington's John F. Kennedy Center, on December 8 at Blues Alley in Washington, and on December 10 in New York City for an arts ball. He then flew to Los Angeles to rest.

*t*ravel for the band resumed on January 15, 1987, at a high school in North Carolina, and one-nighters with few breaks continued across fourteen states before two weeks in California. On March 3, Herman rejoined the band with two guest percussionists for a concert in the Willows Theater in Concord, recorded and made into the Concord album *Woody's Gold Star*. The album opened with Fedchock's treatment of "Battle Royal"—another homage to Duke Ellington (from the latter's 1961 *Paris Blues* film score)—in which the sax quartet played a series of solos, and Herman left behind a few wheezy clarinet notes. Fedchock's "Woody's Gold Star," commemorating Herman's name imbedded in the Walk of Fame, ran for six minutes, featuring walking bass and full-band flashes. "Mambo Rockland," a Puente chart, gave pianist Joel Weiskopf and Tiberi solo time. In his piece called "The Great Escape," Fedchock wrote in solo spots for tenor and trombone saxes. ("Anything that is good jazz to me is a great escape," Herman had sometimes said. "When you're involved in playing or listening to great jazz, no one can get to you.")[17] Fedchock's arrangement of "Watermelon Man" starred five soloists and the percussionists. Another of Fedchock's numbers, based on a Corea piece, finished the album with Dave Riekenberg on flute and a slowly building full-band presence that turned fiery before cooling. As the crowd cheered, Herman identified it as "Samba Song."

Bill Byrne, Herman, Nathan Davidson, who sponsored Herman's last job, and Frank Tiberi, in Minnesota, March 1987. (Courtesy Thomas Cassidy, Inc.)

Herman told Troup he did not know how he had gathered the strength to record *Woody's Gold Star*, and he was failing visibly as the band toured Washington, Oregon, Idaho, Utah, and Colorado. "In Denver, Woody started getting really sick," Fedchock said. "Some decisions about the *Gold Star* album hadn't been made yet. But he said, 'Sorry, all I can do is sleep.'" "The altitude was getting to me," Herman told Troup. "I got some medicine, but felt noticeably weaker. [Then] the tour took us to Grand Meadow, Minnesota, for a concert at a high school."[18] Nathan Davidson, the band director at Grand Meadow High, persuaded Herman to play "Woodchoppers' Ball" that night; Davidson was lucky, as a sideman told him—the band almost never played it any more. "As tired as Woody was," Davidson said, "he stayed around then signed autographs after the concert. What a night to remember."[19] Herman himself recalled that "by the end of that evening, I had nothing left."[20] So there, in the postconcert darkness in an icy northern town of two thousand, his grand career ended on March 23. His next booking was with his doctor, who had him admitted into a Detroit hospital for eight weeks. Fedchock marveled that Herman, with about 25 percent of his lung capacity, "had played on that last album date with virtually no air, and still sounded good."[21] Sick as he was, though, he played, sang, emceed, chose numbers and tempi, directed the band—in charge to the end.

When strong enough, Herman, still needing oxygen, was flown to Hollywood. After several more weeks at Cedars-Sinai Medical Center in Los Angeles, he at last reached his rented Hollywood Hills home. There he languished in a bedroom, hooked to a life-support system, dependent on a wheelchair and a nurse.

Ingrid Reese authorized Tiberi to go on fronting the band and Bill Byrne to handle road business. In New York City during May 11 and 12, the band joined Stoltzman to record the RCA album *Ebony*, which was issued in 1988. In addition to Stoltzman's flawless rendition of "Ebony Concerto," the album contained more mainstream tracks, including Oddo's nine-minute "American Medley," Frank Bennett's "Stories from the West Side," Fedchock's chart of Duke Ellington's "Come Sunday" (from the 1943 suite *Black, Brown and Beige*), a version of "Cousins," and Bill Douglas's short "Waltz for Woody." But the real surprise was a remake of Shorty Rogers's brief and breezy "Igor," transcribed from the 1946 Woodchoppers' record.

During May 16–29, the band played a dozen concerts in Europe with DeFranco and O'Day as guest performers. But Herman was never far from anyone's thoughts. When the band played at Milwaukee's Summerfest on July 2, the *Milwaukee Journal*'s reviewer wrote: "Tell Woody it went fine here. Tiberi gave every band member a chance at solo stardom.

But the real star was the band in unison, delivering those sudden thunderclaps of mass sound to shatter a pensive mood. Woody, you'd have been proud of the boys." In promos sent ahead of the band, Herman responded: "I am proud. Frank Tiberi is one of the great saxophone players, and a fine clarinetist. He's thoroughly familiar with our music and how the band should feel about playing it. The guys have always liked and respected him, so I knew they'd play their hearts out every night." Tiberi said he felt "humbled and honored to have been picked. But mind you now, I'm only the band's director. My job is to help the guys play the music authentically. Make no mistake about it. The leader of this band will always be Woody Herman."[22]

Frank Tiberi playing tenor sax, about 1986. (Courtesy Nick Puopolo)

Bill Byrne and Tiberi visited Herman at home on September 1, while the band was working at Disneyland. He was bedridden, hooked to oxygen with tube and nosepiece. Byrne, knowing Herman had earlier insisted that there be no "ghost band" after his death, asked: "Do you want us to keep the band going, or what?" "Woody took hold of my arm from his bed, and he looked me in the eye," Byrne said. "He then said 'yes!' That was all he said, just the one word, in a very firm voice."[23] *Down Beat* later quoted Herman as adding: "Otherwise there'll be fifteen fewer chairs for tomorrow's great young players to fill."[24]

Disoriented at times and depressed, Herman sank, as his daughter put it, from "indestructible to immobile."[25] Then just before Labor Day, Herman's landlord served eviction papers because Reese, who was drowning in medical bills, had fallen behind on the rent. Word got out, and the news media took an interest. Garment called the Los Angeles firm of Paul, Hastings, Janofsky, and Walker, which let an associate take Herman's case pro bono. In due time, seven volunteer lawyers put in more than $100,000 worth of legal services for Herman.[26] Friends scheduled benefits, Frank Sinatra and Clint Eastwood headed a list of big-name backers, and the National Association of Jazz Educators started a foundation by selling T-shirts that proclaimed "I'm One of Woody's Kids." In Congress, Rep. John Conyers, Jr., of Michigan filed House Resolution 3274—which was never passed—to relieve Herman's tax debt. Herman, he argued, "symbolizes the plight that frequently befalls artists. They're somehow supposed to provide cultural enrichment to our society, while their day-to-day existence is often marked by great sacrifice and a certain amount of suffering. We must not forget the precarious situation we have created for our artists. For a man who has provided this country with such a rich musical legacy, it is the least we could do."[27] KKGO-FM radio in Sherman Oaks broadcast a benefit "rent party" for Herman, raising enough for several payments. The station followed with a benefit concert in October with Clooney, Bennett, Dudley Moore, Doc Severinson and the *Tonight Show* orchestra, McCall, Pierce, and Shorty Rogers. The Blue Note in New York City housed a tribute featuring Urbie Green and Cohn, hosted by disc jockey Al "Jazzbeau" Collins and author Ira Gitler. At the Royal Sonesta Hotel in Cambridge, Massachusetts, Dick Johnson and the Artie Shaw "ghost" band, DeFranco, the Whalin' Herd All Stars with Phil Wilson, Andy McGhee, Fontaine, and McKenna raised $8,500 with a show. Others, famous names among them, worked behind the scenes. The National Academy of Recording Arts and Sciences honored Herman with its Lifetime Achievement Award—at that time only Benny Carter and the Italian singer Enrico Caruso had been so honored.

Regular fans got into the act, too, and letters soon arrived with cash, checks, and greetings:

> The last time I got close to your Great Band was in 1942, at the Hollywood Canteen, when I was a G.I. in the Army, on a pass before going overseas.—Ole Chicago Drummer Ossie

> Enclosed is seven dollars each from a few guys who met you at the bar at the lake in Marion, Ohio, in 1984, and you told us the wonderful story about the bar owner in Buffalo who called you the "Vince Lombardi of Music."

In remembrance of a teenager's before-noon excursions to the Paramount and the Strand. The world was kinder then. I wish that kindness to you.

I remember my first glimpse of Woody Herman—with that slightly malevolent smile that suggested things were going to happen that weren't necessarily what the church had in mind. Thanks to "Woodchoppers' Ball," my ears were tuned for life.[28]

The lawyers found that Herman's landlord had filed 264 eviction notices in Los Angeles Municipal Court, earning him a reputation with the Legal Aid Foundation there; in the blunt words of one staffer, "He became a millionaire on the broken backs of a lot of little people." Little protested: "I don't create the problem that leads to the sale." Then, claiming ignorance of Herman's plight, he softened his eviction demands. Reese had no idea what might have happened had the attorneys not helped: "I was out of options. If I were conventionally religious, I'd say I was living on faith. Let's just say I was Zen-ing it."[29]

$\mathcal{M}$onsignor Parnassus from St. Victor's, in a heart-to-heart bedside visit, offered to work up a musical funeral oriented to Herman's career. But Herman said he wanted the "regular stuff." "It was easy to be his friend," Monsignor Parnassus said. "He was a genuine person, easy to like, who loved his faith."[30]

Word of Herman's death—of heart failure, emphysema, and pneumonia—reached the band on October 29 at Southwestern Community College in Iowa, just minutes before the 7:30 P.M. concert. Southwestern's band director reported that "the talented young musicians were visibly shaken by the loss of their friend and leader. Tiberi dedicated the concert to Woody, and the band responded by playing two hours of inspired big band music. The band is in capable, loving hands, and will continue to bring big band jazz to those who love it. That is the way Woody would want it. Frank Tiberi will see to it."[31]

Friends, fans, and family attended Herman's funeral mass on November 2 in St. Victor's. A writer from Philadelphia noted that "A bunch of kids from the Midwest who borrowed money to fly out, members of a scholastic stage band who met Herman as a visiting clinician" attended.[32] In St. Victor's, Siefert read the eulogy: "Woody was a role model for the young people of today, for he proved that you can still reach your artistic goals and be a nice guy. He was the rarest of all human possessions: he was a true friend. . . . We have just lost the greatest pied piper that American music has ever produced . . . and I have lost the greatest friend any man ever had. May his soul rest in peace."[33]

*f*riend, Pied Piper, Coach, Road Father, 'Chopper—Herman had been different things to different people . . . urbane . . . witty . . . mellow . . . bland . . . fiery. A *Down Beat* writer who had asked Herman what he most wanted to be remembered for said that Herman had replied: "I was completely honest with my music."[34]

And he was, as the numerous accolades from far and wide attest:

> You can have all the technique in the world, but you'd better play from the heart. Feeling transcends technique, as Woody's own playing showed, and as his bands show. Feeling is honesty. That's what great jazz is all about.—Joe Lovano[35]

> Woody always did only what he believed in musically. That's why he could "sell" the band from the stand so convincingly. That's where the power to communicate comes from.—Phil Wilson[36]

Bill Byrne, who was with Herman for a record of twenty-two years, knew him well: "He knew what he wanted musically, and insisted on getting it. He knew his place in music, his standing, knew his place as the band's leader, as The Coach. He was amazingly versatile."[37] Tiberi recalled how sometimes in the middle of a concert neither Herman nor the bandsmen knew what the next number would be. At the last second Herman might call it out or, with his remarks, signal what it would be.[38] According to *Down Beat*, stories and recollections abounded at Berklee, where several alumni taught: Fontaine recalled that often Herman would "volunteer the band to play benefits for musicians in need." Andy McGhee never forgot that "he even gave me a clarinet." And it amazed Phil Wilson how "Woody could sell new music to old audiences; that's how he got fifty years of young geniuses to work for him."[39]

Reese learned from her father "The importance and worth of being an artist. He believed that artists were second to no one, and that a truly successful person is someone who takes the talents given and uses them to their fullest."[40]

Promotional shot of Herman with clarinet, March 1985. (Jack Siefert Collection)

*f*riends continued to rail against "the heartless government who ignores drug profits and business and labor scams, but go full blast after men like Herman."[41] The tax debt, however, went to the grave with Herman. Reese and Keep Swinging didn't need to pay any more. The Woody Herman Foundation received enough to pay Herman's medical bills and establish a fund for destitute musicians and scholarships.

Benefit events continued in Herman's memory—and what memories they were:

> Conversations around musicians' bars, on band buses, wherever else musicians gather, are often about Woody. He had his own cult following. . . . The American Jazz Orchestra played a memorial concert in New York City on December 10. Al Cohn, Milt Jackson and Chubby Jackson performed as guests. Herman made a lot of friends. He only made friends.[42]

And the band played on, owned by Reese, booked by Tom Cassidy, led by Tiberi, and road-managed by Bill Byrne. It turned up at Hilton Head, South Carolina, in March 1988; at Rochester, Minnesota, and Lincoln, Nebraska, in April; at Decatur, Alabama, in July; at Hampton Roads, Virginia, in August. By late 1989, Broadbent had added to the book "Woody 'n Me," a reference to Gillespie's "Woody 'n You." Pay was marginal, bookings hit-and-miss, turnover high. And although the band was still more or .

less intact, something important was missing: as a reviewer for *High Fidelity* mourned: "Who will find and nurture the Ralph Burnses, the Neal Heftis, the Alan Broadbents and the John Fedchocks of the future?"[43]

A "Woody Herman band" worked thirty-three weeks in 1990, but only thirty-seven jobs in 1991, fewer still in 1992, usually in big cities, with Tiberi and Mike Brignola forming the band's nucleus. They picked up other musicians, often band alumni, to fill the chairs. In February 1991, Byrne retired to South Dakota. When a job seemed profitable, Tiberi and Brignola (who doubled as road manager) rounded up musicians to play the old book and a few new charts. Reese, now a college textbook editor in Los Angeles, said that she never became deeply involved in the band's business affairs, although Keep Swinging stayed intact. "But," she said, "the days are gone when you could put a big band on the road fifty-two weeks of the year and make any money."[44] Reese later leased the band to Stew Jackson, of Denver, Colorado. Tiberi led a Herman All-Stars band at the 35th Grammy Awards Party on February 24, 1993, as Jackson kept hunting bookings. In May, Tiberi rounded up alumni from New York City, Chicago, and Los Angeles to play at Jackson's for an eightieth birthday party in Herman's memory. "We had a ball playing and hanging out together," Byrne said.[45]

January 1994 saw the founding of the Woody Herman Society. Reese and A. J. "Al" Julian, a former publicist for Concord Records and other clients, launched a membership drive to keep Herman's memory alive, sustain the band, produce a newsletter, establish scholarships, develop awards programs, and sponsor concerts and clinics by alumni or the band. Tiberi reports that business picked up in 1995. The band tries to get dance dates because that "keeps us going,"[46] but it currently has more engagements doing jazz concerts and still books clinic-concerts at colleges.

More words remain to be written and spoken, more stories and photos published, more concerts played, more audiotape, videotape and film segments marketed about Herman's life in music. And surely reissue will follow reissue of his hundreds of recordings. After all, it is only fitting that although the music stopped for Woody Herman—to paraphrase the 1943 ballad he recorded—we go on dancing.

appendix

significant recordings by woody herman

Woody Herman played on nearly 1,500 performances that have become available to the record-buying public since the 1930s. These included studio recordings, transcriptions, V discs, radio broadcasts, and on-site tapes, occasionally made by amateurs. These selected "significant recordings" may or may not be now available to collectors. They are presented as the best examples of the works of Herman's several bands, of their many styles, of dance music, of swing music, of vocal music, of be-bop, of blues, of big bands and small combos, of popular ballads, of novelties, of experiments, of hits, and of the many good arrangers and soloists, including, of course, Herman himself.

with tom gerun orchestra

1932   Lonesome Me / My Heart's at Ease

with isham jones orchestra

1934–36   Tiger Rag / I've Found a New Baby / Four or Five Times
          Jimtown Blues / China Boy / Sweet Sue / Blue Room
          Black Magic / Blue Lament / Dallas Blues / Panama
          Rock Your Blues Away / Stompin' at the Savoy

with isham jones's juniors

1936   I've Had the Blues So Long / Slappin' the Bass / Nola
          Take It Easy / Fan It / Tormented

woody herman and his orchestra

1937   Dupree Blues / Doctor Jazz / Trouble in Mind / Stardust on the
              Moon
          That Old Feeling / Muskrat Ramble / Jazz Me Blues / Weary Blues
          Royal Garden Blues / Bob White

1938   Calliope Blues / Twin City Blues / Laughing Boy Blues
          Indian Boogie Woogie / Riverbed Blues

1939   At the Woodchoppers' Ball / Big Wig in the Wigwam / Dallas Blues
          Blues Upstairs / Blues Downstairs / The Sheik of Araby / Casbah
              Blues
          Farewell Blues / East Side Kick / Jumpin' Blues / I'm Comin' Virginia
              Blues on Parade

1940   It's a Blue World / Peach Tree Street / Blue Prelude / Cousin to Chris
        Blue Ink / Bessie's Blues / Herman at the Sherman / Jukin'
        Get Your Boots Laced, Papa / Mister Meadowlark
        I Wouldn't Take a Million / Chips' Boogie Woogie / Chips' Blues
        Frenesi / Five O'Clock Whistle / There I Go / Love of My Life
        The Golden Wedding

1941   Bounce Me, Brother, with a Solid Four / Blue Flame
        Fur Trappers' Ball / Fan It / South / G'Bye Now / Night Watchman
        Love Me a Little Little / Hey Doc / Humpty Dumpty Heart
        Bishop's Blues / Woodsheddin' with Woody / Too Late
        Fort Worth Jail / Three Ways to Smoke a Pipe / Ten Day Furlough
        Blues in the Night / This Time the Dream's on Me / Hot Chestnuts
        Yardbird Shuffle / Las Chiapanecas / Even Steven / Rose O'Day
        Someone's Rocking My Dream Boat

1942   Deep in the Heart of Texas / There Are Rivers to Cross / Amen
        Deliver Me to Tennessee / Ooch Ooch a Goon Attach
        Four or Five Times / Down Under / Jingle Bells / I Dood It
            Be Not Disencouraged

1943   The Music Stopped / Do Nothin' Till You Hear From Me / Who
            Dat?
        Basie's Basement

1944   I've Got You under My Skin / I Get a Kick Out of You / Cherry
        It Must Be Jelly / Milkman, Keep Those Bottles Quiet / Irresistible
            You
        Perdido / I Didn't Know about You / G.I. Jive / Red Top
        Is You Is or Is You Ain't My Baby? / 125th Street Prophet
        I Ain't Got Nothin' but the Blues / Jones Beachhead
        I Can't Put My Arms around a Memory / 'Tain't Me / 1-2-3-4 Jump
        Saturday Night

1945   Chubby's Blues / Laura / Apple Honey / I Wonder / Caldonia
        June Comes Around Every Year / Happiness Is a Thing Called Joe
        Goosey Gander / Northwest Passage / A Kiss Goodnight
        I've Got the World on a String / Don't Worry 'bout That Mule
        Good, Good, Good / The Good Earth / Bijou / Black Orchid
        Ah, Your Father's Mustache / Wild Root / Put That Ring on My
            Finger
        On the Atchison, Topeka & Santa Fe / Blowin' Up a Storm
        Atlanta, G.A. / Let It Snow

1946	Great Northern / Panacea / Superman with a Horn / Ee-Ba-Ba-Lee-Ba
	Carnegie Hall Concert / Surrender / Mabel! Mabel! / Steps / Fan It
	Four Men on a Horse / Igor / Nero's Conception / Lost Weekend
	Pam / Ebony Concerto / Sidewalks of Cuba / Stars Fell on Alabama
	Lady McGowan's Dream / Romance in the Dark / Summer Sequence
	Uncle Remus Said / Everywhere / With Someone New / Back Talk
	Wrap Your Troubles in Dreams / Woodchoppers' Ball / Blue Flame
	Non-Alcoholic / The Blues Are Brewin'
1947	Across the Alley from the Alamo / In the Blue of Evening / Natch
	I Got a Right to Sing the Blues / Boulevard of Memories / Civilization
	I Told Ya I Love Ya, Now Get Out / Keen and Peachy / Four Brothers
	I've Got News for You / The Goof and I / Summer Sequence IV
	Swing Low Sweet Clarinet / P.S., I Love You / My Pal, Gonzales
1948	There'll Be Some Changes Made / Berled in Earl / Yucca / Boomsie
	That's Right / Lemon Drop / I Got It Bad / Early Autumn
	I Ain't Gonna Wait Too Long / Keeper of the Flame
1949	The Crickets / More Moon / Not Really the Blues / The Great Lie
	Detour Ahead / Jamaica Rhumba / More Than You Know / Tenderly
	Lollypop / You Rascal You / Rhapsody in Wood
1950	I Want a Little Girl / Spain / Sonny Speaks / Music to Dance To
	Starlight Souvenirs
1951	Life Is Just a Bowl of Cherries / As Long As I Live
	Here Come the Blues / Lonesome Gal / St. Louis Blues / By George
	Leo the Lion / Glory of Love / Cuban Holiday / Hollywood Blues
	Blue Flame / Dandy Lion
1952	Blues in Advance / Terressita / Stompin' at the Savoy / Perdido
	Celestial Blues / Baby Clementine / Moten Stomp / Singin' in the Rain
	In a Little Spanish Town / Mother Goose Jumps / Buck Dance
	No True Love / Blue Lou / Wooftie
1953	Beau Jazz / Men from Mars / I Love Paris / Four Others
1954	Mambo the Most / Mambo the Utmost / Blame Boehm
	Mulligan Tawny / The Third Herd / Autobahn Blues / Pomp Stomp
	Wild Apple Honey / By Play / Woodchoppers' Ball Mambo / Gina

1955	Opus De-Funk / Pimlico / Captain Ahab / I Remember Duke
	Skinned / Skinned Again / Sentimental Journey / Square Circle
	9:20 Special / Broadway / The Boot / Ev'ry Day I Get the Blues
1956	Blues Groove / Smack Dab in the Middle / Pinetop's Blues
	Dupree Blues / Call It Stormy Monday
1957	The Preacher / Wailin' in the Woodshed / Ready, Get Set, Jump
1958	Natchel Blues / Ready, Get Set, Jump / Park East / Gloomy Sunday
	Autobahn Blues / I Cover the Waterfront / Crazy Rhythm
	Black Orchid / Fire Island / Balu / New Cha-Cha / Summer Sequence
	Bamba Samba / Ebony Concerto
1959	Lullaby of Birdland / The Swingin' Shepherd Blues / The Magpie
	Like Some Blues, Man
1960	Darn That Dream / I Can't Get Started / Crown Royal
1961	Pee Wee Blues / Sweet Lorraine / Swing Low Sweet Clarinet
1962	Mo-lasses / Sister Sadie / Sig Ep / Camel Walk / Blues for J. P.
1963	Watermelon Man / Body and Soul / Better Git It in Your Soul
	El Toro Grande / Hallelujah Time / Jazz Hoot / Satin Doll
1964	Just Squeeze Me / Dr. Wong's Bag / Dear John C / Blue Monk
	You Dirty Dog / Pour House Blues / My Favorite Things
1965	A Lot of Livin' to Do / Somewhere / 23 Red / Poor Butterfly
	Greasy Sack Blues / Woody's Whistle / Opus De-Funk
	I Remember Clifford
1966	Sonny Boy / Dinah / San Francisco / April Showers
1967	Tomorrow's Blues Today / Cousins / Woody's Boogaloo
1968	Here I Am Baby / MacArthur Park
1969	Flying Easy / Lancaster Gate
1970	Smiling Phases / A Time for Love / Blues in the Night
1971	Sidewalk Stanley / Hitch Hike on the Possum Trot Line
	Love in Silent Amber / Adam's Apple / After Hours / Proud Mary
1972	Bill's Blues / Watermelon Man / Summer of '42 / The Raven Speaks
	Reunion at Newport
1973	Giant Steps / La Fiesta / Be-Bop and Roses / The Meaning of the
	Blues
1974	Blues for Poland / What Are You Doing the Rest of Your Life?
	Come Saturday Morning / This Time / Brotherhood of Man

	I Can't Get Next to You / Fanfare for the Common Man / Tantum Ergo
	I've Got You under My Skin / Variations on a Scene / Children of Lima
1975	Far In! / 25 or 6 to 4 / King Cobra / Spain / Come Rain or Come Shine
1976	40th Anniversary Concert
1978	Woodchoppers' Ball / I've Got News for You / Fire Dance / Pavane Suite for a Hot Band / Aja / I've Got the News / Easy Livin'
1979	Caravan / I Got It Bad / Countdown / Better Git It in Your Soul Manteca
1981	Things Ain't What They Used to Be / Midnight Run / Lemon Drop John Brown's Other Body / North Beach Breakdown / The Dolphin
1982	Rockin' Chair / The Claw / Peanut Vendor / Greasy Sack Blues Perdido
1983	The Glory of Love / My Buddy / Summer Knows / I Believe in Love
1986	It Don't Mean a Thing / Pools / Blues for Red / Conga / Fried Buzzard
	Central Park West
1987	Battle Royal / Watermelon Man / Woody's Gold Star The Great Escape / The Samba Song

major players in the woody herman bands

An estimated two thousand musicians, singers, and arrangers flowed into and out of the Woody Herman orchestras over the years. The following are those who stayed longest and became, in their times, mainstays of the band. They are listed in the approximate order in which they performed under Herman's baton.

trumpet players

Steady Nelson, Cappy Lewis, Billie Rogers, Neal Hefti, Pete Candoli, Conte Candoli, Ray Wetzel, Sonny Berman, Marky Markowitz, Conrad Gozzo, Shorty Rogers, Al Porcino, Stan Fishelson, Bernie Glow, Ernie Royal, Red Rodney, Doug Mettome, Don Ferraro, Rolf Ericson, Nick Travis, Don Fagerquist, Stu Williamson, John Howell, Reuben McFall, Dick Collins, Bill Castagnino, Johnny Coppola, Danny Styles, Willie Thomas, Nat Adderley, Bill Chase, Don Rader, Ziggy Harrell, Dave Gale, Billy Hunt, Dusko Goykovich, Bill Byrne, Marvin Stamm, Dick Reudebusch, Linn Biviano, Luis

Gasca, Tony Klatka, Bill Stapleton, Dennis Dotson, Alan Vizzutti, George Rabbai, Roger Ingram, Mark Lewis, Ron Stout

trombonists

Neal Reid, Ralph Pfiffner, Bill Harris, Ed Kiefer, Earl Swope, Ollie Wilson, Bob Swift, Bart Varsalona, Vernon Friley, Urbie Green, Carl Fontana, Frank Rehak, Kai Winding, Dick Kenney, Keith Moon, Wayne Andre, Willie Dennis, Bob Lamb, Billy Byers, Phil Wilson, Henry Southall, Mel Wanzo, Bill Watrous, Bob Burgess, Jim Pugh, Birch Johnson, Gene Smith, John Fedchock

saxophonists

Saxie Mansfield, Sam Rubinwitch, Herbie Haymer, Vido Musso, Skippy DeSair, Johnny Bothwell, Georgie Auld, Budd Johnson, Herbie Fields, Sam Marowitz, Flip Phillips, Pete Mondello, John LaPorta, Herbie Steward, Stan Getz, Zoot Sims, Serge Chaloff, Al Cohn, Jimmy Giuffre, Gene Ammons, Buddy Savitt, Don Lanphere, Marty Flax, Buddy Wise, Phil Urso, Sam Staff, Kenny Pinson, Bill Perkins, Arno Marsh, Dick Hafer, Bill Trujillo, Richie Kamuca, Jay Migliore, Joe Romano, Roger Pemberton, Al Belletto, Richie Kamuca, Med Flory, Jimmy Mosher, Sal Nistico, Nick Brignola, Raoul Romero, Andy McGhee, Tom Anastas, Frank Vicari, Joe Romano, Frank Tiberi, Gregory Herbert, Steve Lederer, Gary Anderson, Joe Lovano, Bruce Johnstone, Mike Brignola, Mark Vinci, Dave Riekenberg, Jerry Pinter

pianists

Tommy Linehan, Jimmy Rowles, Ralph Burns, Tony Aless, Fred Otis, Lou Levy, Dave McKenna, Nat Pierce, Norman Pockrandt, Vince Guaraldi, John Bunch, Pete Jolly, Al Planck, Eddie Costa, Bill Potts, Al Dailey, Kenny Ascher, Alan Broadbent, Harold Danko, Andy LaVerne, Pat Coil, Dave Lalama, John Oddo, Brad Williams, Joel Weiskopf

bassists

Walter Yoder, Gene Sargent, Chubby Jackson, Joe Mondragon, Harry Babasin, Jimmy Stutz, Oscar Pettiford, Mert Oliver, Red Mitchell, Red Wooten, Frank Gallagher, Red Kelly, Monte Budwig, Jimmy Gannon, Major Holley, Bill Betts, Milt Hinton, Chuck Andrus, Tony Leonardi, Mike Moore, Carl Pruitt, Arthur Harper, Gene Perla, Tom Azarello, Al Johnson, Wayne Darling, Chip Jackson, Rusty Holloway, Marc Johnson, Mike Hall, Dave Shapiro, Lynn Seaton, Don Gladstone, Dave Carpenter

guitarists

Hy White, Billy Bauer, Chuck Wayne, Jimmy Raney, Ray Biondi, Charlie Byrd, Phil Upchurch, Pat Martino, Joe Beck

drummers

Frank Carlson, Cliff Leeman, Dave Tough, Don Lamond, Shadow Wilson, Shelly Manne, Sonny Igoe, Art Mardigan, Chuck Flores, Bill Bradley, Gus Gustafson, Don Michaels, Karle Kiffe, Jake Hanna, Jimmy Campbell, Gus Johnson, Mel Lewis, Ronnie Zito, John Von Ohlen, Ed Soph, Evan Diner, Joe LaBarbera, Ron Davis, Jeff Brillinger, Dan D'Imperio, Jeff Hamilton, Dave Ratajczak, Jim Rupp, Joe Pulice, Dave Miller

other instruments

Joe Bishop, flugelhorn; Ray Hopfner, violin; Marjorie Hyams, vibes; Red Norvo, vibes; Jerri Ney, vibes; Terry Gibbs, vibes; Milt Jackson, vibes; Sam Staff, flute; Cy Touff, bass trumpet; Victor Feldman, vibes; Tito Puente, Latin percussion; Eddie Costa, vibes; Willie Rodriguez, Latin rhythm; Gus Mas, flute; Gene Roland, valve trombone; Nat Pierce, celesta; Bob Pierson, flute

vocalists

Mary Ann McCall, Elsa Harris, Carol Kaye, Dillagene, Muriel Lane, Carolyn Grey, Anita O'Day, Frances Wayne, Lucille Linwood, The Blue Flames, Lynne Stevens, The Blue Moods, Jerri Ney, Terry Swope, Pat Easton, Dolly Houston, Leah Mathews, Marianne Donne

arrangers

Joe Bishop, Zilmer Randolph, Jiggs Noble, Gordon Jenkins, Bob Mersey, Lowell Martin, Dizzy Gillespie, Dave Matthews, Gene Sargent, Ralph Burns, Neal Hefti, Phil Moore, Eddie Sauter, Roger Segure, Shorty Rogers, Sonny Berman, John LaPorta, Al Cohn, Jimmy Giuffre, Tiny Kahn, Johnny Mandel, Murray Gerlanek, Gene Roland, Nat Pierce, Bill Holman, Manny Albam, Billy May, George "The Fox" Williams, Johnny Coppola, Tadd Dameron, A. K. Salim, Sid Feller, Don Rader, Bill Chase, Bob Hammer, Tom Newsome, Dusko Goykovich, Raoul Romero, Kenny Ascher, Richard Evans, Tony Klatka, Alan Broadbent, Bill Stapleton, Gary Anderson, Joe Roccisano, Dave Lalama, John Oddo, John Fedchock, Chick Corea

notes

introduction

1. Ellington quoted in Herb Wong, notes for Discovery Records album *Woody Herman—The Third Herd*, vol. 1.

2. Basie quoted in ibid.

3. Herman quoted in Ralph J. Gleason, notes for Philips Records album *Swing Low, Sweet Clarinet*.

4. Herman quoted in George Kanzler, notes for Columbia Records album *The Thundering Herds, 1945–47*.

5. Herman quoted in Gary Giddins, "Woody Herman, Winding down a Forty-Six-Year Road Tour," *Esquire*, September 1982, 186.

6. Ibid.

chapter one

1. Woody Herman and Stuart Troup, *The Woodchopper's Ball: The Autobiography of Woody Herman*, 5–6.

2. Herman quoted in Will Friedwald, notes for Columbia Records album *Woody Herman—Best of the Big Bands*.

3. Herman and Troup, *The Woodchopper's Ball*, 8–9.

4. Ibid.

5. Herman quoted in Leonard Feather, "Herman Still Thundering after 50 Years," *Los Angeles Times*, 13 July 1986.

6. Herman and Troup, *The Woodchopper's Ball*, 82–83.

7. Herman quoted in George T. Simon, *The Big Bands*, 247.

8. Herman and Troup, *The Woodchopper's Ball*, 14.

9. Herman quoted in Richard Gehman, "Woody," *Saturday Review*, 11 May 1968, 60.

10. Herman quoted in Giddins, "Woody Herman, Winding down a Forty-Six-Year Road Tour," 186.

11. Herman and Troup, *The Woodchopper's Ball*, 16.

12. John Wilson, notes for Time-Life Books album *Woody Herman*.

13. Decca Records was started by the brothers Dave and Joe Kapp in New York City in 1934. To appeal to the youth market, the Kapps priced their records at thirty-five cents against the industry standard of seventy-five cents. Decca soon profited from the sale of records by Glen Gray's Casa Loma Orchestra, radio singing

star Bing Crosby, and the bands of Isham Jones, Jimmy Dorsey, and Bob Crosby, Bing's brother.

14. Albert McCarthy and Dave Carey, eds., *Jazz Directory*, 5:857.

15. Gunther Schuller, *The Swing Era*, 731.

16. Simon, *The Big Bands*, 277.

17. Herman quoted in John McDonough, "Woody Herman—Fifty Years in the Big Band Business," *Down Beat*, November 1986, 19–20.

18. Basie quoted in Simon, *The Big Bands*, 85.

19. In swing music jargon, "sweet" meant pretty and slow; the opposite was "hot," with emphasis on faster rhythm and improvised solos that veered away from the melody into the unexpected.

20. Herman and Troup, *The Woodchopper's Ball*, 21.

21. Ibid.

22. Herman's remarks from a concert taped at the Herman Park Miller Outdoor Theater in Houston, 17 October 1984, later aired as the PBS Television special *Woody Herman's Big Band Celebration*.

23. Basie quoted in Albert Murray, *Good Morning Blues*, 184–85.

24. Basie quoted in ibid.

25. George T. Simon, *Glenn Miller and His Orchestra*, 16.

chapter two

1. George T. Simon, *Simon Says*, 71.

2. Herman quoted in ibid.

3. Richard Hadlock, notes for MCA Records album *Blues on Parade*.

4. Siefert to author, 26 October 1994.

5. Herman quoted in ibid.

6. Herman and Troup, *The Woodchopper's Ball*, 24–25.

7. Gehman, "Woody," 61.

8. Herman and Troup, *The Woodchopper's Ball*, 31.

9. Riffing is a way of creating interest in music by repeating the same phrases, perhaps with a trace of harmonic change, either as background or main melody. Such repetition is so widely used in jazz, blues, swing, and ballad writing as to be little noticed. The riff is a basic part of the song form. Countless jazz and swing pieces depend on riffs. Glenn Miller's famous "In the Mood" from 1939 builds from a three-note phrase, or riff. A T. D. novelty from 1935, "I've Got a Note," excited with repetition, rhythm breaks, and solos harmonizing with one note. Morton, self-proclaimed "inventor of jazz, blues and stomps," explains: "Slow tunes did more in the development of jazz than any other thing due to the fact that you would always have time to hit a note twice when ordinarily you would only hit it once, and that gave it

a very good flavor. My theory is always [to] have the melody going some way and, of course, your background [should] always be in perfect harmony with what is known as riffs . . . something that gives any orchestra a great background" (quoted in Rex Harris, *Jazz*, 68).

10. Herman and Troup, *The Woodchopper's Ball*, 50.

11. Herman quoted in Simon, *The Big Bands*, 248.

12. George T. Simon, notes for Columbia Records album *The Thundering Herds*.

13. Quoted in Simon, *The Big Bands*, 248.

14. Schuller, *The Swing Era*, 728–29.

15. Herman quoted in Friedwald, notes for *Woody Herman—Best of the Big Bands*.

16. Simon, *The Big Bands*, 249.

17. Hadlock, notes for *Blues on Parade*.

18. Herman and Troup, *The Woodchopper's Ball*, 39.

19. Hadlock, notes for *Blues on Parade*.

20. James Lincoln Collier, *Benny Goodman and the Swing Era*, 187.

21. Herman quoted in Steve Voce, *Woody Herman*, 23.

22. Quoted in Simon, *Simon Says*, 276.

23. Ibid., 262.

24. Herman and Troup, *The Woodchopper's Ball*, 34.

25. Simon, *Simon Says*, 262.

26. Ibid., 268.

27. Herman and Troup, *The Woodchopper's Ball*, 37.

28. Leo Walker, *The Wonderful Era of the Great Dance Bands*, 91.

chapter three

1. Herman quoted in David Patrick Stearns, "Woody Herman," *USA Today*, 1 April 1986.

2. Herman and Troup, *The Woodchopper's Ball*, 40.

3. Gillespie quoted in Ira Gitler, *Swing to Bop*, 123.

4. Herman and Troup, *The Woodchopper's Ball*, 50.

5. Herman quoted in McDonough, "Woody Herman—Fifty Years in the Big Band Business," 20.

6. Herman and Troup, *The Woodchopper's Ball*, 46.

7. Bert quoted in Robert Laber, "Rekindling the Flame,"*Instrumentalist*, December 1993, 25.

8. Jackson to author, 19 January 1994.

9. Young quoted in Gitler, *Swing to Bop*, 91.

10. Herman and Troup, *The Woodchopper's Ball*, 47.

11. Burns quoted in Herman and Troup, *The Woodchopper's Ball*, 44–45.

12. Herman and Burns quoted in Simon, notes for *The Thundering Herds*.

13. Hefti quoted in Michael Ullman, *Jazz Lives*, 48.

14. Herman quoted in George T. Simon, notes for Decca Records album *Woody Herman: The Turning Point (1943–1944)*.

15. Simon, *Glenn Miller and His Orchestra*, 21.

16. Herman and Troup, *The Woodchopper's Ball*, 47.

17. Herman quoted in Kanzler, notes for *The Thundering Herds*.

18. Jackson and Herman quoted in Friedwald, notes for *Woody Herman—Best of the Big Bands*.

19. Tough quoted in Joachim Berendt, *The Jazz Book*, 162.

20. Stearns quoted in ibid.

21. Ibid., 286.

22. Manne quoted in Gitler, *Swing to Bop*, 51.

23. Herman and Jackson quoted in Friedwald, notes for *Woody Herman—Best of the Big Bands*.

24. Herman quoted in Voce, *Woody Herman*, 5.

25. Jackson quoted in Gitler, *Swing to Bop*, 189.

26. Herman quoted in ibid. Since the 1930s, the expressions "head" and "head arrangement" had joined the jazz-band lexicon. With some bands, it was common to write out just the first twenty-four or thirty-two bars of a piece; the remainder would be cooked up in the players' heads, a challenge called "faking." Hefti explains: "When I joined, everything was written out—three-minute charts, pop tunes of the day, etc. If there was a solo in it, it was like a solo around the melody. Very little improvisation. But then guys were drafted very fast. Like you'd change six or seven guys in a week, and a lot of these new guys really couldn't read music very well. Flip Phillips was a good soloist, but really a bad reader. And Bill Harris was another one. I almost had to teach them their parts by rote. And this sort of flustered Woody. He knew they were good musicians while [others] in the band who could read, didn't have the redeeming solo ability that those guys did. So we started faking things on the jobs. After six months of faking 'Flying Home' it became a tune ['Helen of Troy,' eventually recorded as 'The Good Earth']" (Hefti quoted in ibid., 191–92).

27. Simon, *Simon Says*, 199–201.

28. Woody Herman, notes for Columbia Records album *The Three Herds*.

chapter four

1. Kanzler, notes for *The Thundering Herds*.

2. Petrillo quoted in Simon, *The Big Bands*, 54.

3. Ibid.

4. Herman quoted in Simon, notes for *The Thundering Herds*.

5. Chubby Jackson, "Chubby Jackson Speaks Out," *The Herds* 3 (Summer 1994): 2.

6. Herman quoted in Friedwald, notes for *Woody Herman—Best of the Big Bands*.

7. Herman and Troup, *The Woodchopper's Ball*, 58.

8. Herman, notes for *The Three Herds*.

9. Herman and Troup, *The Woodchopper's Ball*, 59.

10. Ibid., 60.

11. Herman, notes for *The Three Herds*.

12. Ibid.

13. Herman quoted in Kanzler, notes for *The Thundering Herds*.

14. Michael Levin, "Record Guide," *Look*, 5 August 1947.

15. Herman quoted in Kanzler, notes for *The Thundering Herds*.

16. Simon, *The Big Bands*, 252.

17. Herman and Troup, *The Woodchopper's Ball*, 60.

18. Leonard Feather, notes for RCA Victor Records album *The 40th Anniversary Concert*.

19. Herman quoted in Simon, notes for *The Thundering Herds*.

20. Rogers quoted in Voce, *Woody Herman*, 46.

21. Herman quoted in Simon, notes for *The Thundering Herds*.

22. Herman quoted in ibid.

23. Herman, Jackson, and Dorsey quoted in Herman and Troup, *The Woodchopper's Ball*, 51.

24. Herman and Troup, *The Woodchopper's Ball*, 64–65.

25. Hefti quoted in Gitler, *Swing to Bop*, 192.

26. Herman and Troup, *The Woodchopper's Ball*, 65.

27. Jackson quoted in Richard M. Sudhalter, notes for RCA Victor Records album *Ebony*.

28. Herman quoted in Gitler, *Swing to Bop*, 195.

29. "Woody's Blues Heaven," *Newsweek*, 31 December 1945, 76.

30. Lamond quoted in Herman and Troup, *The Woodchopper's Ball*, 62.

31. Tough quoted in Gehman, "Woody," 61.

32. Herman quoted in Giddins, "Woody Herman, Winding down a Forty-Six-Year Road Tour," 185–86.

33. Herman quoted in Gitler, *Swing to Bop*, 194–95.

34. Simon, notes for *The Thundering Herds*.

35. Herman quoted in ibid.

36. Herman quoted in ibid.

37. Herman and Rowles quoted in Gitler, *Swing to Bop*, 193.

38. Simon, *The Big Bands*, 252n.

39. Ulanov quoted in ibid.

40. Robert A. Simon, "Musical Events: Including Jazz," *New Yorker*, 6 April 1946, 102.

41. Herman quoted in Simon, *The Big Bands*, 253.

42. Norvo quoted in Berendt, *The Jazz Book*, 197.

43. Leonard Feather, notes for MGM Records album *1946 Carnegie Hall Concert*.

44. Herman quoted in George Kanzler, notes for Columbia Records album *1940s—The Small Groups: New Directions*.

45. Herman quoted in Simon, notes for *The Thundering Herds*.

46. McDonough, "Woody Herman—Fifty Years in the Big Band Business," 19.

47. Herman quoted in ibid.

48. Rowles and Herman quoted in Gitler, *Swing to Bop*, 194–95.

49. Jack Siefert to author, 16 October 1994.

50. Herman quoted in Simon, notes for *The Thundering Herds*.

51. Herman quoted in ibid.

52. Schuller, *The Swing Era*, 743.

53. Herman and Troup, *The Woodchopper's Ball*, 66.

54. Simon, *The Big Bands*, 253–54.

55. Herman quoted in ibid., 254.

56. Herman quoted in ibid.

57. Herman quoted in Kanzler, notes for *The Thundering Herds*.

58. Herman, notes for *The Three Herds*.

59. Barnet quoted in Montgomery Brower, "Woody Herman Plays On to Pay the Piper," *People*, 11 September 1986, 80.

60. Herman and Troup, *The Woodchopper's Ball*, 68–69.

61. Herman, notes for *The Three Herds*.

62. Kanzler, notes for *The Thundering Herds*.

63. Herman, notes for *The Three Herds*.

chapter five

1. Herman quoted in Gitler, *Swing to Bop*, 195.

2. Herman and Troup, *The Woodchopper's Ball*, 71.

3. Eckstine quoted in Gitler, *Swing to Bop*, 127.

4. Quoted in Simon, *Simon Says*, 356.

5. Herman and Troup, *The Woodchopper's Ball*, 72.

6. Herman quoted in Simon, notes for *The Thundering Herds*.

7. Herman, notes for *The Three Herds*.

8. Shorty Rogers quoted in Voce, *Woody Herman*, 55.

9. Herman and Troup, *The Woodchopper's Ball*, 73.

10. Herman quoted in Gitler, *Swing to Bop*, 234.

11. James A. Treichel, *Woody Herman and the Second Herd*, 4–5.

12. Ibid., 6.

13. Herman, notes for *The Three Herds*.

14. Treichel, *Woody Herman and the Second Herd*, 8.

15. Giuffre quoted in Herb Wong, notes for Tall Trees Records album *Keeper of the Flame*.

16. Herman, notes for *The Three Herds*.

17. Friedwald, notes for *Woody Herman—Best of the Big Bands*.

18. Berendt, *The Jazz Book*, 330.

19. Treichel, *Woody Herman and the Second Herd*, 11–12.

20. Quoted in Treichel, *Woody Herman and the Second Herd*, 19.

21. Ibid., 22.

22. Ibid., 23.

23. Ulanov quoted in Treichel, *Woody Herman and the Second Herd*, 23.

24. Getz quoted in Laber, "Rekindling the Flame," 27.

25. Gibbs quoted in Wong, notes for *Keeper of the Flame*.

26. Herman and Troup, *The Woodchopper's Ball*, 75.

27. Gibbs quoted in Bob Davis, "Celebrating Herman's Thunder," *Down Beat*, November 1993, 35.

28. Herman, remarks during 40th Anniversary Concert, November 1976.

29. Cohn quoted in Pete Welding, notes for Capitol Records album *Keeper of the Flame*.

30. Nels Nelson, "Woody Herman: 'Road Father,'" *Philadelphia Daily News*, 6 November 1987, 70.

31. Jackson, "Chubby Jackson Speaks Out," 2.

32. *Down Beat* quoted in Treichel, *Woody Herman and the Second Herd*, 33.

33. Sims quoted in Gitler, *Swing to Bop*, 235.

34. Sims quoted in Gitler, *Swing to Bop*, 235.

35. Red Rodney quoted in ibid.

36. Mel Tormé, *It Wasn't All Velvet*, 171–72.

37. Cohn and Gibbs quoted in Gitler, *Swing to Bop*, 237.

38. Herman and Troup, *The Woodchopper's Ball*, 78.

39. Ibid., 90.

40. Herman and Troup, *The Woodchopper's Ball*, 75.

41. Ibid., 75–76.

42. Gibbs quoted in Gitler, *Swing to Bop*, 243.

43. Herman quoted in ibid., 285.

44. Herman and Troup, *The Woodchopper's Ball*, 80–81.

45. Treichel, *Woody Herman and the Second Herd*, 38.

46. Charlie Barnet with Stanley Dance, *Those Swinging Years*, 148–49.

47. Herman quoted in Treichel, *Woody Herman and the Second Herd*, 49.

48. Leonard Feather, *Inside Be-bop*, 36–37.

49. Herman and Troup, *The Woodchopper's Ball*, 63.

50. Herman quoted in Voce, *Woody Herman*, 11.

51. Treichel, *Woody Herman and the Second Herd*, 44.

52. Herman and Troup, *The Woodchopper's Ball*, 85.

53. Treichel, *Woody Herman and the Second Herd*, 45

54. Ibid., 1.

55. Herman and Troup, *The Woodchopper's Ball*, 86.

56. Herman quoted in Davis, "Celebrating Herman's Thunder," 35.

chapter six

1. Herman and Troup, *The Woodchopper's Ball*, 99.

2. "Conversations . . with Woody Herman," *Sounds & Fury*, October 1965, 43.

3. Quoted in Voce, *Woody Herman*, 56.

4. Herman and Troup, *The Woodchopper's Ball*, 99.

5. Herman and Troup, *The Woodchopper's Ball*, 101.

6. Steve Voce, notes for Verve Records album *Woody Herman, 16.5.1913–29.10.1987.*

7. Herman and Troup, *The Woodchopper's Ball*, 99.

8. Perkins quoted in Herb Wong, notes for Discovery Records album *Woody Herman—The Third Herd*, vol. 2.

9. Pierce quoted in Voce, *Woody Herman*, 67–68.

10. Herman quoted in Wong, notes for *Woody Herman—The Third Herd*, vol. 1.

11. Herman and Troup, *The Woodchopper's Ball*, 74.

12. Wong, notes for *Woody Herman—The Third Herd*, vol. 2.

13. Herman and Troup, *The Woodchopper's Ball*, 100.

14. Ibid., 99.

15. Quoted in Voce, *Woody Herman*, 69.

16. "That Happy Feeling," *Time*, 31 May 1954, 34.

17. Ibid.

18. Pierce quoted in Herman and Troup, *The Woodchopper's Ball*, 101.

19. Francis Davis, "Last of a Breed," *Atlantic*, April 1986, 120.

20. Feather, "Herman Still Thundering after 50 Years."

21. Holley quoted in Herman and Troup, *The Woodchopper's Ball*, 104. Slam

Stewart was a colorful bassist who devised interesting sounds on many recordings made between 1939 and 1946 by humming as he played.

22. Ibid., 102.

23. Holley quoted in ibid., 104.

24. All quotations in Voce, *Woody Herman,* 73.

25. Herman quoted in Steve Voce, notes for Jazz Groove Records album *Woody Herman's Anglo-American Herd.*

26. Herman quoted in Ralph J. Gleason, notes for Atlantic Records album *Woody Herman Live at Monterey.* (An earlier release of the music was in the album *Woody Herman's Big New Herd at the Monterey Jazz Festival.*)

27. Pierce and Herman quoted in Herman and Troup, *The Woodchopper's Ball,* 101.

28. Leonard Feather, *Encyclopedia of Jazz,* 253.

29. Herman and Troup, *The Woodchopper's Ball,* 107.

30. Ibid., 108.

31. Wilson quoted in Voce, notes for *Woody Herman, 16.5.1913–29.10.1987.*

32. Herman quoted in Jack Tracy, notes for Philips Records album *Woody's Big Band Goodies.*

33. Laber, "Rekindling the Flame," 29.

34. Tracy, notes for *Woody's Big Band Goodies.*

35. Ibid.

36. Leonard Feather, *Encyclopedia of Jazz in the 60s,* 156.

37. Ralph J. Gleason, notes for Philips Records album *Woody Herman 1963.*

38. Wilson quoted in Voce, notes for *Woody Herman, 16.5.1913–29.10.1987.*

39. Siefert to author, 16 October 1994.

40. Adderley quoted in Leonard Feather and Ira Gitler, *Encyclopedia of Jazz in the '70s,* 15.

41. "Conversations . . with Woody Herman," 43.

42. Ralph J. Gleason, notes for Columbia Records album *My Kind of Broadway.*

43. Herman quoted in Voce, *Woody Herman,* 21.

44. Bill Byrne to author, 13 March 1990.

45. Gehman, "Woody," 60.

46. Will Friedwald, notes for Stash Records album *Mel Torme—A Retrospective, 1956–1968.*

47. Bill Byrne to author, 16 July 1993.

48. Gehman, "Woody," 60–61.

49. Ed Mulford, "Woody Was a Great Man," *IAJRC Journal* 21, no. 1 (January 1988): 1.

50. Feather, *Encyclopedia of Jazz in the 60s,* 157.

51. Herman and Troup, *The Woodchopper's Ball,* 113.

52. Pierce quoted in Feather, "Herman Still Thundering after 50 Years."

53. Herman quoted in Brower, "Woody Herman Plays On to Pay the Piper," 80.

54. Bill Byrne quoted in Herman and Troup, *The Woodchopper's Ball,* 115.

55. Herman and Lees quoted in ibid.

56. Herman quoted in Donald Clarke, ed., *Penguin Encyclopedia of Popular Music,* 541.

chapter seven

1. Feather, notes for *The 40th Anniversary Concert.*

2. Herman quoted in Leonard Feather, *The Pleasures of Jazz,* 90.

3. John Fedchock to author, 7 January 1995.

4. Hubbard quoted in Feather and Gitler, *Encyclopedia of Jazz in the '70s,* 181.

5. Edward Soph to author, 11 August 1993.

6. Ibid.

7. Ammons quoted in Feather and Gitler, *Encyclopedia of Jazz in the '70s,* 18.

8. Feather, *The Pleasures of Jazz,* 91.

9. Gene Lees, "Woody 'n' Me," *High Fidelity,* September 1969, 118.

10. Barnet, *Those Swinging Years,* 188–89, 194.

11. Edward Soph to author, 11 August 1993.

12. Rehak quoted in Feather and Gitler, *Encyclopedia of Jazz in the '70s,* 281.

13. Frank Tiberi to author, 13 March 1990.

14. Herman and Troup, *The Woodchopper's Ball,* 119.

15. Ibid.

16. Bill Byrne to author, 16 July 1993.

17. Broadbent quoted in Herman and Troup, *The Woodchopper's Ball,* 119.

18. Bill Byrne to author, 16 July 1993.

19. "Out There Forever," *Time,* 11 May 1970, 57–58.

20. Bill Byrne quoted in Herman and Troup, *The Woodchopper's Ball,* 117.

21. Feather, *The Pleasures of Jazz,* 91.

22. John McDonough, "Woody Herman, 1913–87," *Down Beat,* February 1988, 12.

23. Feather, *The Pleasures of Jazz,* 91

24. Bill Byrne to author, 24 July 1993.

25. Herman quoted in "Big Band," *New Yorker,* 9 September 1972, 31.

26. Rudi Blesh, *Combo USA,* 78.

27. Stanley Dance, *The World of Count Basie,* 10.

28. Gene Lees, "The Herman Band at Forty—A Time for Cheering," *Saturday Review,* 30 October 1976, 52.

29. Herman quoted in "Big Band," 32.

30. Broadbent and Lees quoted in Herman and Troup, *The Woodchopper's Ball*, 120–21.

31. Danko quoted in ibid., 122.

32. Bill Byrne to author, 24 July 1993.

33. Danko quoted in Herman and Troup, *The Woodchopper's Ball*, 122.

34. "Big Band," 31.

35. Davis, "Last of a Breed," 120.

36. Herman and Troup, *The Woodchopper's Ball*, 121.

37. Bill Byrne to author, 24 July 1993.

38. Herman quoted in Brower, "Woody Herman Plays On to Pay the Piper," 80.

39. The designation "thundering herd" began appearing in albums, publicity, and music stands. Herman's friend Siefert made and repaired the band's music stands in his home workshop.

40. Bill Byrne to author, 13 March 1990.

41. Bill Byrne to author, 24 July 1993.

42. Ibid.

43. Sinatra quoted in Herb Wong, notes for Fantasy Records album *Herd at Montreux*.

44. Bill Byrne to author, 24 July 1993.

45. Jack Siefert to author, 23 March 1992.

46. Bill Byrne to author, 24 July 1993.

47. Jack Siefert to author, 23 March 1992.

48. Bill Byrne to author, 24 July 1993.

49. Herman and Troup, *The Woodchopper's Ball*, 123.

50. In a ten-year stretch through 1975, Feather counted Herman having played Newport festivals six times; Monterey three; Concord twice, plus Montreux and others abroad (Feather and Gitler, *Encyclopedia of Jazz in the '70s*, 175).

51. Herman's doctor, Stan Levy, had befriended him years before, when Herman needed emergency help with a blocked esophagus. No special fan of jazz, Levy had swiftly become a fan of Herman the man, however. Following Herman by telephone at times to check his health, he prompted Herman to quip that the doctor made "two-thousand-mile house calls" (Stan Levy to author, 8 May 1994). In part payment for such kindness, Herman once took his band to Detroit to play at Levy's wedding reception.

52. Ingrid Herman had become a bluegrass fiddle player and had married Tom Littlefield, a bluegrass guitarist from Alabama. They lived in Nashville as free-lance musicians with Alexandra and son Tommy, who spent time with his grandfather's band and sang a duet with him on "Sonny Boy."

53. Feather, *The 40th Anniversary Concert*.

chapter eight

1. Jackson quoted in Feather, *40th Anniversary Concert.*
2. Mort Goode, notes for RCA Bluebird Records album *Woody Herman Memorial.*
3. Gene Lees, "The Herman Band at Forty—A Time for Cheering," 49, 52.
4. Torme, *It Wasn't All Velvet,* 350.
5. John McDonough, "CD Reviews: Woody Herman," *Down Beat,* September 1988, 41.
6. Herman and Troup, *The Woodchopper's Ball,* 126–27.
7. Ibid., 128.
8. McDonough quoted in Collier, *Benny Goodman and the Swing Era,* 358.
9. Bill Byrne to author, 14 August 1993.
10. Herman quoted in George T. Simon, *Best of the Music Makers,* 270–71.
11. Chuck Stone, "The Greatest Woodchopper of 'Em All," *Philadelphia Daily News,* 3 November 1987.
12. Duke Ellington quoted in Wong, notes to *Woody Herman—The Third Herd,* vol. 1.
13. Bill Byrne to author, 21 August 1993.
14. Woody Herman, notes for Concord Records album *Live at the Concord Jazz Festival.*
15. Annalyn Swan, "The Godfather of Jazz," *Newsweek,* 18 January 1982, 85–86.
16. Giddins, "Woody Herman, Winding down a Forty-Six-Year Road Tour," 186.
17. Herman and Troup, *The Woodchopper's Ball,* 132.
18. Bill Byrne to author, 12 June 1995.
19. Herman quoted in Davis, "Last of a Breed," 119.
20. Jack Siefert to author, 9 March 1994.
21. Stoltzman quoted in Sudhalter, notes for *Ebony.*
22. Brignola and Fedchock quoted in Herman and Troup, *The Woodchopper's Ball,* 140.
23. Reese quoted in Feather, "Herman Still Thundering after 50 Years."
24. Gitler, *Swing to Bop,* 10.
25. Herman and Troup, *The Woodchopper's Ball,* 142.
26. Ibid., 144.
27. Tiberi quoted in Brower, "Woody Herman Plays On to Pay the Piper, 80.

chapter nine

1. Herman and Troup, *The Woodchopper's Ball,* 146.
2. John Fedchock to author, 7 January 1995.

3. Gordon Raddue, notes for Concord Records album *50th Anniversary Tour.*

4. McDonough, "Woody Herman—Fifty Years in the Big Band Business," 19.

5. Stoltzman and Herman quoted in Stearns, "Woody Herman."

6. Davis, "Last of a Breed," 120.

7. Terry Teachout, "Elegy for the Woodchopper," *American Scholar* 58 (Summer 1989): 435

8. Stuart Troup to author, 14 November 1994.

9. Herman and Troup, *The Woodchopper's Ball,* 145–46.

10. Herman quoted in Voce, *Woody Herman,* 8.

11. Bill Byrne to author, 13 March 1990.

12. Brower, "Woody Herman Plays On to Pay the Piper," 79.

13. Teachout, "Elegy for the Woodchopper," 434.

14. Herman quoted in Brower, "Woody Herman Plays On to Pay the Piper," 80.

15. Herman and Troup, *The Woodchopper's Ball,* 148.

16. Nelson, "Woody Herman: 'Road Father.'"

17. Gordon Raddue, notes for Concord Records album *Woody's Gold Star.*

18. Herman and Troup, *The Woodchopper's Ball,* 149.

19. Davidson quoted in James Warrick, "Woody Herman: America Loses Its Greatest Pied Piper," *Instrumentalist,* December 1987, 43.

20. Herman and Troup, *The Woodchopper's Ball,* 149.

21. Fedchock quoted in ibid.

22. *Milwaukee Journal,* Herman, and Tiberi quoted in Thomas Cassidy, Inc., press release, spring 1990.

23. Bill Byrne to author, 4 September 1993.

24. Davis, "Celebrating Herman's Thunder," 36.

25. Reese quoted in Gail Diane Cox, "Even after His Death, Jazzman Gets It Moving," *National Law Journal,* 8 August 1988, 8.

26. Ibid.

27. Conyers quoted in Warrick, "Woody Herman: America Loses Its Greatest Pied Piper," 43

28. Letters quoted in Cox, "Even after His Death, Jazzman Gets It Moving," 8.

29. Staffer, Little, and Reese quoted in ibid.

30. Herman and Parnassus quoted in Burt A. Folkart, "Fans, Friends Bid Goodbye to Woody Herman," *Los Angeles Times,* 3 November 1987.

31. Thomas Cassidy, Inc., press release, spring 1990.

32. Nelson, "Woody Herman: 'Road Father.'"

33. Jack Siefert to author, 21 November 1993, with unpublished typescript of eulogy dated 3 November 1987.

34. Davis, "Celebrating Herman's Thunder," 33.

35. Lovano quoted in ibid.

36. Wilson quoted in ibid.

37. Bill Byrne to author, 13 March 1990.

38. Frank Tiberi to author, 13 March 1990.

39. Fontaine, McGhee, and Wilson quoted in Fred Bouchard, "Herman Tributes Coast-to-Coast," *Down Beat,* January 1988, 11.

40. Reese quoted in Warrick, "Woody Herman: America Loses Its Greatest Pied Piper," 42.

41. Mulford, "Woody Was a Great Man," 1.

42. Mort Goode, notes for RCA compact disc *Woody Herman Memorial—40th Anniversary Concert.*

43. Michael Ullman, "Woody Herman, Bandleader," *High Fidelity,* March 1988, 72.

44. Ingrid Reese to author, 27 February 1991.

45. Bill Byrne to author, 1 June 1993.

46. Frank Tiberi to author, 8 February 1995.

bibliography

Anonymous. Notes for Columbia Records album *Sequence in Jazz*.

Anonymous. Notes for Columbia Records album *Twelve Shades of Blue*.

Anonymous. Notes for Everest Records album *Bamba-Samba Bossa Nova*.

Anonymous. Notes for Fantasy Records album *Children of Lima*.

Balliett, Whitney. "Herd after Herd." *New Yorker,* 12 October 1963.

Barnet, Charlie, with Stanley Dance. *Those Swinging Years.* New York: Da Capo Press, 1992.

Berendt, Joachim. *The Jazz Book.* New York: Lawrence Hill, 1975.

"Big Band." *New Yorker,* 9 September 1972.

Blesh, Rudi. *Combo USA.* New York: Chilton, 1971.

"Blow It Down." *Time,* 8 April 1946.

Bouchard, Fred. "Herman Tributes Coast-to-Coast." *Down Beat,* January 1988.

Brower, Montgomery. "Woody Herman Plays On to Pay the Piper." *People,* 1 September 1986.

Buck, George H., Jr. Notes for Circle Records album *Woody Herman and His Orchestra First Session, 1937.*

Chilton, John. *Who's Who of Jazz.* Philadelphia, Pa.: Chilton, 1978.

Clarke, Donald, ed. *Penguin Encyclopedia of Popular Music.* New York: Viking, 1989.

Collier, James Lincoln. *Benny Goodman and the Swing Era.* New York: Oxford University Press, 1989.

Conover, Willis. Notes for Philips Records album *Woody Herman: 1964.*

"Conversations . . with Woody Herman." *Sounds & Fury,* October 1965.

Corea, Chick. Notes for Century Records album *Chick, Donald, Walter & Woodrow*.

Cox, Gail Diane. "Even after His Death, Jazzman Gets It Moving." *National Law Journal,* 8 August 1988.

Dance, Stanley. *The World of Count Basie.* New York: Charles Scribner's Sons, 1980.

Davis, Bob. "Celebrating Herman's Thunder." *Down Beat,* November 1993.

Davis, Francis. "Last of a Breed." *Atlantic,* April 1986.

Delaunay, Charles. *New Hot Discography.* New York: Criterion, 1948.

Driggs, Frank. Notes for Circle Records album *First Session, 1937.*

Elwood, Philip. Notes for Concord Records album *World Class*.

Esposito, Bill. Notes for Fanfare Records album *Woody Herman—The First Herd*.

Fagen, Donald, and Walter Becker. Notes for Century Records album *Chick, Donald, Walter & Woodrow*.

Feather, Leonard. *Encyclopedia of Jazz.* New York: Bonanza Books, 1960.

———. *Encyclopedia of Jazz in the 60s.* New York: Da Capo, 1966.

———. "Herman Still Thundering after 50 Years." *Los Angeles Times,* 13 July 1986.

———. *Inside Be-bop.* New York: J. J. Robbins & Sons, 1949.

———. *Jazz Times,* December 1986.

———. Notes for MGM Records album *1946 Carnegie Hall Concert.*

———. Notes for RCA Victor Records album *The 40th Anniversary Concert.*

———. *The Pleasures of Jazz.* New York: Horizon Press, 1976.

Feather, Leonard, and Ira Gitler. *Encyclopedia of Jazz in the '70s.* New York: Da Capo, 1976.

Folkart, Burt A. "Fans, Friends Bid Goodbye to Woody Herman." *Los Angeles Times,* 3 November 1987.

Friedwald, Will. Notes for Columbia Records album *Woody Herman—Best of the Big Bands.*

———. Notes for Stash Records album *Mel Tormé—A Retrospective 1956-1968.*

Garrod, Charles. *Isham Jones and His Orchestra.* Zephyrhills, Fla.: Joyce Record Club, Inc., 1992.

———. *Woody Herman and His Orchestra.* Vol. 1, *1936–1947.* Zephyrhills, Fla.: Joyce Record Club, Inc., 1985.

———. *Woody Herman and His Orchestra.* Vol. 2, *1948–1957.* Zephyrhills, Fla.: Joyce Record Club, Inc., 1986.

———. *Woody Herman and His Orchestra.* Vol. 3, *1958–1987.* Zephyrhills, Fla.: Joyce Record Club, Inc., 1988.

Garrod, Charles, Ken Crawford, and Dave Kressley. *World Transcriptions Original Series.* Zephyrhills, Fla.: Joyce Record Club, Inc., 1992.

Gehman, Richard. "Woody." *Saturday Review,* 11 May 1968.

Giddins, Gary. *Riding on a Blue Note: Jazz and American Pop.* Oxford: Oxford University Press, 1982.

———. "Woody Herman, Winding down a Forty-Six-Year Road Tour." *Esquire,* September 1982.

Gitler, Ira. *Swing to Bop.* New York: Oxford University Press, 1985.

Glaser, Martha. Notes for Columbia Records album *Music for Tired Lovers.*

Gleason, Ralph J. Notes for Atlantic Records album *Woody Herman Live at Monterey.*

———. Notes for Capitol Records album *Blues Groove.*

———. Notes for Columbia Records album *My Kind of Broadway.*

———. Notes for Fantasy Records album *Brand New.*

———. Notes for Philips Records album *Swing Low, Sweet Clarinet.*

———. Notes for Philips Records album *Woody Herman 1963.*

———. Notes for Verve Records album *Concerto for Herd.*

Goode, Mort. Notes for Columbia Records album *Jazz Hoot.*

———. Notes for RCA Bluebird Records album *Woody Herman Memorial.*

———. Notes for RCA compact disc *Woody Herman Memorial—40th Anniversary Concert.*

Gottlieb, William P. *The Golden Age of Jazz.* New York: Simon and Schuster, 1979.

Hadlock, Richard. Notes for MCA Records album *Blues on Parade.*

Hall, George. Notes for Hep Records album *The V Disc Years, 1944–45,* vol. 1.

———. Notes for Hindsight Records album *Woody Herman, 1937.*

‒‒‒‒‒‒. Notes for Hindsight Records album *Woody Herman*. Vol. 2, *1944*.

‒‒‒‒‒‒. Notes for Jass Records album *Northwest Passage*.

‒‒‒‒‒‒. Notes for Jass Records album *Woodchopper's Ball*.

Harris, Rex. *Jazz*. London: Penguin, 1953.

Hentoff, Nat. "Indigenous Music." *Nation*, 21 May 1977.

‒‒‒‒‒‒. Notes for Everest Records album *The Herd Rides Again*.

‒‒‒‒‒‒. Notes for Everest Records album *Herman's Heat and Puente's Beat*.

Herman, Woody. Notes for Century Records album *Chick, Donald, Walter & Woodrow*.

‒‒‒‒‒‒. Notes for Columbia Records album *The Three Herds*. November 1954.

‒‒‒‒‒‒. Notes for Columbia Records album *The Thundering Herds*, 1963.

‒‒‒‒‒‒. Notes for Concord Records album *Live at the Concord Jazz Festival*.

Herman, Woody, and Stuart Troup. *The Woodchopper's Ball: The Autobiography of Woody Herman*. 1990. Reprint, New York: Proscenium Publishers, Inc., 1994.

Jackson, Chubby. "Chubby Jackson Speaks Out." *The Herd* 3 (Summer 1994): 2.

Kanzler, George. Notes for Columbia Records album *1940s—The Small Groups: New Directions*.

‒‒‒‒‒‒. Notes for Columbia Records album *The Thundering Herds, 1945–47*.

Laber, Robert. "Rekindling the Flame." *Instrumentalist*, December 1993.

Lees, Gene. "The Herman Band at Forty—A Time for Cheering." *Saturday Review*, 30 October 1976.

‒‒‒‒‒‒. "Woody 'n' Me." *High Fidelity*, September 1969.

Levin, Michael. "Record Guide." *Look*, 5 August 1947.

Liska, James A. Notes for Concord Records album *My Buddy*.

Marlo, John. Notes for Crown Records album *The New Swingin' Herman Herd*.

McCarthy, Albert. *The Dance Band Era*. New York: Spring Books, 1971.

McCarthy, Albert, Dave Carey, and Ralph Venables, eds. *Jazz Directory*. Vol. 1. London: Cassell, 1955.

McCarthy, Albert, and Dave Carey, eds. *Jazz Directory*. Vols. 2, 3, 4. Fordingbridge: Delphic, 1950–52.

‒‒‒‒‒‒. *Jazz Directory*. Vol. 5. London: Cassell, 1955.

McDonough, John. "CD Reviews: Woody Herman." *Down Beat*, September 1988.

‒‒‒‒‒‒. "Woody Herman—Fifty Years in the Big Band Business." *Down Beat*, November 1986.

‒‒‒‒‒‒. "Woody Herman, 1913–87." *Down Beat*, February 1988.

Mulford, Ed. "Woody Was a Great Man." *IAJRC Journal* 21, no. 1 (January 1988):1–3.

Murray, Albert. *Good Morning Blues*. New York: Random House, 1985.

Nelson, Nels. "From a Splinter, a Woody Friendship." *Philadelphia Daily News*, 1 May 1963.

‒‒‒‒‒‒. "Woody Herman: 'Road Father.'" *Philadelphia Daily News*, 6 November 1987.

Nicotera, Frank. "Herd Corralled." *Down Beat*, August 1981.

"Out There Forever." *Time*, 11 May 1970.

Pirie, Christopher A. Notes for First Heard Records album *It Pours*.

———. Notes for First Heard Records album *Juke Box—Woody Herman and the First Herd.*

Raddue, Gordon. Notes for Concord Records album *50th Anniversary Tour.*

———. Notes for Concord Records album *Woody's Gold Star.*

Ramsey, Doug. Notes for Trip Records album *Encore—Woody Herman 1963.*

Reed, B. Mitchell. Notes for Cadet Records album *Woody.*

Roberts, Alan. Notes for Sunbeam Records album *Woody Herman & His Orchestra.*

Schuller, Gunther. *The Swing Era.* New York and Oxford: Oxford University Press, 1989.

Simon, George T. *Best of the Music Makers.* New York: Doubleday, 1979.

———. *The Big Bands.* New York: Macmillan, 1967.

———. *Glenn Miller and His Orchestra.* New York: Crowell, 1974.

———. Notes for Columbia Records album *The Thundering Herds.*

———. Notes for Decca Records album *Woody Herman: The Turning Point (1943–1944).*

———. *Simon Says.* New York: Arlington House, 1971.

Simon, Robert A. "Musical Events: Including Jazz." *New Yorker,* 6 April 1946.

Stearns, David Patrick. "Woody Herman." *USA Today,* 1 April 1986.

Stone, Chuck. "The Greatest Woodchopper of 'Em All." *Philadelphia Daily News,* 3 November 1987.

Sudhalter, Richard M. Notes for RCA Victor Records album *Ebony.*

Swan, Annalyn. "The Godfather of Jazz." *Newsweek,* 18 January 1982.

Sylvester, Robert. Notes for Forum Records album *Woody Herman Sextet at the Roundtable.*

Teachout, Terry. "Elegy for the Woodchopper." *American Scholar* 58 (Summer 1989).

"That Happy Feeling." *Time,* 31 May 1954.

Thomas Cassidy., Inc. Press release, spring 1990.

Tormé, Mel. *It Wasn't All Velvet.* New York: Kensington Publishing, 1988.

Tracy, Jack. Notes for Philips Records album *Woody's Big Band Goodies.*

Treichel, James A. *Woody Herman and the Second Herd.* Zephyrhills, Fla.: Joyce Record Club, Inc., 1978.

Tuttle, Anthony. Notes for Columbia Records album *Woody Live East and West.*

Ullman, Michael. *Jazz Lives.* Washington, D.C.: New Republic Books, 1980.

———. "Woody Herman, Bandleader." *High Fidelity,* March 1988.

Voce, Steve. Notes for Jazz Groove Records album *Woody Herman's Anglo-American Herd.*

———. Notes for Verve Records album *Woody Herman, 16.5.1913–29.10.1987.*

———. *Woody Herman.* London: Apollo Press Ltd., 1986.

Walker, Leo. *The Big Band Almanac.* Rev. ed. New York: Da Capo, 1989.

———. *The Wonderful Era of the Great Dance Bands.* New York: Doubleday, 1972.

Warrick, James. "Woody Herman: America Loses Its Greatest Pied Piper." *Instrumentalist,* December 1987.

Webman, Hal. Notes for Coral Records album *Woody Herman Souvenirs.*

Welding, Pete. Notes for Capitol Records album *Keeper of the Flame,* 1992.

White, Bozy. *AFRS Basic Music Library, P-1 to P-1200.* Zephyrhills, Fla.: Joyce Record Club, Inc., 1988.

———. *AFRS Basic Music Library, P-1201 to P-2399.* Zephyrhills, Fla.: Joyce Record Club, Inc., 1988.

Wilson, John. Notes for Time-Life Books album *Woody Herman.*

Wong, Herb. Notes for Cadet Records album *Light My Fire.*

———. Notes for Century Records album *Road Father.*

———. Notes for Columbia Records album *Woody's Winners.*

———. Notes for Concord Records album *Woody and Friends.*

———. Notes for Discovery Records album *Woody Herman—The Third Herd,* vol. 1.

———. Notes for Discovery Records album *Woody Herman—The Third Herd,* vol. 2.

———. Notes for Fantasy Records album *Herd at Montreux.*

———. Notes for Philips Records album *The Swinging Herman Herd Recorded Live.*

———. Notes for Tall Tree Records album *Keeper of the Flame,* 1984.

"Woody's Blues Heaven." *Newsweek,* 31 December 1945.

index

Broadbent, Alan, 197, 201, 203–4; and "Blues in the Night," 198, 200; and "Variations on a Scene," 211; and "Woody 'n Me," 249

Brown, Les, 35, 116, 121, 161

Burns, Ralph, 62, 65, 89, 100, 111, 145, 215; arranging touches of, 67; as combo leader, 114; Herman's appraisals of, 72, 87, 88, 216–17; leading backup bands, 120, 121, 124

Byrd, Charlie, 169

Byrne, Bill, 182; about Dionne Warwick, 198–99; about Herman archive, 210–11; about Herman's last wishes, 245; about Herman's place in jazz, 248; about Mel Tormé, 184; pictured, 243; as road manager, 185

*C*adet Records, 192, 193

Caiazza, Nick, pictured, 31

"Caldonia," 87, 167, 168, 217

Calloway, Cab, 36, 66

Campbell, Jimmy, 170, 173

Candoli, "Conte," 71, 216, 240

Candoli, Pete, 71, 72, 77, 98, 119, 216, 240

Capitol Records, 48, 59, 135, 144, 161

"Captain Ahab," 163, 165

Carlson, Frankie, 10, 25, 29, 45; pictured, 19

Carmichael, Hoagy, 28, 121, 150

Carnegie Hall concert (1946), 103, 104–5; record album of, 105–6

Carter, Benny, 30, 36, 59, 116

"Casbah Blues," 23, 26, 37

"Celestial Blues," 155

Century Records, 220

Chaloff, Serge, 124, 130, 141

Chase, Bill, 166, 173, 176, 181, 183

"Chips' Blues," 33, 35, 84

"Chips' Boogie Woogie," 33, 35

Christy, June, 129, 143

"Chubby's Blues," 84

Clinton, Larry, 21, 24, 35

Clooney, Rosemary, 202, 229, 230

Cohn, Al, 126, 131, 139, 161, 216; pictured, 217

Cole, Nat "King," 75, 133, 138, 143, 145, 146

Coltrane, John, 181

Columbia Records, 59, 81, 85, 105, 110, 121, 154, 160, 179

Columbo, Russ, 4, 18

"Concerto for Herd," 187

Concord Records, 226, 228, 230

Continental Artists, 119, 120, 133

Copland, Aaron, 209

Coppola, John, 163, 178, 217

Corea, Chick, 222

Costa, Eddie, 170

"Cousins," 178, 185, 217, 244. *See also* "Blues Groove"

"Cousin to Chris," 29, 31, 34

"Crickets, The," 139–40, 141

Crosby, Bing, 20, 29, 33, 42, 44, 45

Crosby, Bob, 20, 21, 23, 24, 25, 30, 50

Crown Records, 166, 173

*D*allas Blues," 25, 28

Davidson, Nathan, 243–44; pictured, 243

Davis, Miles, 112, 134, 179, 184

Decca Records, 7, 9, 26, 34, 59, 69, 79, 82, 142

DeFranco, Buddy, 219

"Detour Ahead," 142

Dillagene, 30, 33, 34, 35, 36

Direct-to-disc recording, 220, 222

Discovery Records, 155, 157; Trend-Discovery Records, 232

"Doctor Jazz," 16, 22

"Do Nothin' Till You Hear from Me," 59, 61, 64

"Don't Worry 'bout That Mule," 90, 92

Herman, Woody, life of: automobile accident, 219; and Charlotte Neste, 6, 11; childhood, 3–4; financial problems, 189–90, 207–8, 235, 241, 249; funeral, 247–48; heart disease, 242; and Jack Siefert, 16; marital problems, 116; sense of humor, 90; surgeries, 46, 213

Herman, Woody, musicianship of: on alto saxophone, 29–30; and artistic stubbornness, 23; and art versus profit, 34; compared to Barnet, 62; compared to Bob Crosby, 20–21; compared to Ellington, 61; early influences on, 4; Ellington's influence on, 4, 59–60, 101; innovations, 191; Latin American influence on, 169; and leadership traits, 202–3; and longevity, 202–3, 236, 237; and musical freedom, 229; and repertoire, 198; and rock music, 192; on soprano saxophone, 181; and style changes, 25; swinging, 124, 234

Herman, Woody, opinions about and honors: archive, 210; of Basie, 1; Big Band Hall of Fame, 232; of Dick Haymes, 122; of Ellington, 1; of Fedchock, 243; of Giddins, 2; Grammy awards, 177, 207, 212; honorary degree, 219; Lifetime Achievement Award, 246; in magazine polls, 50; scholarship fund, 213; of Schuller, 31. See also Balliett, Whitney; Feather, Leonard; Lees, Gene; Simon, George T.

Herman, Woody, opinions of: about band business, 2; about Chubby Jackson, 69–70; about Dave Tough, 71; about Dizzy Gillespie, 56; about "ghost bands," 215; about jazz, 1, 124, 243; about nostalgia, 204, 224; about Ralph Burns, 72

Herman, Woody, performances and recordings of: and ASCAP ban, 37; with Bing Crosby, 42; "Caldonia," 87; in Cuba, 147; and Columbia, 82, 85, 106–7, 112, 135, 154; and Decca, 11, 21, 69, 82; "Ebony Concerto," 99, 101, 104, 110, 113; in Europe, 159; "Fan It" and "South," 38; fiftieth anniversary concert, 240; first jobs, 5; fortieth anniversary concert, 215–18; "Four Brothers," 136, 140, 146; with Frank Sinatra, 209–10; "Goosey Gander," 88; with Gus Arnheim, 7; with Harry Sosnick, 7; with Houston Symphony, 211; with Isham Jones, 7–9; with Isham Jones's Juniors, 9; jazz cruise, 213; with Krewe of Zulu, 224; last performance, 244; "Let It Snow, Let It Snow, Let It Snow," 97; and Mars Records, 155; movies, 22, 41–42, 58; "Non-Alcoholic," 115; "Northwest Passage," 88; with Richard Stoltzman, 233–34; on the road, 185–86; in South America, 169; with Tom Gerun, 5–6; vaudeville, 3; as "Wally Hayes" 17–18, 19; "We the People Bop," 134; Wildroot series, 94–95; "Woodchoppers' Ball," 25, 26, 103, 115; *Woody Herman and His Orchestra,* 22; workshops, 191–92; "Your Father's Mustache," 92

Herman, Woody, pictured, 8, 19, 57, 75, 111, 135, 176, 182, 188, 192, 224, 243, 245

"Herman at the Sherman," 30, 35

Hines, Earl, 4, 6, 121

Hodges, Johnny, 69, 181

Holiday, Billie, 110, 142

Holley, Major Quincy "Mule," Jr., 168, 169, 170, 171

Holman, Bill, 154, 187, 227

"Hot Chestnuts," 44

Houston, Dolly, 151